Feeding the Mouth That Bites You is ⎡...⎤ does a wonderful job guiding parei ⎡...⎤ of raising adolescents so they can make their way into adulthood. Ken has a deep heart of compassion for both parents and adolescents given how hard this process is, and his engaging sense of humor helps lighten the tone along the way. *Feeding the Mouth That Bites You* has already ministered to countless thousands of parents, and I know this new edition will be helpful to so many more. If you are looking for a book to help you more deeply understand how to raise adolescents to live healthy and flourishing lives, this is the one. I highly recommend it!

    DR. CHRIS THURMAN, psychologist and bestselling author of *The Lies We Believe*

In parenting, like most things, we tend to surround ourselves with advice that lines up with what we want to hear rather than what we need to hear. This makes Ken Wilgus an absolute essential for all of us in the throes of parenting kids in this fast-paced, ever-changing culture. Dr. Ken's second edition of *Feeding the Mouth That Bites You* is practical, straightforward, and extremely timely. If there was ever a one-size-fits-all parenting handbook, this is it!

    CYNTHIA YANOF, author and host of the *MESSmerized* podcast

I am a father of teenagers and a pastor to teenagers. I don't think I have read anything that's as important for parents and leaders as *Feeding the Mouth That Bites You.* I asked my daughter recently what has been most helpful in keeping our relationship and communication strong. She said, "Freedom." She loves that we trust her. We learned this concept from Dr. Ken.

    DUSTIN TAPPAN, senior director of Next Gen at Christ's Church of the Valley in Phoenix, Arizona

KENNETH WILGUS, PhD

Parenting Teenagers into Adulthood

FOCUS
ON THE FAMILY.
A Focus on the Family resource
published by Tyndale House Publishers

To my wife, Sally—
My greatest friend and one true life's companion;
and to Alex, Anna, and Frances—
who make us look good every day

Contents

Foreword

One of the great blessings of hosting a daily radio program devoted to helping families thrive in Christ is that I often have the privilege of interacting with guests who have encouraged and equipped *me* in my own roles as a husband and father. Beyond our radio, podcast, and online audiences, I'm often the beneficiary of wise counsel from our guests that empowers me as a parent and spouse and bolsters my faith. In those moments, I'm reminded of the old Hair Club commercials, during which the spokesman testifies, "I'm not only the Hair Club president—but I'm also a client!"

This was especially true in 2019, when Dr. Ken Wilgus first appeared on our broadcast to talk about his book, *Feeding the Mouth That Bites You.* Focus on the Family received a great deal of positive feedback from our listeners about that program, but it was also definitely one of those occasions when I benefited *personally* from what our guest had to say during the course of our interview. Dr. Wilgus made so many excellent points about the importance of releasing your teenager into adulthood and how to make the "Planned Emancipation" process run smoothly.

After the recording session concluded, I pulled Dr. Wilgus aside and asked if he'd be willing to take a phone call from me and my wife, Jean. You see, at the very time that broadcast was recorded, Jean and I were grappling with some serious emancipation challenges of our own with one of our teenage sons. Put simply, our son wanted more autonomy, and we were struggling to let go. It was creating no small degree of stress and confusion in the Daly household.

Dr. Wilgus graciously agreed to take our call, and the conversation was tremendously helpful. In fact, when we implemented some of his tips and suggestions, it's not an exaggeration to say that it fundamentally changed our relationship with our son and moved it in a much more positive direction. We're eternally grateful for Dr. Wilgus and his practical plan of Planned Emancipation. As I said, I'm not just the president of Focus—I'm also a client!

This book has an important message for Christian parents. As moms and dads, we're admonished in Scripture to bring our children up in the fear of the Lord. Involvement in our children's lives is a good thing; they need our presence and our attention. And especially for Christian parents, there is added pressure to provide *protection*, not only from physical dangers and threats but also from our immoral culture and from ideologies that can damage them spiritually. If you're feeling a sense of urgency to take an active role in these pursuits with your children, those are good instincts!

But we also have to grapple with the truth of the popular adage "You're not raising children; you're raising adults." No one wants his or her children to grow up too fast, especially in this age when our culture seems bent on robbing them of their innocence before they're even old enough to go to kindergarten. Nevertheless, with each passing year that our children are with us, we need to be relinquishing a bit more control and empowering them to make decisions for themselves.

This will look different for every child, but make no mistake: *Every* child needs to go through this process. "Letting go" of our children isn't a one-time event that happens when they graduate from high school or college; it's a yearslong process that happens gradually, intentionally, and with much prayer.

That's why I'm such a firm believer in Dr. Wilgus and his common-sense methodology of Planned Emancipation. And that's why Focus on the Family is proud to be publishing this updated and expanded version of *Feeding the Mouth That Bites You*. We want as many parents as possible to benefit from this book and its excellent message.

Our world is teetering on chaos, and we desperately need future generations of citizens who have the confidence, skills, and spiritual maturity to step up and lead. If you want your own children to be among them, I encourage you to read this book and take it to heart.

Jim Daly
President, Focus on the Family

Acknowledgments

As I write a second edition of *Feeding the Mouth That Bites You*, I am particularly grateful to Jim and Jean Daly, who have been great supporters of the message this book teaches. Because of them, I have come to know many members of the team at Focus on the Family who have carried this project forward. Particular thanks to Larry Weeden and Jesse Lange, who edited and held my hand when I needed it.

Thirty-five years of professional experience do not happen alone. I am forever grateful to my colleagues—Greg Gore, Guy Chandler, Sandi Frost, Jo Lynn Wilburn, and David Nicholson—with whom I shared many years of practice. Above all, I am eternally grateful to Paul Warren, my friend and mentor whom I miss every day.

Special thanks to Jessica Pfeiffer, my podcast cohost, who represents and advocates for parents of teenagers around the world.

Finally, I am grateful to my own parents, Robert and Sandra Wilgus, whom I miss and love dearly. Their success in parenting my brother, sister, and me is the basis for much of the content of this book.

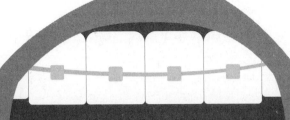

PART ONE

We Created
This Mess

Why Our Understanding of Teenagers Is New
and Why Not All Cultures Have Problems
with Their Adolescents

CHAPTER 1

A Revolution in Parenting Teenagers

There are times when parenthood seems nothing
but feeding the mouth that bites you.
PETER DE VRIES

This isn't just another parenting book. For thousands of parents, *Feeding the Mouth That Bites You* has lifted their burden, not added to it. That's important to me. How did the job of being a parent get to be so hard? So many articles, books, and podcasts comfort parents with the message that "it's okay. No one knows what they're doing when they have kids." Really? How is it that despite having an explosion of resources for parents, we still have this deep insecurity about how well we're doing the job?

When my oldest was five years old, I remember calling my mother and saying, "Alex walks around the house complaining that he's bored. What did you do when we were bored?"

After a thoughtful pause, my sweet mom said, "Kenneth, I don't think we cared that much if you were bored."

Her answer kind of clicked for me. My parents did a good job raising my brother, sister, and me, but I don't remember expecting them to take care of all my discomforts.

I fear this new onslaught of parenting information isn't helping the way we need it to. For comparison: Becoming an adept driver isn't useful if you don't know where you're going. I picture today's parents as drivers in cars. These parents/drivers are worried about the kid/car they're trying to drive. "Does it pull to the left?" "What's that noise under the hood?" "Make sure we don't crash into anything!" Many parents are sort of driving/navigating their kids' lives while sifting through piles of user's manuals that have conflicting information. Parents are stressed, and they desperately want to know if they're driving well. But almost all these parents/drivers have one thing in common: They *never* look at the map. All those manuals may help you understand the vehicle, but they don't necessarily help you reach your destination.

We have become so focused on the task of parenting that a growing percentage of our young-adult children aren't going anywhere in life. They're like cars stalled on the side of the road. They may be shiny, healthy, well-loved cars, but they're stuck nonetheless.

Feeding the Mouth That Bites You is designed to help you—the parent or guardian—as you help your teenager follow the road map of adolescence. Let me be clear: This is not a map of the road you think they *should be* on. It's the road that leads from childhood to independent adulthood. Your teenager is on this path whether you like it or not.

The impact the first edition of this book has had on moms and dads has been exciting to watch. For so many parents already, reading *Feeding the Mouth That Bites You* has been like finding a lost map of the path through the wilderness. I love it when I meet parents who have implemented the cultural shift in their families that I call Planned Emancipation. Planned Emancipation is the one foundational shift in your role as a parent that can maximize your effectiveness in influencing your teenager. It will be the primary subject and theme of this book.

We have become so focused on the task of parenting that a growing percentage of our young-adult children aren't going anywhere in life. They're like cars stalled on the side of the road.

So why do we need a second edition? First, it's stunning how much the world has changed for adolescents since the initial release. Issues related to social media, social isolation, and identity were not even on the radar when the book was first published. Additionally, the rapidly multiplying number of books on brain science, "neurodiversity," and other topics can bury parents deeper than ever in the pit of confusion over what path to take with their teenagers.

Another reason for writing this second edition is to clarify commonly misunderstood elements of *Feeding the Mouth* parenting. On our *Feeding the Mouth That Bites You* podcast, I've been able to hear from many readers. While it's been great to hear the positive responses, some parents continue to misunderstand the basic elements of Planned Emancipation. In this volume, I will try to clarify more of what *Feeding the Mouth* parenting is and also what it isn't. Spoiler alert: There is no inside scoop that guarantees your teen will turn out well, and Planned Emancipation is no exception. However, it can make a huge difference in how you parent.

Finally, in this edition, I hope to provide even more encouragement to struggling parents. Parents of teens today are burdened with the heavy self-consciousness of whether they are parenting well. My parents never thought about their parenting; they just thought about the job of raising their children. The use of the word *parenting* is similar to how we use the new term *adulting*. When people feel overly self-conscious and insecure, the normal things that adults do become *adulting*, just as the normal things parents do with their children now carry the self-conscious term *parenting*.

With all this pressure on parents, is it any wonder that an alarming number of teens and young adults say they have no desire to have children? Who would want to take on such a stressful task that seems to reap little reward? *Feeding the Mouth That Bites You* lays out a clear path for parents so you can know whether you're following the right path for being effective with your adolescents. It outlines the starting and finishing lines that teenagers need to see throughout their transition from childhood to adulthood.

Planned Emancipation is a path for parents to follow that is distinct from chasing fleeting milestones of whether your teenager is excelling in all areas of life, or even whether your teenager is happy. *Feeding the Mouth That Bites You* simply lays out the path from childhood to adulthood. That path is probably easier than you think.

CHAPTER 2

The Invention of Teenagers

We have created a new disorder: Extended Childhood
Disorder, characterized by feelings of hopelessness,
anger, and a lack of control over one's life.

ROBERT EPSTEIN, PhD

"I don't understand why you've been so hostile to us lately, Noah."

Noah reacted like so many of the adolescents I see in my office: He didn't.

"And your grades? They're not what they used to be, are they, honey?" his mother said.

The dad butted in: "We just want to find out if this is normal teenage behavior."

I looked at Noah and asked, "What do you think? Is what you've been doing normal teenage behavior?"

He averted my gaze and looked to the ceiling, then glanced at his parents. With a sneer, he answered my question with a question: "What *is* normal teenage behavior?"

Mom and Dad both rolled their eyes and answered in sync, "See?"

I nodded my head in affirmation, but not because I saw what they thought I saw. Without always realizing it, teenagers can ask some important questions.

The New Normal in Adolescent Behavior

How would you answer Noah's question? What words do you think describe normal teenage behavior? If you're like most parents, your list may include the following:

- *rebellious*
- *passive-aggressive*
- *emotional*
- *lazy*
- *sneaky*

The first thing you need to know is that whatever you've included in your list, the way we all think about the teenage years is very new.

When I started studying adolescent psychology, one of the first things I learned was that our current understanding of adolescents is about 120 years old. The word *teenager* only started being used around 1941. This was stunning to me. Imagine going to your first day of study to be an ear, nose, and throat doctor and hearing, "Now, people didn't have noses until a little more than a hundred years ago, and we didn't even start calling them noses until after the Second World War." Wait . . . what?

I'm telling you this because I want you also to be a little stunned by this historical fact. Think about it. The understanding you have of your teenager wasn't even thought about 120 years ago. If you asked someone in America two hundred years ago a question about parenting his teenager, he wouldn't understand what you meant—not because young people around the ages of thirteen to eighteen did not exist, of course, but because there was nothing unique about that particular age group.

> The understanding you have of your teenager wasn't even thought about 120 years ago.

Our current way of defining *adolescence* was first used by the American psychologist G. Stanley Hall in 1904 and was described as a period of "storm and stress."[1] In his view, physiological and psychological changes in adolescents led to three basic characteristics: conflict with parents, mood disruptions, and risky behavior. But Hall's assumptions about such characteristics as an inevitable part of adolescence have been called into question. Why weren't these features characteristic of this age group in centuries past? Why is this description not universal in other cultures?

In his book *The Case against Adolescence*, Dr. Robert Epstein, professor and former editor-in-chief of *Psychology Today*, presents an excellent history of this development:

> Adolescence is the creation of modern industrialization, which got into high gear in the United States between 1880 and 1920. For most of human history before the Industrial Era, young people worked side by side with adults as soon as they were able, and it was not uncommon for young people, and especially young females, to marry and establish independent households soon after puberty. It wasn't until the turn of the twentieth century that adolescence was identified as a separate stage of life characterized by "storm and stress."[2]

Did you get that? Everyone knows that the years from about thirteen to eighteen bring significant physical and psychological changes, but these didn't become big, stormy problems until our society changed. Somewhere along the way, we lost track of who teenagers are and where they fit in our communities.

Cultures without Teenagers

Another important fact to consider is that even today, there are more than one hundred societies that do not have adolescents as we understand them. Most of these cultures don't even have a word for adolescence. Members of these tribes in their teen years have no significant levels of antisocial behavior, depression, or drug use.[3] These are not teenagers who spend most of their time away from adults but young members of the community who are actively being incorporated into full-member status with other adults. There is even evidence that when these societies adopt more-Western practices, problems with the adolescent age group begin to emerge.[4]

The human stage of development called *childhood* comes to its natural end around the age of thirteen. This has been universally acknowledged throughout human history until just recently. This general age limit is related to puberty. The physical transformation that prepares the human body for reproduction is a universal human experience that cannot be ignored. When your baby can have babies, she's not your baby anymore.

In a simple agrarian culture, thirteen- and fourteen-year-olds are ready to assume their place in the workforce along with older adults. Historically, ceremonies like the bar mitzvah marked the transition into adulthood. One could be a child yesterday and a man today.

In the sixteenth century, William Shakespeare did not write *Romeo and Juliet* about a couple of infatuated children. These were young adults, aged about thirteen or fourteen, with responsibilities, servants, and enough authority to be secretly married and held liable for murder. By many estimates, Mary, the mother of Jesus, might well have been around thirteen or fourteen years old when she conceived and then proclaimed possibly the greatest words of praise to God the world has ever heard (see Luke 1:46-55).

Throughout most of human history, a thirteen-year-old was old enough to have learned self-management and was expected to begin contributing to the community as an adult. In the late 1800s, our post–industrial revolution society required a longer period of education and training before a young adult was ready to function independently. The more complex the society, the longer the training period was required. The resulting gap of time between the onset of puberty and readiness for independence created a population of young people who looked and felt physically mature but had to wait several years before reaching the status of adulthood.

The postwar baby boom of the 1950s brought an unusual amount of prosperity to American parents eager to provide whatever their children needed. Instead of being recognized as young adults finishing necessary training before independence, adolescents began to be viewed as a distinct group separate from children and adults. A large amount of disposable income made these young people a marketing category, with fashions, music, magazines, and movies targeted directly to teens. By the mid-1950s, many in this increasingly entitled and aimless group would be described as "rebels without a cause."

Their parents encouraged this problem by treating them like large, recalcitrant children. In *Escaping the Endless Adolescence*, Joseph and Claudia Allen lament, "The period of preparation has expanded so boundlessly that many teens no longer have any realistic sense of what they're ultimately preparing for, or even that they *are* preparing for something. Their motivation, morale, and character all ultimately take hits."[5]

Today, we are three or four generations removed from a normal cultural memory that tells us the proper time when childhood should come to its natural end and adulthood truly begins. It's not only today's parents who are confused about this transition; their parents and grandparents were too. This cultural confusion is so ingrained and multigenerational that it's difficult for us to see it today.

If you're having problems with your teenager, it's not that *you* are doing it wrong, so to speak. It's more likely that *we're all* doing it wrong and have been for a long time. In our culture, the significant differences between children (birth to thirteen) and adolescents (thirteen to end of high school) are ignored or minimized. Children may be disobedient, but they don't misbehave for the same reasons teenagers do. Even a strong-willed six-year-old does not regularly announce, "Just twelve more years and I'm outta here!"

Our modern, scientific age has emphasized individual differences at the expense of obvious categories. Our culture has forgotten what all previous cultures knew instinctively: that human offspring are children for only the first twelve or so years of life, and after that they're adults. A complex society renders these young adults in need of several more years of training. *This means that our teenagers are best understood as adults-in-training.*

9

Where Are the Grown-Ups?

To add even more confusion, we view adolescents as overgrown children, but we also live in a culture that worships youth. The same mother who nags her teen daughter today may come asking to borrow some of her daughter's clothes tomorrow. As one author put it, "Our society has passed from a period which was ignorant of adolescence to a period in which adolescence is the favourite age. We now want to come to it early and linger in it as long as possible."[6]

My grandfather was born in 1901, and I'm pretty sure that if he ever wore blue jeans, it was only while herding cattle in New Mexico when he was fifteen. Trying to stay young looking didn't use to be important to adults. Just for fun, take a look at some high school yearbooks from the 1940s. See those teachers? Do they look funny to you? Those are called grown-ups. They may look odd because they were not trying to look like teenagers.

And just to add one more piece to this confused culture puzzle, the average age of the onset of puberty has been dropping steadily for decades. The result of these changes is that we live in a culture where the average teenager looks more adult at earlier ages while his parents are trying to look younger. Ever notice how many movies and television shows portray teenagers who display greater maturity than the adults who are supposed to be in charge? We're seeing a generation of adolescents who are maturing physically faster than ever but are being treated like children by parents who are themselves trying to look like their own teenagers! Where did all the grown-ups go, and why is no one even aspiring to be one?

Where did all the grown-ups go, and why is no one even aspiring to be one?

If you ask twenty-, thirty-, or even some forty-year-olds whether they feel grown-up, many will answer, "Not really." When I started practicing as an adolescent psychologist, most of the parents I worked with had found at least one way to feel grown-up: by becoming parents.

CHAPTER 3

The Burden of Parenting

Motherhood is an early retirement position.
Your children do grow up.
COLLEEN PARRO

"I just want to know what I did wrong!" The tearful woman reached for the tissue box in my office.

Amy was the mother of two adult children, and like so many mothers who come to see me, she felt like a failure as a parent. Her daughter (the older of the two) had just filed for divorce. This was particularly hard for Amy because she and her husband had spent years and thousands of dollars combatting their son's addictions. Unknowingly, Amy had divided her children into the *problem* one and the *good* one. Now, to Amy, it seemed that even her good child was failing.

"Maybe I shouldn't have worked when they were young. I just don't know," she said, sobbing.

I asked her why she felt her adult children's choices reflected on her as a mother. She looked a little astonished.

"I can't help feeling that if I did a better job, my children wouldn't be making these mistakes."

I have met many mothers like Amy. I want so much to offer comfort to them. Sometimes I make the observation that, logically, if a child's bad choices are because of their mother's actions, then her bad parenting must be the fault of *her* mother, and so on. And the response from the mother is . . . crickets.

One thing I've noticed, however, is that fathers rarely come to my office fretting that they messed up their kids. When I asked Amy why she didn't place part of the blame on her husband, she gave a sort of knowing smile and said, "Well, Chris did his best." Regardless of the circumstances, this burden of parenting well is felt almost exclusively by moms.

The Invention of *Parenting*

In the last chapter, I pointed out that the word *teenager* wasn't used until about 1941. I find it interesting that only a few years later, around 1959, the word *parenting* entered the dictionary. The word picked up use in the 1980s and 1990s. Like that annoying word *adulting*, *parenting* should mean simply what it is—"the activities of a parent."

Today, *parenting* has taken on a whole new, heavily burdensome meaning. Alison Gopnik, professor of psychology at UC Berkeley, outlines the problem this way:

> The promise of "parenting" is that there is some set of
> techniques, some particular expertise, that parents could
> acquire that would help them accomplish the goal of shaping
> their children's lives. . . . There is almost no evidence that any
> of this has much predictable effect on what children will be like
> when they grow up.[1]

No one is saying parents don't play an important role in children's lives. Parents who are abusive and neglectful can cause serious harm to children's development. Children who are raised with the secure love of both parents, fed, protected from undue harm, and instructed in life skills will flourish significantly better than children without these necessities.

But how much credit can we parents take for a remarkably successful adult child? When so-called experts start telling pregnant mothers that infants who listen to classical music in utero have better-developed brains (this was never validated, by the way), it puts pressure on moms to either fall in line or secretly worry that they're *doing it wrong*. Thousands of books, podcasts, and videos seem to carry the message that there's a new or secret technique or product that guarantees your child will turn out happy, well-adjusted, and confident.

This kind of parenting guilt seems to be experienced mostly by middle- and upper-class moms, usually ones who are white. Ylonda Gault Caviness, in her 2015 *New York Times* article titled "What Black Moms Know," says:

> I feel sorry for . . . those mothers: the highly informed, professionally accomplished—usually white—women who, judging by the mommy blog fodder, daytime TV, and new parenting guides lining store shelves, are apparently panicking all day, every day, over modern child rearing and everything that comes with it.[2]

It was and is a privilege to be able to sit and obsess over every interaction with your children. In centuries past, mothers dealt with numerous pregnancies throughout their contraception-free lives. And if the mother survived childbirth, her children often didn't live past the age of five. Mothers with a dozen kids, living in poverty or out on the frontier, didn't have time to be burdened with the expectations most mothers carry today.

Caviness describes a significantly different set of goals that she learned growing up in a black community in Buffalo, New York:

> Thankfully, I am a black mom. Like many of my fellow sisters, I don't have time for all that foolishness. Our charge is to raise—notice I did not say "parent"—our children in a way that prepares them for a world that, at best, may well overlook their awesomeness and, at worst, may seek to destroy it.[3]

When I started practicing as a psychologist, the 1980s and 1990s seemed to be part of a golden age of parenting. Young parents were eager to provide loving, safe environments in which their children could thrive. Books on parenting sold millions of copies. Dr. James Dobson's Focus on the Family ministry enjoyed a huge community of devoted followers. Parents attended all-day seminars, perfectly willing to give up countless hours to be educated on how to best parent their children.

While these parents were busy setting up their homes as havens for their beautiful children, no one reminded them of the goal of child-rearing: to produce adults who are contributing members of the community.

A few particularly zealous parents seemed to be preparing their homes, marriages, and personal lives to become permanently child friendly. Parenting books treated adolescence as just a hormone-crazed, older stage of childhood. These parents were in it for the long haul, and no one talked much about how and when to bring the job of parenting to a screeching halt.

> While these parents were busy setting up their homes as havens for their beautiful children, no one reminded them of the goal of child-rearing: to produce adults who are contributing members of the community.

Many of these parents now come to my office and are devastated or angry that these "older children" are no longer interested in reaping the benefits of the sacrifices they've made. They feel they have so much more to give to kids who, after the onset of puberty, no longer want what their parents have to offer. In a culture that has lost its understanding of childhood and adulthood, a generation of well-meaning, motivated, and loving parents may be inadvertently making things worse for themselves and their adolescent children.

The Need for Significant Change

Feeding the Mouth That Bites You isn't a parenting book in the contemporary sense of the word. I don't have techniques that will guarantee a certain outcome—no one does. The cultural confusion that has created many of the problems we have with adolescents has also placed an unrealistic, overwhelming burden on parents. If we think of adolescents as big, argumentative children, then a parent's job has now become at least five years longer than before, with the added bonus that these final parenting years are often the most turbulent of all.

This is the problem: We live in a culture that has no universally accepted means of transitioning children into adulthood. This never-ending childhood has spawned an entire industry of parenting material that exaggerates a parent's capacity to influence their children, especially during adolescence.

Robert Epstein explains, "*For the first time in human history, we have artificially extended childhood well past puberty.* Simply stated, we are not letting our young people grow up."[4] What's worse is that we have no memory of having gone through such a transition in our lives, and our parents don't either. We have lost the ability to differentiate adolescence from childhood and adulthood from adolescence.

As a culture, we started seeing and identifying the teenage years as a separate season when it started giving us problems. Adolescence became a stormy period when we changed how we treated this age group in our families and communities. Our society stopped giving these young people what they needed. For the most part, we've even forgotten what adolescents need most. We've become like people who have cut off the oxygen from our teenagers' air hoses and then stand around wondering, *Why do they flail around like that?*

At the same time, parents are feeling the increasing burden of parenting that seems to prescribe a continual task of making their children happy and successful, no matter their age. This confusion has led to too many unhappy young adults living with guilt-ridden, frightened parents.

This book offers a rational approach to correcting this confusion. You're probably doing a better job as a parent than you think, and your teenagers aren't bad kids. Rather, they're young adults who may choose to behave in ways that you taught them not to. Even teenagers know their bad behavior isn't your fault.

I have sat in my office many times with parents and their teenager who has been kicked out of school or something for bad behavior. The mother may be tearfully telling me, "We feel this is mostly our fault for not providing what he needed to make better choices!"

That's where I usually stop and ask the kid, "Do you agree that this is mostly your parents' fault?" It's a safe question because adolescents always say the same thing.

"No. It's my fault!"

"I agree with him," I usually say. "This is his fault, not yours."

Parents who blame themselves for the poor choices of their young-adult children overburden themselves and indirectly disrespect their teenage children. When teenagers *do* blame their parents for their bad behavior, it's usually just to goad their guilt-ridden parents.

As I've said, Planned Emancipation is not a guaranteed method for getting your teen to act a certain way. This approach attempts to correct a cultural anomaly that has burdened parents and frustrated our adolescent children for decades.

Although I hope the purpose and effectiveness of this approach will make sense to you, it won't necessarily make sense to everyone around you. Parents who start implementing the plan often encounter confusion and even criticism from well-meaning family, friends, and other counseling professionals. Just remember, you're not the only one who is confused. We've been muddleheaded about this stuff for more than a hundred years.

The first step in correcting this cultural confusion is to understand what adolescents need. Our culture continues to fluctuate in how we define ourselves and relate to each other, but the developmental needs that accompany puberty remain relatively predictable. Understanding these needs can go a long way in understanding stormy teenage behavior.

CHAPTER 4

What Adolescents Need and Why They Act This Way

You know your children are growing up when they stop asking you
where they came from and refuse to tell you where they're going.

P. J. O'ROURKE

"They're always telling me what to do, Dr. Wilgus, like I'm still a kid. And they always want to know where I'm going, who I'm going there with, and when I'll be back."

Hannah was sixteen and capable of that unique sixteen-year-old glare—a mix of anger, bitterness, frustration, and confusion. She'd yelled at her parents the night before, venting her feelings, but she didn't believe they'd heard her. Hannah was generally well-behaved, but I surmised that if something didn't change, she might not stay that way.

"Why does it bother you so much that they want to know where you're going? You usually go where you say you're going, right?" I asked.

"I do, but that's not the point." She splayed her arms out in a gesture of helplessness. "Why do they have to know? Shouldn't it be enough that *I* know where I'm going? Shouldn't they trust me just a little bit more now that I'm older?"

"So, it's not that you're doing secret stuff. It sounds more like you don't like that your parents don't trust your judgment to handle these things yourself."

Hannah let out an immense sigh. "Yes! Exactly. I feel like I've spent all these years being a good girl, and for what? I mean, sometimes I think I might as well have done drugs or something. Not that I want to do drugs—but look what being responsible has gotten me! They treat me like a prisoner."

Hannah's story is the same as that of almost all the teenagers I've worked with. Her words reveal an inner struggle that most teenagers can't quite voice. Even though it's what they're trying to talk about all the time, teenagers are often frustrated with being unable to explain what they need. When this gap between their words and needs gets too wide, they shut down communication altogether.

Hannah's mother would ask, "If you're not doing anything wrong, why do you need to hide where you're going and who you're with from your parents?"

Like most adolescents, Hannah struggled to explain the difference between her need for autonomy and her growing desire to be sneaky. She would shut down and practice her eye-rolling and sighing—which she was getting good at, as I recall. Sadly, Hannah's mother thought she'd made a good point to her daughter.

It's funny how often parents come to my office and quote their own elaborate, rational speeches they've given to their teenagers. The passionate way they recount these diatribes displays how much these parents want to get their message across to *somebody*. When they finish, I usually ask, "So how did he answer?" Then comes the truth.

They always answer with something along these lines: "Well, he didn't say anything, but you could tell he knew I was right." Unfortunately, parents often interpret silence from their teenagers as a sign they're getting through to them. But Hannah's eye-rolling and sighing revealed something different: She felt a huge, rational need that wasn't going away, but she didn't know how to express it to her parents. The problem wasn't that Hannah's mother wasn't getting through to Hannah. The problem was that Hannah wasn't getting through to her mother.

Individuation: What Adolescents Really Need

"Everything goes fine in our house until we say no," frustrated parents often tell me. With teenagers who don't know how to articulate what they need, parents are left to guess their needs from their behaviors, and most of the time, they seem to want only to be left alone and do what they want (probably something bad or dangerous, in their parents' minds). And yet many times, saying yes to some requests doesn't seem to help either.

Have you ever said yes to something your teenager asked for that was against your better judgment because you felt worn down?

"Okay, fine. If this is such a big deal, I'll let you go, but just this once!"

You sit there feeling like a bad parent as your adolescent happily goes off to that movie you didn't think she should see or spends the night with that one friend who makes you uneasy. You think, *Well, at least she'll be a little happier with me for a while.* But is she?

Only two days later, she asks to get a ride home with a friend, even though your rule is no riding with first-year drivers. "Oh, come on!" she snaps, and then you pull your "Get out of jail free" card and say, "Hey, I let you see that movie, didn't I? I think you should give me a little slack here."

Pop quiz: Does she calm down and give you the appreciation you deserve for having given in before? Answer: No! (You knew that, right?) Even when parents give in to what their teenagers want, it doesn't seem to help. That's why it's important to know what teenagers are asking for.

Although adolescent demands and disagreements seem to center on where they're allowed to go, when they must be home, or whether they have to do homework, their frustrations betray something deeper that's motivating these battles. If you could listen in on my therapy sessions with teenagers, you'd see the energy and interest released when they hear their real needs articulated.

In my conversation with Hannah, did you notice the key word I used that caused her to light up? *Judgment.* Hannah wasn't trying to keep her parents from knowing the evil deeds she was planning, and she didn't feel better when they gave in. She wanted to know when her parents would realize she was ready to *use her own judgment* in deciding where to go and whom to go with.

What Hannah needed was the answer to the question her adolescent heart was constantly asking: *When will I be fully an adult, and how will I know that I've gotten there?* Her need to find the answer to that question is called *individuation.* Individuation is a teenager's primary need.

I cannot emphasize this enough: The need for individuation is essential to all adolescents; it is not equal to other needs teenagers have. All the other things they need—success in school, social connections, athletic achievement, spiritual growth, and so on—can and will be sacrificed by adolescents if they don't sense that they're on a clear path toward adulthood.

I've seen star athletes give up the sport they love because pressure from well-meaning parents interfered with their need to feel that it was *their own* sport. I've lost count of the number of teenage girls who seemed to automatically gravitate to dating the very boys their parents warned them about just to *feel ownership* of their dating choices. When alone with me in my office, teenagers will express sincere concern about their poor grades, but they will lie and vigorously battle any of their parents' attempts to help because they can't stand being treated like a child. Numerous studies have shown that, when asked confidentially, teenagers admit that the primary reason they're drawn to drink alcohol and smoke is to *feel grown-up.*

> Knowing how to meet your teenager's need for individuation is the key to effective parenting during his or her adolescent years.

Let that statement sink in for a moment.

Knowing how to meet your teenager's need for individuation is the key to effective parenting during his or her adolescent years.

What Is Individuation?

Individuation equals autonomy plus attachment.

It's important to note that an adolescent declaring herself to be an adult is not individuation. Although teenagers desire autonomy (self-rule), they need those who know them best (parents) to reassure them that they're ready to use their own judgment. In other words, teenagers want the freedom to make their own choices, but they want that freedom to be given by their parents or guardians. They want to be separate, but they're still emotionally connected and need reassurance.

Why do you think your adolescent gets so defensive about issues you bring up with her? Because she cares what you think about her.

She probably cares more about what *you* think than what her friends think. For example, have you ever casually told your daughter to grab a sweater before going out on a cold day only to hear "Oh, come on, Mom! I know I need a sweater"? Although you may have meant it as innocently as possible, her adolescent ears translated your suggestion into criticism: "You're not old enough to know if you need a sweater, so let me as your parent remind you, my child, to get a sweater."

Individuation requires both autonomy and attachment. Without attachment, autonomy is meaningless. As I've said before, parents tend to think their teenagers want to be left alone to do whatever they want. These parents haven't seen what I've seen. I've seen adolescents who had almost complete autonomy at a young age but not given to them by involved parents.

I specifically recall a group counseling session at an adolescent day hospital. The teens were complaining that their parents always hounded them or wouldn't let them do this or that. One chronically depressed fourteen-year-old girl, who rarely spoke, peeked out from behind her dark bangs and shut down everyone's complaining. She said, "I have everything most of you want. I wish someone would ask me what I was doing or where I was going. I'd love to be asked about my day when I get home. I just wish someone would *be* there when I get home." Talk about heartbreaking.

She was between households, and her parents were overwhelmed by almost everything else aside from their daughter's life. She was given enough money to live on, but that was the only support she received from them. She had the total freedom adolescents crave, but it came from a place of neglect, not from a place of affection and respect.

In other words, she was forced to become an adult without the blessing or leading of those whom she most wanted to love her. This is a sad reality for many adolescents today, but her plight serves as an insightful illustration. For adult-level individuation to be achieved, autonomy is best granted to an adolescent by a loving, involved parent or guardian.

"When Will I Be an Adult?"

It's a reasonable question for adolescents to ask. By the age of thirteen, numerous changes are well underway inside every teenager. These changes come on like a confusing whirlwind that signals one thing: Childhood is over.

Physical Changes

At the age of twelve or so, adolescents' bodies start to look more and more like adults' and less like children's. Even if your teen isn't developing so quickly, her friends are, and trust me, all the kids notice it.

The early stages of adolescent physical development are particularly awkward. A boy's voice deepens, signifying that other parts of his anatomy have likewise dropped. A girl develops breasts and endures her first, often embarrassing, menstrual period. These are inescapable mile markers on the journey to adulthood. Dozens of other physical changes accompany the transition, too, such as hair in strange new places and faces riddled with acne.

Let me put it this way: How often do you show your seventh-grade class photo to your friends today?

Young adolescents look like old children who've been overtaken by some force that's transitioning them into something else. Their appearance is awkward precisely because they look like a weird mix of childhood and adulthood. The only hope we can give younger teenagers for this appearance-altering disease is "Don't worry. You'll grow up," which means *Your body is becoming adult.* It's only natural that on some level they begin to ask, "When will I be an adult?"

But physical changes aren't the only thing driving a teenager's need for individuation.

Cognitive Changes

In addition to dealing with their new (and sometimes undesired) physical changes, adolescents must also navigate the new mental territory of *formal operational* thinking. This scientific terminology describes their cognitive development from a child to an adult-in-training. As a child, they use *concrete operational* thought patterns. As the phrase says, they see and interact with the world as it is, in concrete, literal ways.

But after puberty strikes, they become capable of abstract thought and begin to question the whys of the world around them. No longer does your daughter ask, "Why is the sky blue?" Now she asks, "Why does my older sister get to stay out later than I do?"

For example, a five-year-old can learn not to take a cookie that doesn't belong to him because his parents said so and because he knows he might get in trouble. However, a thirteen-year-old learns not to take a cookie because he or she understands what would happen if *everyone* took things that didn't belong to them. This is also why *Because I said so* doesn't work with your teenagers. It may be an appropriate answer for a child, but it's an inadequate answer once formal operational thought develops.

This cognitive change also helps explain why many adolescents suddenly become lawyer-level debaters, especially regarding issues they're passionate about, like social media apps, school, and their friends. They will defend their choices to the death—not because they're trying to be rebellious but because they're now capable of abstract reasoning. They're flexing their mental muscles and trying to make sense of their world while discovering their identity. Sure, some of their persistent arguing may reveal a bit of rebelliousness, but you should also remember that they are reasoning in a new way.

To make matters more confusing, both for adolescents and parents, there's yet another layer of change all teenagers must face.

Social Changes

First their bodies seem to be turning against them; then their minds start expanding at such a rapid rate that it's no wonder they may sometimes seem like deer caught in headlights. The ups and downs of their emotions further complicate their daily lives.

But those significant changes wreak havoc in one area that is foundational to *all* of us: identity. Adults-in-training don't know who they are yet. They try on identities like they do clothes. (As you probably well know, what they wear can often be an expression of their identity.)

For now, you need to know that the word *identity* is derived from the word *identical*. Teenagers' internal sense of themselves fluctuates widely. Abstract thought leads to a painful awareness of how teenagers believe they're seen by others. With such intense internal analysis, adolescents naturally become increasingly self-conscious. They worry about being scrutinized and often complain they're being judged unfairly. This behavior reflects the powerful judgments they are now able to make about themselves.

Consequently, identity and social behavior are inextricably linked. The struggle for a stable sense of identity strongly affects adolescent social behavior. Our culture does not offer much opportunity for teenagers to be identified with adult groups. As a result, adolescents' relationships with other teenagers become *extremely* important.

You've likely witnessed this in your teenager or his friends. The people in his peer group probably wear the same clothing, like the same music, and hang out at the same places. You may have also noticed a wholesale identity exchange, where your son or daughter suddenly has all new friends, wants different clothes, and starts listening to different music.

To put it simply, she's trying to fit in. If you recall your adolescent days, no doubt there are dozens of examples where you trod a similar path to what she's currently walking. Even if you worked hard at not fitting in, you were still looking to fit in with those who didn't want to fit in.

When your teen pulls away from spending time with the family in favor of spending time with his friends, this isn't necessarily a reflection of a lack of gratitude or appreciation. His need for social growth is an inevitable part of his development. While you don't have to celebrate such a cutting of the apron strings, you should recognize that his identity seeking and exploration of new social circles is proof of his transition into adulthood.

This is where recent cultural changes become important. I was cautioning parents about the growing amount of social isolation in the lives of teenagers long before the COVID-19 pandemic. If there's anything worse than a surly teenager who resists being treated like a kid and only wants to be with her friends, it's a teenager who *doesn't* resist being patronized by parents because they're her only social connection. I'll say more about this later. For now, an adolescent who avoids social groups because she's in her room staring at electronic devices is in greater danger of developmental stagnation than those struggling through social transition.

> Even if you worked hard at not fitting in, you were still looking to fit in with those who didn't want to fit in.

With so many physical, cognitive, and social changes marching them toward adulthood, it should come as no surprise that adolescents want to know, *When will I fully be an adult?*

A Rite of Passage

As noted before, our culture is woefully inept at helping adolescents answer that question. Broadly speaking, we do not have common rites of passage to mark this transition. The ones we used in the past seem to have less meaning than they once did.

When I was a teenager, my friends and I were beyond excited to get our driver's licenses. Not only would those small pieces of plastic give us a license to drive, but they would also give us a license to *freedom*. Even more so, it was our ID for adulthood, proof that we'd (mostly) graduated from at least early adolescence.

Today's teenagers often put off getting driver's licenses. They do this because they're too busy with school and extracurricular activities; or because they know that getting a license means they'll become chauffeurs for younger siblings. Some parents seem relieved by this (it's one less thing to worry about). As an adolescent psychologist, however, it worries me. It's a sign that an increasing number of adolescents aren't even pushing for autonomy.

Some may point to high school graduation as another agreed-upon rite of passage for today's adolescents. But even there, thousands of graduated seniors walk off the podium and directly into their parents' basements, where they remain for the next year, or three, or ten. Are they adults? They may have become adults in the eyes of society, but they lack the inner motivation to leave home, get a job, and, well . . . grow up.

Without a cultural road map to mark a path to adulthood, today's adolescents are more like vagabonds than rebels. Their souls may have moved out of their parents' camp, but they don't seem too interested in setting up camp for themselves. Physical maturation and cognitive development may have given them enough determination to overcome much of their parents' ability to control them, but for some, it wasn't enough to push them to set up their own independent lives.

What's needed is a radical approach to parenting adolescents, one that corrects our current confusion and provides a meaningful answer to the question *When will my parents say I'm fully an adult?*

I call this approach Planned Emancipation.

PART TWO

Planned Emancipation

How to Make an Essential Cultural
Correction in Your Home

CHAPTER 5

Understanding Planned Emancipation

Parents can only give good advice or put them on the right paths, but the final forming of a person's character lies in their own hands.

ANNE FRANK

Let's rethink how to parent adolescents. As explained in previous chapters, many parents have taken on a parenting role that doesn't tell them when the job is done. Consequently, adolescent children push back against what they perceive as constant patronizing and disrespect from well-meaning parents. Planned Emancipation clarifies the endpoint of parenting and outlines a clear and orderly transition from parents' authority to their young adult's authority.

I want to emphasize that this transition is not a technique, it's a reality of life that happens whether parents or their children recognize it. The only thing parents can control is how the transition is made.

Take a minute and answer this question:

When will you consider your adolescent to be an adult? That is, when will you say he or she deserves all the rights and privileges of an adult, just like you?

Did you think about it? Do you have your answer? Let me congratulate you for having spent some time thinking about it! Your adolescent needs an answer to this question, and yet, as discussed earlier, we live in a time where parents rarely ponder it.

When I ask this in parenting seminars, I invariably receive three general responses:

1. The age response: "When my teenager is eighteen [or twenty-one], I'll know he's an adult."
2. The under-my-roof response: "As long as she lives under my roof, she's not an adult."
3. The know-it-when-I-see-it response: "When he starts acting like an adult, I'll treat him like an adult."

How did you answer? Are you surprised we don't all have the same answer? Of course not, because you read chapter 1.

Let's consider the first answer. If you based your adolescent's entrance into adulthood entirely on his age, what age would that be and how did you arrive at that age? Most of the time, parents choose an age that complies with the legal system. But when does your state say someone is legally an adult?

For instance, consider these legal milestones in the state of Texas, where I live:

- At sixteen, a teenager can drive, just like an adult.
- At seventeen, a teenager can leave home without her parents' consent, just like an adult. (I know, right? But that's true here.)
- At eighteen, a teenager can vote, just like an adult.
- At twenty-one, an extended adolescent can drink, just like an adult.

While these laws certainly serve their purposes, they're terrible at answering the question of when your adolescent becomes an adult.

The next two answers are more common, but they're also more

problematic than you might think. Both answers depend on your adolescent telling you when it's time for him to be granted adulthood. In other words, your recognition of his adulthood depends on his displaying certain behaviors. It's like that scene from the old *Kung Fu* TV show when the Shaolin monk holds out a pebble in the palm of his hand and announces, "When you can take the pebble from my hand, it will be time for you to leave."[1]

For example, if you answered in the "under my roof" group, what if your son or daughter has no desire to get out from under your roof? For those who answered in the "I'll know it when I see it" category, do you know someone in her twenties, thirties, or even older who still doesn't display the critical adult characteristics you're looking for? What happens if your *Kung Fu* kid never gets fast enough to snatch the pebble? What if she's not trying?

So if legal standards are confusing, we can't make financial independence a marker, and we can't just wait for our teenagers to show us responsible adult behavior, how do we clearly show them when they're adults?

The answer is what I call Planned Emancipation, a rational approach to answering our teenagers' need for individuation. Planned Emancipation allows you to take control of your adolescent's inevitable drive toward adulthood and provides a reasonable progression of autonomy that eventually ends in confidently giving your teenager the message: "You are now an adult in our eyes." Planned Emancipation allows the teenager in your house to know he or she has grown up and not just gotten away.

The Diplomatic Relations of Planned Emancipation

Believe it or not, rational and effective parenting of teenagers is a lot like negotiating foreign policy. I know that may sound weird, but I've thought about it a lot, and it's a good way to understand the goal of Planned Emancipation. Consider the following conversation from the movie *Gandhi* (emphasis mine):

Mahatma Gandhi, leader of India's independence movement, speaking to a British official: "We think it is time you recognized that *you are masters in someone else's home.* Despite the best intentions of the best of you, you must, in the nature of things, humiliate us to control us. . . . *It is time you left.*"

British official: "With respect, Mr. Gandhi, without British administration, this country would be reduced to chaos."

Gandhi: ". . . I beg you to accept that there is no people on earth who would not prefer *their own bad government to the good government of an alien power.*"

[. . .]

British official: ". . . You don't think we're just going to walk out of India?"

Gandhi: "Yes. In the end, you will walk out. Because *100,000 Englishmen simply cannot control 350 million Indians if those Indians refuse to cooperate.*"[2]

Do you hear something hauntingly familiar in that scene? (Okay, I probably think about this stuff a little too much.) In the 1982 movie *Gandhi*, there's this great scene where a little man in a wrapped white cloth sits across a huge table from all the representatives of England's power over India, and he's calmly telling them, "It's time you left."

I think of this scene often when talking to adolescents and their parents. The story of England's departure from India in 1947 can give you essential insight into maintaining a close and influential relationship with your teenager. The only bad news is that in your family's story, the hero (the guy in the white dhoti and shawl in the movie) isn't you . . . it's your teenager!

India had been a British colony for *three hundred years.* In 1946, Mahatma Gandhi and other Indian leaders made their request clear: "We must be free from British rule." The British viceroy of India at the time couldn't handle the mounting pressure of a likely revolution. He was replaced by Lord Louis Mountbatten, who quickly took control of a dangerously unruly situation. Understanding how he did this is key to effectively managing your teenager. Lord Mountbatten took control *by relinquishing control in an orderly fashion.*

As soon as Mountbatten stepped off the airplane in India (before he'd even left the runway), he announced that he had come to serve as the last viceroy of India. Although occupying the same hated position of authority held by his predecessor, Mountbatten and his stated goal (as far as Indian leaders believed him) changed everything. He was still in charge, but he was in India to oversee an orderly transition from British rule to Indian self-rule.

Mountbatten's approach is a perfect example of effective adolescent parenting.

Like Mountbatten, parents need to announce to their teenagers that they are still in charge, but not for long. Parents need to demonstrate a commitment to an orderly transfer of authority from themselves to their adolescents. This is the only way to allow adolescents the necessary time to clarify their priorities and prepare to deal with weaknesses they see within themselves.

> Parents need to demonstrate a commitment to an orderly transfer of authority from themselves to their adolescents.

This kind of parenting means sometimes giving bad news, such as having to say, "Sorry, you still have to do this my way now, but soon it will be your decision. Have you thought about how you'll handle this then?" However, the real missing piece is that good adolescent parenting must also include providing some clear good news: "That's up to you now. You know what I think, but now you should do what you think is right."

Did you get that? I am *not* talking about letting your teenagers do whatever they want. Parents who focus too much on controlling their kids often set up this sort of false dichotomy.

Effectively parenting adolescents means setting a middle course between holding on until your teenager wrestles control out of your cold dead hands, or handing over your car, house, and credit cards to let him go wild.

Here's the other important point. Effective parenting of teenagers also means addressing the question *Who's in charge of this?* up front rather than shying away from it.

How does this reverse revolution work? By withdrawing your troops one state at a time.

Withdrawing Your Troops

It's important that you understand the overall strategy and goals of this handover of power before proceeding to the mechanics of Planned Emancipation. Parents who understand this have reported immediate calming of tensions with their adolescents. Parents who *don't* grasp or get behind the overall goal of Planned Emancipation may follow some of the steps outlined in the chapters to follow, but their teenager can feel his or her parents' reluctance.

Autonomy is what feeds the biting mouth of teenagers. An adolescent who is offered freedoms from reluctant or resentful parents doesn't feel like he or she is being fed at all.

The pictures that follow may help you get an idea of what the overall goal of Planned Emancipation looks like.

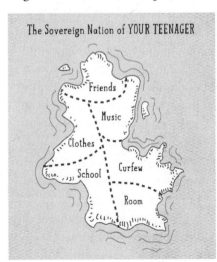

Image 1

Start by thinking of your teenager as a sovereign nation—the Sovereign Nation of [your teenager's name]. (Lord knows that's how your teenager sees herself!) Image 1 illustrates your adolescent as a country divided into territories. These territories represent discrete areas of choice that need to be managed in an adolescent's life.

In this example, the adolescent's life choices are divided into territories—friends that are okay

33

for this teenager to have, music that's good for this teenager to listen to, and so on. As we shall see, our map is far from complete. You can probably think of many other territories that need to be considered. Each territory can be viewed as either under your authority or under your teenager's authority. As we've learned, adolescents are keenly aware of who seems to be in charge of these choices—just like a nation seeking independence.

Now color in the territories that you retain authority over. Remember that autonomy has nothing to do with how generous you are with limits. A teenager's real issue is not "Can I wear this to school?" or "Can I make a D in English?" She's concerned with the issue of *who decides* what clothes she wears or *who decides* how she handles school. Trying to appease her by arguing that you mostly leave her alone on these issues is like the viceroy of India trying to tell Gandhi, "Our troops are nice and don't shoot much." Teenagers are frustrated by the fact that they do not have autonomy, not that your occupying troops are mean. Are you starting to see the pattern now?

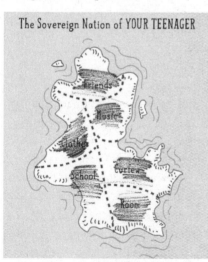

The Sovereign Nation of YOUR TEENAGER

Image 2

Image 2 illustrates the way many teenagers see their lives. This is a teenager who thinks, *My parents control everything!* While this is the way things should be during childhood, it becomes a growing problem for adolescents. Older adolescents who still perceive their lives like this are frustrated and feel as though they're getting nowhere. Remember, it does no good if *you* feel your teen has some control. It's a matter of how your *teenager* perceives it.

There is nothing wrong with maintaining control over large parts of your teenager's life, especially for young teenagers. However, the goal of Planned Emancipation is *to display your willingness* to systematically withdraw your authority from more and more territories as your adolescent gets older. Giving over autonomy in stages allows adolescents time to confront problems they may have in managing these aspects of their lives.

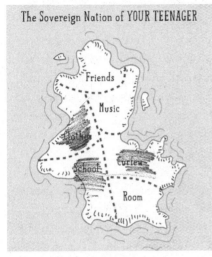

The Sovereign Nation of YOUR TEENAGER

Image 3

Image 3 illustrates a stage in the parent-teenager relationship that is all too rare. There comes a point in mid-adolescence when parents have released control over what music their adolescent listens to, what friends he hangs with, and whether she cleans her room. This teenager will likely still feel some frustration with his parents' monitoring of school grades, clothes, and curfew, but these will be *much* easier to stomach because he has obtained some autonomy. He knows he can look forward to continued independence as he gets older.

Your end goal is for her map to ultimately go back to looking like image 1. In almost every case, the time for reaching this end goal is the end of high school. In other words, your troops should have made a complete withdrawal by then. At that point, your adolescent should have complete freedom of choice when it comes to his room, music, friends, schoolwork, bedtime, clothing, and curfew. For an adolescent to be ready for life after high school, she needs at least some time to exercise her judgment in all aspects of her life while she's still at home with her parents. Otherwise, her first practice at managing these things by herself will come after she's away from you.

> The goal of Planned Emancipation is *to display your willingness to systematically withdraw your authority from more and more territories as your adolescent gets older.*

Now take a breath. If your teenager is still young, this ultimate goal may seem overwhelming. You may even think your current adolescent may never be ready for such full autonomy. That's one of the reasons I advocate for a *progressive* withdrawal that begins with comparatively easier territories like rooms, music, and friends. We'll cover each of these territories in depth in the following chapter.

It's also important to note that giving over control does *not* mean giving up influence! When adolescents know you're leaving a matter to their judgment, they usually become much more communicative and will even seek out your advice. We'll say more about this in chapter 9, on communication.

Freedom Always Comes with Responsibility

Parents are often surprised to find that their teenagers want the freedom to make their own choices, but they also want their parents to pay for those choices. These are phrases I've heard before, and I'm willing to bet you've probably said a version of these yourself:

- "I understand giving my son freedom to choose his music, but he thinks it's fine to charge it on my Amazon account!"
- "Okay, so I stopped nagging her in the mornings, but now we leave so late that she's making her brother late to school, and I'm late to work!"
- "Well, I bit my tongue when I saw what he was wearing to school, and sure enough, I got a call and had to stop what I was doing to bring him a different shirt!"

A teenager's expectation to do what he wants without having to pay for it shouldn't be such a surprise. It isn't a character flaw in adolescents; it's human nature. I'll be honest with you, I like my job, but if my mom and dad started paying for everything I want, I'd probably still come to work—but I might have a little more trouble getting here on time.

So a key principle of Planned Emancipation is that teenagers' increasing freedoms should not be allowed to be a burden on their parents or the rest of the family. For example, letting them choose what music they listen to doesn't mean you have to buy that music or even listen to that same music in the car. After all, it's *your* car. Freedom to get themselves ready in the morning must come with a contingency plan for getting to school after Mom's taxi has already left. An adolescent old enough to decide her own style of dress must be left to suffer the consequences of defying her school's rules about clothing.

Interestingly, most teenagers accept limits for the stated purpose of safeguarding other family members from being inconvenienced much better than they accept limits established for their own good. Teenagers who *don't* understand this distinction might angrily demand that their parents cover for their misjudgments. They may be perfectly happy inconveniencing the rest of the family. In such cases, teens are displaying serious entitlement problems. These adolescents need to be rescued even less, not more, and this should start now, not later.

Releasing your authority in each area requires a perspective shift. You move from seeing your teenager as being accountable to you to seeing him be accountable to other forces in his life. Letting go means you'll be allowing whatever natural consequences may come if he handles things poorly.

If you think about it, we exercise parental authority because we're trying to protect our children from the harsh natural consequences of their poor choices. We don't punish children for running out in the street because we wish to add pain to their lives. The punishment attempts to teach them to avoid the natural consequence of getting run over by a car!

When parents continue to doggedly stand in the gap, always shielding their adolescents from any real consequences long after childhood is over, their teenagers develop a sort of unrealistic distance from experiencing their own lives. I've seen adolescents who are at risk of failing in school sit in my office next to crying, upset parents. The parents desperately ask me, "What are we going to do?" while their teenager sits, gazing around the room in mild boredom. The odd thing is that the only person in the room who's at risk seems to think, *School? Oh yeah, I have people who take care of that for me.*

Now that your teen's childhood is over, it's your job to relinquish the constant responsibility of protecting and teaching your adolescent. You can find creative ways to do this, but it's time to allow your teenager to feel the consequences of his or her actions. When it comes to younger adolescents, give them autonomy in areas of life where the natural consequences are not huge. Keep in mind you have only about five years to give over complete autonomy.

Eventually, you will be giving over autonomy in areas that have serious, natural consequences for your older adolescents. The reality is that this is happening anyway. Some parents console themselves by giving long speeches on the dangers of speeding and other typical teenage temptations. But in the end, an adolescent who drives away from home is already shouldering the responsibility that comes with how he or she chooses to drive.

When choosing areas of autonomy to relinquish, ask yourself, *Can I give this over to my teenager without the likelihood of devastating consequences?* If the answer is yes, give it to her. Remember, the goal is to let go, not fearfully hold on to all the control you have.

Teenagers need to begin experiencing the real risks that their behavior can and will cause. As parents, be aware of the autonomy that your adolescent is naturally gaining. For example, unless you're willing to hire a private detective, you can't tell your teenager, "I don't want you talking to that boy at school." That's not something you have control over. If you can't control something, wrap it up and make an autonomy gift out of it, such as saying, "Of course, at your age, it's up to you whether you talk to him at school."

They know you can't stop them, but they like *knowing that you know* you can't stop them.

Granting Freedom Doesn't Mean Giving Up Influence

I'll expand on this much more in chapter 10, but I need to clarify one important point: Giving freedom in an area of your teenager's life does *not* mean you will no longer influence that area. The effect is just the opposite. Giving over freedom allows for much greater communication between parents and adolescents.

When parents define their influence over their children strictly in terms of their ability to control them, handing over freedom may seem like giving up any chance of influencing their teen. What these parents miss is the significant influence they can have through open communication and advice giving, a skill we'll discuss at length in chapter 10.

> Giving freedom in an area of your teenager's life does *not* mean you will no longer influence that area.

As adolescents get older, they gain further mobility and spend more time on their own. Parents' control naturally diminishes. As we've seen, often a freedom that is granted through Planned Emancipation is a freedom the teenager already has. In such cases, being proactive in acknowledging freedom is the only way to maintain any kind of influence.

Withdrawing your troops displays acceptance of your adolescent's eventual freedom from your control. These freedoms are food for the biting mouth of your teenager. They allow him to grow up in your home, not feel as if he's just escaped.

So how can you feed teenagers freedom without getting bitten too much?

CHAPTER 6

Implementing Planned Emancipation

A hero is someone who understands the responsibility
that comes with his freedom.
BOB DYLAN

When parents begin implementing Planned Emancipation, amazing things happen. Take a look at what I've heard from parents about their teens:

- "When we first started reading the list, he stopped us and said, 'Wait, these are things I don't have to do?'"
- "She just sat there silent for a long time. We asked if she had any questions, and she just said, 'Uh, no . . . that'd be great!'"
- "He asked us if this was a trick!"

Since adolescents get so used to fighting their parents for autonomy, it's often a shock when they first hear Mom and Dad freely giving it to them. They're like emaciated animals, cautiously sniffing the food being handed to them, warily eyeing the hand that feeds them.

Implementing Planned Emancipation is the fun part for parents. Seeing a surly, know-it-all teenager in stunned silence is always amusing to watch.

By the end of this book, you will have created two lists: a Freedoms list and an Expectations and Consequences list. We're about to dive headlong into the Freedoms list, and we'll discuss the Expectations and Consequences list in chapter 12.

You must think through the Freedoms list *before* you worry about the Expectations and Consequences list. As your adolescent ages, the Freedoms list should grow while the Expectations and Consequences list shrinks. When giving over these freedoms to your adolescent, keep in mind the international diplomacy metaphor: You're the occupying troops in his sovereign nation, and he wants you out—the sooner the better.

The Freedoms List

The first step in this systematic transfer of authority is to consider the areas of responsibility in your adolescent's life you release. Weigh all the aspects of her life—things she's required to ask your permission for or that you regularly need to remind her about. There are many ways to divide these territories, and I encourage you to be creative about this.

As mentioned in the last chapter, since you're giving over freedom in stages, boundaries must be set for each freedom. Since your adolescent probably lives in your house, it's perfectly reasonable to expect that your teenager's freedom shouldn't burden other members of the family. Boundaries also protect you from having to pay for any poor choices your teenager makes. Adolescents usually accept these boundaries without issue. Being told his music shouldn't keep everyone else awake is much easier to swallow than being told he can't listen to it at all.

This list offers a starting point for giving over freedoms and setting limits, but it is by no means exhaustive:

FREEDOM	BOUNDARIES
Use your own judgment in keeping your room as clean or dirty as you see fit.	• Do your laundry. • No food in your room. • No odors beyond your room.
Use your own judgment in the choice of music you listen to.	• Must guard access by younger siblings. • Use headphones when asked.
Use your own judgment in deciding when to go to bed.	• In your room and quiet by __:__. • All screens off by __:__. • Wake yourself up and be ready on time. • Parents will not help with fatigue-related problems.
Use your own judgment in handling school as long as minimum grades are maintained.	• Privileges may be suspended if grades drop below minimum.
Use your own judgment in style of dress.	• Parents may still limit provocative dress. • Parents won't pay extra for objectionable clothes.
Use your own judgment in where to attend church.	• Parents may still require attendance at a Christian church. • Find your own transportation.
Use your own judgment in choosing friends.	• Certain friends may not be allowed in our home. • Friends are not an excuse for being late, etc.
Use your own judgment in deciding when to come in at night.	• Respect parents' and household's need for sleep.

Carefully look at this list. Do you see its logic? Do some of these examples scare you?

If adolescents desire autonomy, parents can meet this need by giving over pieces of responsibility to their teenagers. As young adults, adolescents can and must learn life lessons through the natural consequences of their choices. Planned Emancipation allows parents to come alongside their teenagers as advisers and supporters, without feeling like constant nags or teachers to deaf ears. The Freedoms list boldly announces to adolescents that their parents are transitioning out and that independence is nigh.

> As young adults, adolescents can and must learn life lessons through the natural consequences of their choices.

Planned Emancipation Example

Let's walk through one example here to show the thinking behind giving over freedoms. There are several more examples with implications in appendix 1. Hopefully, these examples will show you how to hand over freedoms while still holding your teenagers accountable for their choices. But let's look at this one specifically: *Use your own judgment in the choice of music you listen to.*

It may seem like just yesterday your son or daughter was listening to music specifically geared toward children. You didn't have to monitor the music because it was harmless. But then your child became an adolescent. He started talking with other adolescents, and his interest in music changed. Now he listens to a genre of music you don't even know how to describe.

The territory of music within the Sovereign Nation of Your Teenager is a prime battleground where both sides can sit entrenched for years. This often holds especially true for Christian parents who would prefer their adolescents listen exclusively to Christian music. Because it has its own genre, contemporary Christian music offers a viable alternative to what's played on the radio or streamed online. But your adolescents' worldviews are expanding, and they're meeting other teenagers whose tastes in music drastically differ from yours.

One important criterion to consider when deciding which freedoms to give over to your teenager is whether this is something you can effectively control. Freedom to choose music is an important example of giving a freedom that you have little ability to control anyway. With as many ways as adolescents can hear music today, there's no way you can effectively monitor everything they listen to. If you could, it would be your full-time job. I'm not suggesting you shouldn't know what they're listening to; I am suggesting that you reexamine the best way to maximize your influence on your adolescent's music choices.

Since your ability to control music choices is weak, turn the tables and make sure you get full credit by formally acknowledging that you will respect their judgment in this area. Doing this does not decrease your influence over their music choice. It increases your influence through communication and eliminates control battles you cannot win.

When Should I Recognize This Freedom?

If your nine-year-old wants to listen to rap music about killing cops and taking drugs, you should absolutely forbid him from doing so and explain why you made that decision. But if your thirteen-year-old wants to listen to that same kind of music, should you let her?

When you frame the question as whether you should *let her*, you're forgetting the ever-weakening control you have. The question to ask yourself at that point is *Can I give this over to her judgment without major consequences?* If the answer is yes, give over as much as you can.

> Giving over autonomy in music choice isn't just about relinquishing control. . . . It's also an opportunity to increase your ability to honestly talk to your teenagers about their decisions.

Giving over autonomy in music choice isn't just about relinquishing control over audio input. It's also an opportunity to increase your ability to honestly talk to your teenagers about their decisions.

In the chapter on communication, we learn that the most common reason adolescents avoid talking to their parents is their resistance to parental control. Your teenager won't talk to you about the music he likes if he knows you're going to make him delete objectionable songs from his playlist. And if he deletes those songs, he could still stream them from another source, get the music from a friend, or find it on YouTube. Putting your foot down in this area can end up making you look silly.

Giving freedom over music means shifting your efforts to increasing communication. If you've granted your daughter autonomy in music, ask to listen to her favorite playlist. Remind her that nothing you hear will get her into trouble. Show her you're interested in knowing what she likes. Don't be afraid to gag if you don't like it. Your respectful vocal disapproval emphasizes that autonomy doesn't require you to like what she likes. If something you hear disturbs you, ask if it disturbs her. If you can't have this kind of discussion without showing disgust or resentment, don't talk to her about it. Maybe your spouse would be better at this, or a friend or student minister at your church.

What Are the Boundaries of This Freedom?

Since this adult-in-training still lives in your house, this freedom should have reasonable boundaries. Let's take a closer look at the boundaries mentioned on the Freedoms list:

- *Do not allow younger siblings to hear objectionable music.* Your adolescent's choices shouldn't be a burden to you or your household. Most adolescents will understand this. You can say, "I don't care that your brother took your iPhone without asking. You've been given the responsibility to handle this like an adult, and now we will have to [insert appropriate consequence here]." We'll talk more about consequences in chapter 11.
- *Use headphones or turn the music down when asked.* This limit respects her choice while still respecting your house. It's also how adults would respond to each other if one person's music distracted or annoyed another.

Don't get me wrong—violent and obscene music is a problematic issue. But when you release control to gain communication, you may discover a secret avenue toward learning more about your adolescent than you thought possible. Think of it this way: As you withdraw your troops from the territory of musical decisions, you're leaving an emissary behind. You become someone who can meet your teen on their turf to discuss why you would avoid listening to a certain song or a popular singer's album.

I hope this one example of music freedom provides a way for you to think through freedoms for your adolescent. I've included a long list of freedom examples along with relevant implications in appendix 1.

Freedom Is Not Privilege

It's important to think of freedoms as areas of your adolescent's life that you *recognize* as under his control. This is different from letting him make his own choices in each area—that's called *privilege*. Privilege says, "This thing is still under my control, but I'll let you go it alone for a while." Freedom says, "I recognize you are in control of this thing, not me." Do you hear the difference? Your teenager certainly does.

Adolescents will accept privilege, but it doesn't satisfy their desperate need for freedom. I've known parents who thought they were generous with how much they let their adolescents do, only to be surprised by the level of resentment that remained.

If parents say a teenager can choose his music "as long as it's [fill in the blank]," they're granting privilege and forgetting the reality that they have no real control over their teen's choice of music. Freedom is recognized, not given, and it must not be withdrawn just because an adolescent is handling things differently from what his parents would want. Too often, when they don't like their teenager's choices, parents resort to worn-out efforts to control him.

Planned Emancipation Can Set You Both Free

In a culture that has forgotten adolescents aren't children and autonomy is the food they're starving for, this first feeding is often met with cautious optimism. Commonly, teenagers don't believe their parents will follow through with giving them these freedoms. Sometimes they're right. You must follow through with what you say. When the Planned Emancipation is implemented correctly, there's no need to withdraw a freedom once it has been given. Let the natural consequences and boundaries you've set do the work of training your teenager.

The Planned Emancipation process begins when you sit down with your adolescent and give her the first list of freedoms. It's a *first* list because you will need to add freedoms about every six months, or at least every year until adolescence is finished, which (for most teens) should be at the end of high school. If you think of an area of freedom your teenager has functionally gained but you forgot to place on the list, put it there. Don't miss a chance to get full credit!

The freedoms discussed in this chapter are suggestions, although they do represent the issues I hear from parents and teenagers in my office. My goal is not to provide an encyclopedia but to give guidelines for you to be able to list the freedoms that make sense to you. Feel free to be creative in finding your ways to feed the mouth that bites you.

> When the Planned Emancipation is implemented correctly, there's no need to withdraw a freedom once it has been given.

Though I've covered common freedoms at length in appendix 1 and beyond, I encourage you to set other freedoms (and boundaries) that you feel are appropriate for your teen. Read over the following list of suggestions:

- Thirteen-year-olds and older may see any PG-13 movie they choose.
- Seventeen-year-olds and older may see any R-rated movie they choose.
- Adolescents may opt out of family night or some family nights. (This freedom is made even more effective when you firmly deny any younger siblings this same choice. The little ones won't like it, but they'll remember when they get older.)
- Adolescents may/must get a job. (This is usually accompanied by cutting off any allowance and is more constructive than trying to make a teenager get a job.)

You can make your family's list in any form you wish. However, I recommend that you keep it short, like the freedoms and boundaries table earlier in this chapter. Adolescents' eyes tend to glaze over if you start with a long preamble introducing freedoms, and then conclude with yet another grand speech.

Since you're progressively withdrawing, your teenager will still not have total freedom—and I'm sure he'll remind you of that fact as you relinquish more freedoms. "You're letting me choose my music. Why can't I choose my clothes yet?" That's why the Freedoms list is accompanied by the Expectations and Consequences list, which we'll discuss in depth in chapters 11 and 12.

CHAPTER 7

The Endpoint of Planned Emancipation

*We cannot always build the future for our youth,
but we can build our youth for the future.*
FRANKLIN D. ROOSEVELT

When does parenting end? In 2018, a New York Supreme Court judge sided with Mark and Christina Rotondo in a lawsuit filed against their son Michael to force him to move out of their home. He had lived with them for eight years after losing his job, and he did not appear to be looking for another one. Michael paid no rent and did not contribute to household maintenance. Michael was thirty years old. He called the judge's ruling ridiculous.

Public reaction to this failure-to-launch story was uniformly outraged. For me, this story was simply an extreme example of a true, logical problem for parents and their adult kids. When are a child's problems no longer his parents' problems? When is it appropriate to say to your child, "That's your problem now, not mine"?

The Rotondos (like many of us) didn't know the answer to that question, and neither did their son. Even the parents' eviction notice came with $1,100 cash and a list of parental advice that ended by saying, "If you want help finding a place your Mother has offered to help you."[1]

Ironically, much of their son's pushback came from his contention that he needed to stay for the sake of *his own son*, with whom he had recently lost visitation rights.

When the value of "parents should always help their kids" takes the constant moral high ground, it becomes difficult to find teenagers who see themselves as independent adults who should be held responsible for their own choices.

For Planned Emancipation to be effective, you *must* think seriously about the endpoint of your parenting job. Now, before you get upset and start repeating your favorite platitudes, such as "Once a parent, always a parent," I'm *not* saying parents eventually stop being parents in their children's lives. I'm talking about the time when you no longer *force* your parenting on unwilling children. I want you to feel the relief of a true endpoint to the parenting burden.

> For Planned Emancipation to be effective, you *must* think seriously about the endpoint of your parenting job.

For you to reach this endpoint, you need the confidence of knowing when your children's problems are no longer your obligation. By any community standard, parents have completed their obligation when their child finishes high school.

At that point, you are done. Congratulations! Take a holiday. Your adult child's problems are now her problems. As her parent, you will certainly wish the best for her. You may even be open to helping her, especially if there's a disability of some kind involved, but you must recognize that her life is no longer resting on your shoulders.

Clarifying this finish line isn't just to help parents. It's an essential message for adult children. Parents who continue past this point, blithely instructing, worrying, and making demands exactly as before, are not succeeding in going the extra mile for their children. Instead, they deliver a powerful, sometimes crippling, message that they do not believe their adult children can handle their own lives.

Readers outside the US usually know their equivalent of the high school graduation milestone. In most places, parents provide for their children until the end of some sort of secondary education. In the US, high school graduation is actually more important than turning eighteen years old.

I've heard so many seventeen-year-olds angrily declare, "Once I'm eighteen, you can't tell me what to do!" It's always disappointing when I remind these adolescents that as long as they're living with their parents and relying on their financial support, they don't have the rights they hope for. When parents take in the reality that their child's turning eighteen means they're no longer obligated to support this adult, the power balance returns to normal. "Happy eighteenth birthday. The good news is that we're willing to let you continue living here until you finish high school!" (This could be a fun—if not passive-aggressive, slightly inappropriate—birthday card inscription to give an entitled teenager.)

Implementing Planned Emancipation effectively requires that you put your teenager's graduation date somewhere in your mind in bright, bold font, like one of those countdown timers. You should refer to this point often. Instead of dreading this endpoint, you should embrace it and regularly refer to it. This does not mean you can have no more involvement in your adult child's life post-graduation. Knowing when your job as a parent ends can go a long way toward ensuring your adult kid will welcome your input and help.

The Benevolent Bank

Once your adolescent has reached the endpoint of high school graduation, what does your relationship look like then? A good relationship starts with a realistic assessment of the power dynamics at work. What can you expect from this adult child of yours? What can you demand of this person?

I recommend that you think of yourself as a benevolent bank. In most situations, your real influence will be wielded by the financial resources you are willing to provide. We will discuss more about living with adult children in chapter 34, but for now, it's important to conceptualize this endpoint relationship so you can prepare for what's ahead.

For parents who struggle just to make ends meet, a post–high school relationship is easier to define. Low-income parents don't fret over updating their kid's iPhone to the latest model. Adult children in these homes aren't so demanding and may work to provide money for their younger siblings. Ironically, no one would wish harsh financial circumstances on anyone, but these homes often produce young people who know they are adults and wouldn't conceive of demanding more from their parents.

I once had a young couple referred to me because they were considering marriage and the boy's parents weren't happy about it. The boy and girl were both eighteen or nineteen at the time. I saw the boy first, and it was obvious he didn't want to be there. He slouched and gave one-word answers until we got to the topic of how much he hated his wealthy parents' meddling in his life. He was angry that his parents didn't approve of the marriage because his girlfriend came from a single-parent home and didn't have much money. When the session ended and I asked about payment, he stared blankly. I told him I'd bill his parents. He got in his almost new sports car and drove away.

The next week I saw his girlfriend. Although she was the same age as her boyfriend, she acted about five years older. Before we even started, she asked how much the session would cost. When I told her I thought the boy's parents were paying, she seemed relieved and grateful, even though she hadn't felt his parents treated her particularly well. Since graduating high school, she had worked two jobs to help her mother and younger sister.

The boyfriend was still looking for a job. He'd been fired from delivering pizzas for coming to work late too many times. He complained that his parents were always nagging him about getting a job.

By the end of these sessions, I was more concerned about the imbalance of this mature young woman considering marrying this same-age boy. His parents felt the burden of guiding their son in his dating choices and were constantly battling his resistance. They never noticed that this girlfriend was displaying the kind of responsible choices they wished for their son. I'm sure this girl's mother had just as much love and concern for her daughter's choices as the boy's parents. She simply didn't have the financial leverage to try to dictate her adult daughter's choices. Her daughter felt the weight of her own life, and she was responding admirably.

For parents with financial resources, the lines of responsibility can get blurry. The image of a benevolent bank can help draw those lines. As a bank, you might be willing to invest in your adult child's future. You may consider supporting him, for a time, with things like a place to live, insurance, a phone, transportation, and so on. I say "may consider" because there is no longer any reason for you to feel responsible to pay for these things. If you and your assets disappeared tomorrow, do you think your eighteen-year-old, high school–graduate kid couldn't figure out a way to go on living her life? Your answer reveals a lot about your level of respect for your adult child.

> If you and your assets disappeared tomorrow, do you think your eighteen-year-old, high school-graduate kid couldn't figure out a way to go on living her life?

What a Bank Does

You're a bank. What would that look like? A bank would certainly have a spreadsheet of all expenses it's paying out to support the adult it's investing in. I encourage you to do this and include health insurance, phone, and all monthly expenses. A bank would also clarify what kind of expenditures it would consider underwriting. Think of these examples:

- "We are willing to pay for an accredited college, university, or trade school tuition and living expenses up to [X amount of money]."
- "We will be happy for you to live in our house as long as you're working full-time, going to school full-time, or some combination of the two."
- "We're willing to continue paying for the items on the spreadsheet while you're in school."

You get the idea. There's no reason to express this kind of clarity in a spirit of anger or guilt. Avoid speeches that include the phrase "Now is the time for you to . . ." Banks don't make speeches. When you ask a bank to pay bills you should take care of yourself, the bank respectfully declines without judgment. It's just not their problem. You can see the importance of communicating this future living arrangement change long before your teenager graduates from high school.

What a Bank Doesn't Do

With adult children, support and financial discussions should be about you, not your child. Your son or daughter needs to know where your support stops so they can clearly understand what part is on their shoulders. Banks don't lecture their clients, and they certainly have no reason to lose their temper.

Let's look at specific things banks don't say and alternative options for parents. Banks don't say:

- "If you go off to that college and mess around, we're gonna come get you and drag you back home." It's better to state that you will pay only for passing grades and require repayment for failing grades. Also, what home are you going to drag her back to? It's all yours now, and you are not required to let her live there.
- "It's October, and you still don't have a job. Now turn off that Xbox and go apply for more jobs!" It's better to calmly announce that he must find another place to stay after a specified date.
- "We're not gonna let you [go to College X; pledge that fraternity; go out of state; and so on]." This is only effective if your adult child doesn't realize she can go to college without your support. Her resentment of your overcontrol renders this approach far less effective than if you had offered her these options as advice from one adult to another.

Clarity and real influence can come from parents who are willing and able to offer financial support after high school. However, respectful communication of limits to your support can only come once you accept that you're not required to take care of all your adult child's needs. Communicating clear boundaries around what you will and won't support is essential in giving your child self-respect and helping her take responsibility for her life choices and develop independence.

CHAPTER 8

When Planned Emancipation Doesn't Work

Sometimes I'm left with the distinct feeling that
I am outnumbered by my only child.

COLLEEN FERRARY BADER

Occasionally, parents will complain to me that they tried to implement Planned Emancipation, but it didn't work. Since Planned Emancipation is not a parenting technique, that's a bit like saying, "We didn't like the road bumps, so we threw the map away." Planned Emancipation may not have the desired effect immediately, but you shouldn't give up on the whole thing. In this chapter, we'll review the most common examples of when Planned Emancipation appears to be ineffective and what you can do about it.

What Were You Expecting?

Consider your expectations when you began the process. If "didn't work" means that Planned Emancipation didn't make your teen more successful and happier, please reread chapter 3. I can't emphasize enough: *Planned Emancipation is not a parenting technique that will guarantee a certain outcome for your teenager.* No parenting advice can do that, and I want to encourage you to take the pressure off yourself.

For example, when your fifteen-year-old who is struggling in school argues and undermines your attempts to force help on him, you should recognize his freedom to manage schoolwork himself. I didn't say "let him"; that's privilege. Giving this freedom is waving the white flag and announcing the truth that you *can't* make this young adult accept your help.

Letting go in this area doesn't mean he'll suddenly start making good grades. You back off because your efforts are becoming counterproductive. Your son needs to gain insight into what he needs academically, not improve his skills in fighting with you. You should still give consequences for poor grades, but this is closer to natural consequences (e.g., "I can't make you study, but you're not going to spend time on electronic games if your grades are bad."). By doing this, you also avoid the perception of being patronizing.

When parents implement Planned Emancipation, *the main evidence that it is working is a significant reduction in conflict and a teenager who is less defensive with her parents.* Yet even after implementing Planned Emancipation, there are still times when an adolescent appears unchanged in her tension with her parents. Let's look at some common causes of ineffectiveness.

Problem 1: You Haven't Gone All In with Planned Emancipation

I have had the following conversation countless times:

Me: "So did your parents go over the Freedoms list?"

Teenager: "Oh, that. . . . Yeah, I guess."

Me: "You don't seem very excited about it. Weren't some of those freedoms the very things you wanted them to leave up to you?"

Teenager: "Yeah, but I know they won't do it."

When teenagers tell me they don't believe their parents will follow through with the freedoms given, they are too often correct. Our kids sometimes know us better than we know ourselves.

Planned Emancipation can be scary, but half-hearted efforts are often useless or worse. Many parents who tell me they're implementing *Feeding the Mouth* strategies aren't doing it at all. Implementing Planned Emancipation isn't just adding a few freedoms to the otherwise continuous directing, teaching, and monitoring you've always done. If you continue with the same style of parenting, Planned Emancipation will not make any difference. *Feeding the Mouth* parenting requires that you recenter all aspects of parenting on the reality that your teenager is an adult, not a large child. Effectiveness stems from your teen's trust; he needs to believe you see him in this way.

The Freedoms list should be your starting point in communicating this change, but it's not the whole thing. There can and should be countless other ways to show that you respect your child's status as a young adult and that your time as the controller of his life will be coming to an end. Remember, Planned Emancipation never means you must let your teenager do whatever he wants. In chapter 11, we'll discuss how you can set and enforce limits while still making an orderly withdrawal from controlling your teen's life.

> Celebrate your teenager's young-adultness loudly and often.

When parents give more freedom to their teenager, the adolescent will, almost always, fail to manage her freedom well in some way. Parents who rush in and take control again have forgotten why they let go in the first place. They started this process because their young adult needed to master these things herself, and because their efforts to control her weren't working.

Once you've given freedoms to your teen, do not retake control when you don't like the outcome. Let your teenager suffer consequences without your protection. (We'll discuss what to do in some tough situations in part 5.)

Let me be blunt here: If you're not sure about this whole Planned Emancipation thing, don't do it. There are other methods of parenting adolescents that don't place so much emphasis on clarifying freedoms.

It's better that you don't try Planned Emancipation at all rather than give it a try and then take it all back when you're afraid.

If you're all in, however, make a party out of it. Celebrate your teenager's young-adultness loudly and often. In doing so, you are increasing your influence and connection with him. But a message that communicates to him you are only *trying out* this treating-him-as-an-adult thing will backfire spectacularly.

Problem 2: You're Not Getting Full Credit for Planned Emancipation

When parents have implemented Planned Emancipation, but their teenager remains as sullen and defensive as ever, this sometimes signals that these parents aren't getting full credit for the freedoms they have given over. Getting full credit means that the message of increasing freedoms being handed over has been received. Parents can help make this happen by emphasizing the shift that has occurred in how they view their teenager. The teen needs to understand that his parents now consider him an adult.

It may feel awkward to make some big ceremony out of a Freedoms list. Your teenager may just stare at the list and not know what to say. But it's still important that you communicate that these freedoms are not just you being nicer. I strongly recommend the language that I use in the Freedoms list. There's a big difference between the message "You can keep your room dirty if you want" and "Use your own judgment in how you choose to keep your room."

Not getting full credit can also happen when parents have implemented Planned Emancipation during a crisis in the adolescent's life. What if your teenager is caught smoking marijuana right after receiving a Freedoms list? The message of "You're an adult now" can be dulled significantly during a lengthy grounding. Restating the freedoms is usually necessary. (See chapter 22 for more on dealing with alcohol and other intoxicants.)

"I haven't seen Omar lately. Are you guys still friends?"
"Yes, Mom! I've just been busy lately!"

"Okay, 'Mr. Touchy,' I've already told you that who you choose to be friends with is up to you now. I was just asking. Remember the Freedoms list?"

At this point, you'll want to listen carefully to his response. If he backs off, that's good. But he may tell you why he doesn't perceive he has the freedoms you've given him. You can't expect the Freedoms list to be effective if your teenager doesn't believe he has those freedoms.

Problem 3: You're Giving Adult Freedoms but Communicating As If Your Teen Is Still a Child

One of the more subtle reasons Planned Emancipation may not reduce tension is that the parents continue to use language patterns they've used since their teenager was a small child. I've seen this often. This can be some parents' way of coping with the fear of having a full-blown young adult in their house. Sometimes it's just an attempt to stay connected.

This is also something you can discover by asking your teenager why she's still defensive. Even if she's not talking, you can probably tell when something is wrong. You may feel you didn't say anything to upset her, but she perceived your words as laced with disrespect. Remember, when your teen says you talk to her like she's a little kid, it doesn't mean she's *right* in some objective way. She's expressing her perception. Certainly, by now you know that any speech of yours that begins with "Listen, we give you plenty of respect around here" is *not* going to end well. It helps to make an effort to *sound as if* you see her as a fellow adult.

Language to avoid:

- "So he's got a little girlfriend now."
- "*We* did fine our sophomore year, but *we* had a little trouble with algebra last year, didn't *we*?"
- "Honey, don't eat that. Sit down and let me make you something decent!"
- "I know it's up to you, but just tell me what your plans are with that history project. Have you started yet?"

These comments are from parents who have committed to the Planned Emancipation process but have a bad habit of speaking in patronizing ways. Often, they can't hear it themselves. Here's how I counsel them in my office:

> Parent: "So he's got a little girlfriend now."
>
> Me: "What? He's dating little girls now?"

Another example:

> Parent: "We did fine our sophomore year, but we had a little trouble with algebra last year, didn't we?"
>
> Me: "You're going to the same high school as your kid?"

You get the idea. (I'm always ready to be helpful.)

Planned Emancipation should lead to a significant increase in your ability to influence your teenager's life. This begins with the most important interaction you'll have with him: communication.

PART THREE

Harnessing the Power of Planned Emancipation

How Respecting Your Teenager
as a Young Adult Increases
Your Effectiveness

CHAPTER 9

The Priority and Problems
in Communication with Teenagers

Don't look at me in that tone of voice.
DOROTHY PARKER

Maintaining good communication with teenagers can be tricky business. Some teens are naturally good communicators, leaving parents feeling confident they have a good sense of what's going on in their lives. But many adolescents seem sullen and withdrawn. See if you can relate to this interaction:

"Hi, sweetie. How was your day?"
"Fine."
"How was your math test?"
"Fine."
"Who was that girl you were talking to when I drove up?"
"Just a girl! Could you stop asking me all these questions?"

Even if your teenager used to be more talkative, you can wake up one day and suddenly realize you've lost the connection you once had. You may find yourself not wanting to put in the effort to reconnect with your surly, uncommunicative teenager, but I assure you it's worth the effort.

I remember when my wife told me my fourteen-year-old daughter was upset by something I had said to her. (My kids tell me I have a habit of being snarky. Can you imagine?) On our next one-on-one outing together, I asked my daughter about it. Before we addressed the thing that hurt her feelings, I asked, "Why didn't you just tell me directly instead of your mom? I want to know anything that makes it hard for you to be direct with me." While it's not easy to hear why your teenager doesn't feel comfortable talking with you, it's better to know the problem than just push through with your ears closed.

Communication Is More Important Than Control

By now, you've learned that you won't always be able to control your adolescent. You should be actively working toward controlling him less and less as he ages. In time, you will have little control over his choices and actions. Monitoring and disciplining your teenager's behavior, no matter how good you are at it, is only going to help until the end of his senior year at best. And even then, your attempts at control won't mean much.

Sometimes a teenager's behavioral problem is a parental communication problem. For instance, if a dad tells his adolescent daughter to be home at a reasonable hour and she returns at two o'clock in the morning, the dad may believe his daughter was acting irresponsibly. But in digging deeper into the issue, the dad might discover that his daughter had quite a different definition of *reasonable*. In that example, she didn't intend to disobey. She just didn't understand because the father failed to clarify *reasonable*. In this case, a specific expectation ("Be home before midnight.") would have served the relationship much better.

I purposefully placed this chapter before the chapter on setting limits because communication is so essential to the health of your parent-adolescent relationship. Parents who fear losing control of their adolescents often fail to realize that a better and longer-lasting avenue of influence can remain open to them for the rest of their lives:

communication. You can place as many or as few limits as you'd like on your teenager, but it's all for naught if your communication avenues aren't open and clear. You may know (or even have) parents who still try to use financial support or guilt to control their children's lives long after they've passed adolescence. At best, these controlling old people seem funny to their adult children. At worst, their children visit them as little as possible. Only through good communication can you hope to remain relevant and have any influence in your children's lives as they pass into adulthood.

> Only through good communication can you hope to remain relevant and have any influence in your children's lives as they pass into adulthood.

As Control Leaves, Communication Moves In

I hope one point is becoming clear to you: Strategically letting go of control does not mean you are giving up on influencing your teenager. We're talking about changing from one type of influence—control—to a much more prolific and useful way of influencing: communication. Once you've granted teenagers autonomy over their lives, you will no longer have direct control, but you will have influence by way of healthy communication.

I've seen wide-eyed parents return to my office after giving over particular territories of autonomy. They say the same things, just in different ways: "He started talking to me about his music. I didn't even have to ask. It was the strangest thing. I still don't care for his music, but at least now I have a better understanding of why he likes it."

Built into Planned Emancipation is the expectation that when an adolescent is given autonomy in a given area, there should be a noticeable increase in his willingness to talk freely about that subject.

For example, when you give over the freedom for your adolescent to choose his friends, this does not mean you can no longer say anything on that subject. On the contrary, now that you're not a cop in that territory, it's time to make the effort to start a dialogue with your teenager. This is particularly true in those areas we've discussed where parents have little ability to control their teenager's behavior, like his choice of music or friends. See this example:

"He canceled on you at the last minute *again*?"

"Mom, I told you. He forgot he had to do some stuff for his dad. He's a good guy."

"Hey, who you're friends with is up to you. I have no idea if he's a good guy or not. Besides, you're way too old to have your mom tell you who's a good guy. I'm just saying if it were me, I think I'd feel a little blown off."

"It does bug me a little."

"Well, I'm sorry it happened again. What about that guy on your soccer team, Carlos? He seems pretty cool."

"Yeah, he's great, but he lives twenty minutes away."

"Wow, that's a long way!"

If you've given over a particular freedom but your adolescent remains defensive or quiet, ask him about it. Remember, it's possible he doesn't believe you won't swoop back in and take control when he chooses a path you don't agree with. Planned Emancipation is not a process of reducing your controlling influence; it's a process of *increasing* your influence through communication.

Your Teenager Wants to Communicate with You

Parents I counsel are sometimes shocked to learn that their reticent teenager desires to talk with them. (I see some of you rolling your eyes and thinking, *Not my kid!*) Teenagers may not be particularly good at talking to their parents. There may be problems in the relationship that discourage them from sharing, but adolescents always desire good communication with their parents.

Most of the time, teenagers tell me the problem is that their parents don't listen to them. This may be true to a degree, but teenagers tend to underestimate their limitations in expressing themselves. Although adolescents are striving for adulthood, their ability to verbally communicate their viewpoints and longings often remains underdeveloped.

This is especially true in early adolescence when their verbal skills rarely keep pace with their strong emotions. Middle schoolers can't articulate what they are feeling: "I'm frustrated and hurt right now by the things you're saying to me, so I'd like to wait and discuss this another time." Instead, they typically opt for the more popular teenage response and spout, "Whatever!" At other times, teenagers may attempt communication but become overwhelmed with emotion. When that happens, their words are usually drowned out by anger or tears.

Lecturing Isn't Communicating

In contrast, I find that parents often overestimate how much their teenagers are listening to them. Let's be honest: Making impassioned speeches to teenagers can feel good. One father confessed to me that although he had tried to control himself after his daughter came in well past curfew, he felt he had to let her have it. Loudly, he lectured his daughter for nearly an hour, outlining the late-night risks of physical harm or sexual assault.

When asked how she responded, he gave a very common answer: "She didn't say anything, but I could tell she was taking it all in." Later, when I asked his daughter about this intense lecture, she barely remembered it. Parents can easily fall prey to the belief that *just one more* lecture is all that's needed to get through to their teenager. I can assure you that when they look like they're not listening, they aren't.

I know I certainly enjoyed some of my speeches when my kids were teenagers.

I once interviewed my own (now adult) kids on my podcast and said, "I advise parents to avoid making speeches. Did I make speeches?"

Without hesitation, they answered, "Yes, you did!"

So, grasping at straws, I asked, "Were the things I said in my speeches helpful?"

My sweet, older daughter looked me in the eye and said, "I don't remember the content of any of your speeches. I just remember that there were speeches."

Ouch! Well said.

Some adolescents won't engage in discussions with their parents because they're afraid they'll just be told they're wrong. What you may think is a friendly discussion may feel like an overwhelming challenge to your teen. Remember that their cognitive abilities are still developing in tandem with their search for an identity. While you should engage with them on important topics, be careful not to go overboard, as seen in this example:

Teenager: "I just think religion is responsible for most of the wars and hatred in the world. Religious people go around thinking they're better than everybody because they have God on their side."

Parent: "Where did you get that? From that left-wing history teacher you keep talking about? If it weren't for religion, we wouldn't have this great country! And what's wrong with saying so if you know that God *is* on your side!"

Teenager: "Never mind!"

Parent: "Why don't you go ask that teacher of yours who he thinks founded this country, atheists?"

Teenager: "Leave me alone!"

Teenagers' cognitive ability to comprehend greater implications is still new to them. Although passionate about their beliefs, they can still feel insecure about them. This leaves them feeling defensive and easily shut down. Parents must be gentle in encouraging their teenagers to discuss their ideas and beliefs, no matter how off base they may sound. Consider the following conversation:

Teenager: "I just think religion is responsible for most of the wars and hatred in the world. Religious people go around thinking they're better than everybody because they have God on their side."

Parent: "I've heard other people say that same thing. Sort of like people just use their absolute beliefs about God to justify their hatred?"

Teenager: "Yeah, something like that. I just think history is full of people who justify killing and violence because God told them to."

Parent: "Well, you're too old for me to just talk you out of that view, especially since a lot of other people agree with you. I just can't say I agree."

Teenager: "What do you mean?"

It may seem strange to put "You have the freedom to choose what you think and believe" on a list of freedoms, but you need to clarify that you understand you *can't control* your teenager's beliefs and opinions. Remember, when you emphasize your powerlessness to change your teenager's mind, you increase your ability to influence him through communication. By announcing your unwillingness to enter a battle over his thoughts (a battle you cannot win), you should enjoy much more and healthier communication on the subject. We'll discuss influencing faith in chapter 28.

How Can I Talk with My Teenager and Persuade Her to Talk to Me?

Even though they want to be able to talk and reach an understanding, adolescents need their parents' help to bridge gaps in communication. To do that, parents first need to pay attention to and correctly diagnose the communication problems that exist. Not all teenagers have the same problems in communicating with their parents. Parents can't simply start applying techniques without knowing the problem.

Careful observation of your interactions with your teenager should suggest what's going on and how best to respond. Although each family is unique, there are commonalities in many communication problems that surface. We're going to dig deeper into some of those problems.

Control Battles: "You Can't Make Me Talk!"

By now, it should come as no surprise that the battle for control is the foundational issue behind most communication breakdowns. See the following example:

> "I got an email from your teacher today, Nathan. Anything you want to tell me?"
>
> ". . ."
>
> "She said your grades are slipping and that you seem unhappy all the time."
>
> "She hates me."
>
> "She doesn't hate you! Mrs. Miller is just concerned, and so am I. It's time for you to tell me what's going on with you and why you seem so unhappy all the time!"
>
> "I'm fine, Mom."
>
> "We'll just see how fine you are when I take away those video games you're always playing!"
>
> "I knew you'd bring up my games!"
>
> "Well, if you won't tell me what's wrong, then maybe that'll give you some time to think about how you trea—"
>
> [Nathan storms away.]
>
> "Don't you walk away from me while I'm talking to you . . . Nathan! Nathan!"

For adolescents who feel little personal control over their lives, the ability to exercise control over how, when, or even *if* communication will occur is a strong temptation. As we discussed in chapter 4, adults-in-training want to know when they'll be old enough to oversee their own decisions. Behind the communication control battle lies one essential thought: *You can't make me listen or talk with you!* Because communicating with you is a choice they control, adolescents will assert that independence quite often.

All attempts at strong-arming them into sharing (e.g., "We're not leaving this room until you tell me what's wrong!") usually result in either greater distancing (e.g., they lie) or the adolescent feeling resentful at having been treated disrespectfully.

> Because communicating with you is a choice they control, adolescents will assert that independence quite often.

As a father, I specifically remember making speeches to my son when he was a teenager. (Knowing this stuff doesn't mean I didn't make mistakes.) I can still see the facial expression he had mastered while silently enduring my erudite speech (at least I thought it was). His face was a stiff mask that seemed to say, *You know that I know that you know that I'm not listening—but you can't prove it!* In the end, his silence won the battle. I couldn't make him listen to me.

A different and particularly painful example of this same struggle for control happened to parents who caught their teenager off guard one night. They pushed their way through a confrontation and reached what they thought was a tender moment of connection with their adolescent. The mother told me that after confronting her son for a long time, "He finally broke down and tearfully told us about feeling disconnected from his friends and us. It was great. But the next morning, he acted as though nothing had happened and was even surlier than usual!" Again, *you cannot force communication with adolescents.* The cost of the confrontation to get through to them far outweighs the benefits.

Control Battles: Winning by Surrender

Communication is *always* by invitation. To counteract the control struggles, parents need to boldly wave the white flag of surrender.

You may know you can't force your teenager to talk, but does your teenager know you know this? Does this conversation sound familiar?

"Katy, are you texting Brandon again?"

"Mmhmm."

"He seems to be spending a lot of time communicating with you. Do you think he likes you?"

"C'mon, Mom! Can you just leave me alone?"

"You know your dating life is completely up to you, so you don't have to tell me anything. I just like knowing what's going on with you. Sorry if I sounded like I was prying."

"I'm sorry, Mom. I just don't know what he thinks of me. He's so weird about it."

It's not enough to stop trying to push them into sharing. Parents should announce that they know they can't force openness. Too often we hate to admit when we're wrong or when we need to change course with our teenagers. This can lead to an adolescent feeling stuck in the great battle for control of communication long after her parents have conceded.

Make sure you get full credit for recognizing their freedom to communicate by reminding them that you know you can't make them open up to you. If you relinquish (your perceived) control of their communication, you'll likely be rewarded with the one thing you've been seeking all along: communication.

Emotional Immaturity: Looks Can Be Deceiving

We tend to forget that our adolescents are still growing into their bodies and growing into their emotions. Some adolescents fail to communicate well with their parents because they're intimidated and unable to express themselves as well as the adults. Parents often overlook this possibility because adolescents may appear quite mature on the outside. But for even the most adult-looking fifteen-year-old, "I don't know" may be the most honest answer they can give to a question about their feelings. It's not purposeful disrespect; it's an honest statement from a place of emotional immaturity.

"I was just trying to remind you to make sure your coach knows you're going to miss Saturday's practice. Is that so bad?"

"No."

"Then why do you snap at me like that? You do the same thing with your mother. Do we annoy you so much that we can't give you a simple reminder?"

"..."

"There's got to be a reason you act like this. Are you using drugs?"

"Oh c'mon, Dad!"

"Don't c'mon Dad me! If it's not drugs, it's got to be something that makes you act like this. What's gotten into you?"

"Whatever."

Teenagers experience a jumble of emotions and often don't know what it all means. They don't know how to explain their feelings, and such an internal mess may threaten their needed development into adulthood. Consequently, they may say, "I don't want to tell you that" rather than admit they don't know *how* to tell you. Because of their emotional immaturity, they simply don't have the words to adequately articulate their feelings.

For instance, you'll never hear a teenager tell you, "I'm feeling some very powerful and confusing feelings right now, and I need time to sort them out, okay?" But this phrase is underneath their favorite replies: "yeah," "fine," and "whatever." Note that *whatever* tends to stand in for what teenagers are unable to verbalize.

The best way to find out if emotional immaturity is a problem is to listen in on how your teen talks to friends. Don't eavesdrop, but when he's talking with his friends in your vicinity (like on the ride home from school), casually overhear what they're saying.

Let's say your teenage daughter is chatting with her friends and says, "No, I was just *down* this morning, you know? I hate that class, especially since it's first thing." This kind of talk suggests you are not having problems with emotional immaturity. But if you overhear her talking with a friend and it sounds more like what you hear regularly ("Uh-huh. Yep. Don't know. 'kay. See ya."), then you may have a communication issue due to emotional immaturity.

Emotional Immaturity: Communicating on Their Level

Improving communication problems due to emotional immaturity can be challenging. Sometimes it just takes patience until your son's or daughter's emotional maturity catches up to his or her physical maturity. However, there are a few strategies you can take right now to help communication despite your adolescent's emotional immaturity.

The first step is to take a step back: Back off! We'll discuss specific techniques for enabling better communication shortly, but emotionally immature teenagers *don't* need to be goaded about their emotional immaturity and lack of communication skills. Deep down, they know they're not communicating well. Pressing the point will turn them further away from you and result in an even wider communication gap. For now, take solace in realizing that this kind of struggle isn't all about you.

The second suggested step is to ask them less emotionally involved questions. For example, emotionally immature teenagers are better at talking about concrete things: "Where did you go?" or "How does that work?" It may even be difficult for them to answer internal preference questions such as "Did you enjoy that movie?" Pay particular interest to the kinds of questions your teenager answers at length versus questions that elicit an "I don't know" response.

If you can tell your question has stumped your teenager, try making it into a multiple choice. Instead of asking, "Why are you talking to your sister like that?" you might say, "So is she annoying you, or are you just tired?" As long as you don't press the point, giving optional emotions for a teenager to choose from may even help in his or her emotional development.

If you're careful about it, you can also model a healthy emotional response. Instead of asking a deep, emotional question like "Are Mondays difficult for you?" you might start by saying from your own experience, "I used to hate Monday mornings, you know what I mean?" I mention being careful because using catchphrases or baiting language when you're trying to encourage openness can be tricky business. Teenagers hate when parents sound like therapists, and even though they may not be able to fully understand their own ways of communicating, they're often not too keen when you're trying to impart a lesson to them.

Trust Issues: "Who Told You, and Who'd You Tell?"

As you may have already found out, breaking your teenager's trust can occur in a split second with even the most innocent of questions.

> "Christie's mom told me she had no idea she was dating Tyler."
> "You told Christie's mom?"
> "Well, yes. I think her mother ought to know if her daughter's dating someone!"
> "But she didn't want anyone to know. Now Christie's gonna hate me for telling!"
> "Maybe Christie should think twice about keeping such important things a secret from her mother. Is she still dating him?"
> "..."
> "Honey, are they still dating?"
> "..."

If parents don't take their teenagers' need for privacy seriously, their teenagers will stop sharing with them. In other words, the fastest route to obtaining a silent and brooding adolescent is to breach his trust and invade his privacy. Talking to other family members or friends about what your teenager has told you can also disrupt his or her ability to trust you with further information. While young children often don't mind (and sometimes even enjoy being talked about while they're not around), adolescents will likely feel their privacy has been violated or that you don't take them seriously. Neither is conducive to establishing a trustworthy relationship.

To communicate respect to your teenager, check with her before sharing private information with someone else. Even if you think your adolescent won't mind, go ahead and ask, "Do you mind if I tell Grandmom about your boyfriend?" It never hurts to check, and the question can be a comforting reminder that you are taking her privacy seriously.

Some parents view their teenagers' desire to keep their communications secret as prime evidence that they must be up to no good. I know of one mother who regularly reads her son's text messages, incorrectly believing that if he isn't doing anything wrong, he shouldn't mind. Adolescents' efforts to establish their own lives separate from their parents (i.e., *individuation*) bring on a natural need for privacy that is rarely if ever motivated by clandestine activities.

Under the guise of worry, parents can rationalize breaching their adolescents' privacy to ensure they're safe or behaving appropriately. Parents may grant themselves carte blanche access to their adolescents' lives and carry out all kinds of schemes, from calling their friends without their knowledge to searching their rooms when they're not home, to poring over cell phone records to see who they're talking to.

> If parents don't take their teenagers' need for privacy seriously, their teenagers will stop sharing with them.

Building and maintaining trust with your adolescent should be of the utmost importance to you, as the risks of not doing so far outweigh the parent-centered rewards of safety and control. There are exceptions, of course, when particular situations occur. Even as the parent of an adult-in-training, you still have the right to exert control when control is necessary.

Exception to Trust Issues: Criminal Behavior

If you have *real* evidence that your adolescent is involved with drugs or alcohol, you have every right to investigate. Even then, however, you should try to demonstrate sensitivity to your teenager's violation. If possible, you should also reassure your teen that you will cease snooping as soon as you have reason to believe your suspicions are false. While alcohol and drug issues occur somewhat often (which is why that topic is covered at length in chapter 22), criminal behavior happens less so. The consequences of your trust-violating actions must be carefully weighed. Establishing trust with a teenager who feels his privacy isn't respected is a challenging, if not impossible, task.

Exception to Trust Issues: Splitting

Splitting occurs when your teenager begs you to exclude your spouse from important information related to you in private. For example, if your son calls from jail and pleads, "Don't tell Dad! He'll kill me!" it's not a good idea to promise parental confidentiality. Although not all information your teenager tells you needs to be immediately texted to your spouse, an important rule of thumb is to ask yourself, *If I don't share this, how will my spouse feel if he [or she] finds out later?* If the answer is "He'd be fine not knowing" (e.g., mother-daughter discussions about menstruation), then keep it to yourself.

If a parent has chronic, unaddressed issues with his or her spouse, those parents are at a greater risk of splitting. Depending on the unresolved issue, a parent may even feel justified in agreeing with her adolescent about how frustrating the other parent can be. These sorts of discussions may make the parent feel better as an unhappy spouse, but they only harm the teenager and the marriage. (How your marriage, singleness, or divorce affects your parenting is covered in chapters 30 to 32.)

Adolescents need good relationships with both parents. Don't let your marital problems discourage your teen from maintaining a healthy relationship with both of you. If your adolescent complains to you about their other parent, it's best to suggest that your teen talk directly to the parent causing so much grief. Because of limited communication skills, the teenager may respond, "It won't do any good," but this is often wrong. To agree with her hopelessness is also to imply that your teenager doesn't have the resourcefulness to communicate more effectively. In some cases, you may need to jump-start the process by telling your spouse what your teenager told you. This will give your spouse a chance to address the issue.

In the rare circumstance that you aren't sure if your adolescent is safe in speaking with your spouse for fear of verbal abuse, seek marriage counseling (or counseling for your teen if you're divorced). If your teenager is *physically* afraid of your spouse and you agree, outside help *must* be sought.

Under normal circumstances, you should always be careful about telling other people what your adolescent has told you in private—but you must *never* give assurances that you won't tell his other parent. To promise confidentiality is tempting, because it seems like a quick way to gain his trust, but often such trust will be broken when you inevitably have to tell your spouse about the issue at hand. By telling your teen up front that anything he says will be related to your spouse, you no longer run the risk of losing his trust in the future—at least over the issue of parental confidentiality.

Exception to Trust Issues: Your Support System

When something traumatic or worrying is going on in your teenager's life, it's a reasonable response to want to tell the one or two people whom you count on for support. This is particularly true for mothers since women often have close friends who offer helpful support.

To ensure you're maintaining your adolescent's confidentiality, tell your teenager exactly what you'll be sharing and with whom. Like before, even if you think she'll be okay with it, make sure she is. In doing so, you're modeling respect for her privacy. Additionally, make sure the friend you're sharing with is trustworthy. The last thing you want is for your teenager to see her name on the church's prayer list for healing from an unknown STD.

Now that we've taken the time to understand the main sources of problems in communication with your teenager, let's look at actions you can take to improve this communication.

CHAPTER 10

Tools for Effective
Communication with Teenagers

The single biggest problem in communication
is the illusion that it has taken place.
ATTRIBUTED TO GEORGE BERNARD SHAW

Take a moment and reconsider the three major communication problems we discussed in the last chapter: control battles, emotional immaturity, and trust issues. Your relationship with your teenager may suffer from one or all three. Keep these issues in mind as you read through this chapter on specific techniques you can use to open the iron-gated doors of communication.

By now, you know there are no methods to *make* an adolescent talk to you. Trying to force that is one of the more hair-pulling stressors in a parent-adolescent relationship. So what *can* you do to increase the likelihood of your teenager's opening up to you (without the risk of going bald)? First, you can become more aware of the ways your adolescent may already be trying to communicate with you. Following that, you can try a few simple methods to open the conversation channels.

Agreeing to Disagree

Some of the worst arguments between teenagers and parents occur in close families. In close families, parents talk things through with their kids. They feel comforted when a mutual understanding is reached, and their kids often feel the same way. The arrival of adolescence brings a big problem: formal operational thought. Remember when we talked in chapter 4 about cognitive development in teenagers and how their *why* questions change? They now think more in terms of *what if?* Although this marks growth in adolescents, it can also create an impasse between parents and children.

When small children don't like a rule Mom and Dad set, the parents can often explain their views in ways that help the child understand. Even if they don't like the rule, children still carry an assumption that parents know things they don't. But adolescents are too old for that to work. Teens don't think their parents' perspectives need to be explained. They just think their parents are wrong. That's when the trouble starts.

I've heard numerous stories of loud, sometimes out-of-control arguments that started as sincere attempts, by the parent or the teenager, to explain why the other person's view was wrong. These discussions escalate as both parties' rationale fails to convince the other. Neither the parent nor the teenager can comprehend that their old way of coming to a mutual understanding just isn't working. Both parties begin accusing the other of not listening, or even of refusing to admit when they're wrong.

> Parents of teenagers must learn how to agree to disagree [with their teens].

Parents of teenagers must learn how to agree to disagree. Instead of seeing these impasses as dangerous deteriorations in the relationship, Mom and Dad should view them as signals that their teenager is growing up.

I remember the day when I reminded my thirteen-year-old son that we had agreed he should mow the whole backyard and not just the upper half, as he thought. I could tell he didn't like being reminded of this, but he walked back to the mower in a huff. When I looked out the back window a few minutes later, I saw something I hadn't expected. Instead of starting the mower, he was pacing, talking to himself. The next thing I knew, he came back into the house and angrily confronted me, saying that I was mistaken and that he had done what we had agreed on.

We went back and forth for a few minutes, our voices escalating each time we explained where the other was getting it wrong. He had never stood up to me like this, and none of my words seemed to have an effect. I suddenly realized I wasn't talking to my boy anymore. This was a young adult who felt just as strongly about his perspective as I did about mine. As an adolescent psychologist, I had known this day was coming, but it hit me like a ton of bricks.

I started to get choked up with emotion. (Do you see how weird it is to have a psychologist for a father?) With tears in my eyes, I said, "Son, we're just going to have to agree to disagree on this. I can tell you're too old to just take my word for it. I'm sorry we don't agree, but if you don't finish the yard, I'm not going to pay you."

He didn't like that at all, but the argument stopped. (He might have stopped arguing because he saw he was talking to an emotional nut of a father, but that's not the point!)

When you have disagreements with your teenager, it's good to explain your view and listen to hers. But after you've both done this a few times with no new information being added, you probably need to simply agree to disagree. Don't be afraid of a teenager walking away from you having demonstrated that she thinks you're wrong. That's okay. Adults don't always agree. Besides, you think she's wrong too.

Agreeing to disagree conveys an important message to a teenager: "You are free to think your own thoughts. I know I can't make you change your mind." Of course, freedom to think isn't a freedom you *give* to teenagers. They already have it. Still, they like to know that you know it.

Advice Giving

Besides agreeing to disagree, another important skill you need to master when implementing Planned Emancipation is the art of giving advice.

Many parents complain to me that their teenager doesn't allow them to say anything without the teen getting angry. "If I said the sky is blue, she'd argue it's green!" This pattern escalates as parents try to push back with louder voices, or even threats, in a futile effort to force their teenager to listen to them.

From our previous discussion, you've probably guessed the underlying struggle here. This is a control battle, and it's one of the silliest and most anemic battles parents continually fall into. Using intimidation tactics ("You can't leave until I'm finished.") or trick questions ("Do you understand me, young man?") succeeds only in keeping a teenager's carcass in your presence while you prattle on. Her mind and soul are far away. What's a parent to do? How can you get her to listen?

Implementing Planned Emancipation helps a great deal. As stated earlier, as control leaves, communication moves in. The type of communication that needs to move in is advice, not directions from on high. You need to master how to advise so your words have an impact on the life of your teen. The hardest thing about advice giving is that it's counterintuitive. Feedback that's hard for your teenager to hear, or something you know he's likely to disagree with, needs to be made *smaller*, not bigger. In other words, if you want an adolescent to swallow a bitter pill, chop the ends off.

Chopping the Ends Off a Bitter Pill

You chop off the front end of a bitter pill for your teenager by labeling the words you're about to speak as optional and as only your view. That is, your teen needs to hear *up front* something that lets him know you're not about to give him orders or directions—that this is just your opinion. You may know you're not going to make him do something, but your teenager doesn't until you say so.

"Hey, I thought you were going to the movies with Morgan."

"She just called and said she forgot she already agreed to go to the game with Lacey."

"Didn't she cancel on you last weekend too?"

"She just forgets sometimes, okay? It's no big deal!"

What do you say? You want to give some helpful input. Driving to Morgan's and punching her in the face is probably not a good idea, so what can you do?

First, chop the front of the pill off: "I'm so sorry, sweetheart. Can I mention something you'll probably think is stupid? And this may be just me—you know how touchy I can be sometimes. But . . ."

Did you see that? As an upset and protective parent, you'll be tempted to make your words bigger (e.g., "You know, I haven't said anything before, but I've just gotta say . . ."). But you need to make your words smaller. Individuation causes adolescents to hear your feedback as criticism of their judgment (e.g., whether they know how to pick their friends), rendering them deaf to the real feedback you're trying to give.

The message you're about to deliver has now been labeled as both *advice* and *my opinion* versus *you have to*.

Your last step is to chop off the back end of the pill. Be sure to finish your advice with a quick reminder that there's no control battle here: "I'm so sorry, sweetheart. Can I mention something you'll probably think is stupid? And this may be just me—you know how touchy I can be sometimes. But I think Morgan doesn't seem as interested in your friendship since she made the dance team. If it were me, I'd think she's giving out signals that you're not as close as you used to be. But again, it's your friendship, and there's probably a lot I don't know."

Does this kind of message feel wrong to you? Do you think the parent is pandering or she's weak? I would argue that this kind of talk displays respect for a young, insecure adult-in-training. The goal, of course, is to *increase* your influence. Smaller pills are much easier to swallow.

You Must Initiate Conversation

Sometimes frustrated parents take a defensive position: "Fine, if he doesn't want to talk, I'll just wait around until he decides he wants to say something to me!" Those parents run the risk of waiting a *very* long time. Being available when and if your adolescent wants to talk is not enough. You must be proactive and initiate conversation.

Adolescents are still emotionally immature, and talking about their inner thoughts and feelings is as desirable to them as taking their clothes off in front of the entire student body. If communication is waning, or if it has completely stopped, you must try to initiate communication by regularly and respectfully asking them to talk with you.

Making the effort to increase communication with a moody teenager can be unpleasant. Even so, parents must take the initiative to invite their adolescents to speak with them. These talks should not always go deep, and parents should try not to have a particular agenda. It's all too common for an adolescent to assume something is wrong any time a parent calls her name. Instead, parents should sprinkle in invitations to get together for no specific purpose other than to talk. The goal of these invitations is to demonstrate your desire to be together and communicate, even if she doesn't want to.

> Being available when and if your adolescent wants to talk is not enough. You must be proactive and initiate conversation.

"Hey, Abi, I've got to run to the store to get a filter for the kitchen exhaust fan. Why don't you come with me so we can talk? I'll buy you that strawberry lime drink you like at Sonic."

"Am I in trouble?"

"Not at all. We just haven't talked in a while, and I miss spending time with you."

"Yeah, well . . . no, thanks."

"Okay. Maybe we can do it another time."

"You could get me that strawberry limeade though."

"Sorry, you gotta be present to win. Maybe next time."

These invitations must be respectful and regular. Allow your teenager to decline your invitation without consequence or irritation from you.

(Withholding free soft drink delivery doesn't count as a consequence.) Notice that even if your teenager declines your offer to talk, you have still communicated you would like to spend time with her. No matter what her response looks like, she likes knowing you want to communicate with her. However, the hard part is that no one likes to be rejected, especially by their teenager.

Even with the poorest of teenage conversationalists, parents must take the initiative to invite their teenagers to talk. It takes a confident mom or dad to offer a kind invitation, only to be continually turned down, but this kind of regularity and respect is hard for teenagers to ignore. Remember, *they want to talk to you* but don't know how. It's the rare teenager who can endure five or six honest invitations without eventually giving in.

"The bank's right across from that lime soda place you like. Wanna ride along and talk for a few minutes?"

"A large strawberry limeade?"

"Sure, why not?"

"Well, I guess I'll go then."

Note: If your teenager has said no a dozen times before, don't make a big deal out of finally receiving a yes. Though such a yes is important to you, he still needs to feel as if this is just a casual, no-consequences, just-talking outing—which it is! Don't make it weird for him and lose your opportunity to connect.

Be Flexible with Time and Place

Parents and adolescents often differ on when and where is the best place to talk. Adolescents may choose times that are highly inconvenient for their parents, like ten thirty on a Sunday night. You're comfortably in bed, only to hear a loud knock on the bedroom door and your teenager announcing, "I'm failing algebra!" If you insist on having conversations at the proper time and place *as you see it*, you risk having little interaction with your teenager.

Sometimes teens are ready to talk when you least expect it. For example, many parents have noticed there's something slightly magical about being alone in the car with their adolescent. A parent is driving along, and suddenly their sullen teenager starts going on and on about school, religion, dating, or any number of topics, all without parental prodding. With silent breathing and hands frozen to the steering wheel, these parents are fearful of saying any word that might bring such a moment of candor and vulnerability to a halt.

It's hard to say what causes this phenomenon. Some say it's because the adolescent knows the conversation is time limited: *I know I can quit talking once we get to our destination.* But because these conversations almost always occur while the parent is driving, I believe adolescents subconsciously take advantage of their parent's split-focused attention. Many teenagers can't handle the eye-to-eye intensity of most of the conversations with their parents, but when an adolescent sits next to or behind a parent while in the car, the parent is half-focused on driving, and the attention intensity decreases to a more acceptable (and less vulnerable) level for the teenager.

More often, your adolescent is *not* ready to talk when you are. You may be an up-and-at-'em Saturday morning talker, but I'm willing to bet your teenager is not. Most teens are up at the crack of lunch, and words don't arrive in their brains until after two thirty in the afternoon. Parents may have to adjust their timetables to optimize when they talk with their teenagers. This is not always possible, but parents shouldn't be rigid about when discussion occurs.

Then there are the times when you think you should do a lot of talking, but it's better if you don't. For example, never try to teach during a crisis. When your daughter calls following her first car accident, that's not the time to scold her and say, "Why were you driving so fast?" She needs a calm and caring reaction: "Are you okay? I'll be there as fast as I can." Because of the crisis and your teenager's heightened emotions, whatever point you try to make will be completely lost. Adolescents learn more from experience than through words. Waiting to talk about the personal consequences of her accident is a better plan.

But when there's no crisis and no inconvenience, when should a parent seek to speak with his or her teenager? Anytime and anyplace the teenager seems willing.

Whatever the reason, parents *must* pay attention to both the time and place where their teenagers tend to open up. These conversations can take place anywhere but may *not* be best in their room. Unless you've been invited there, a parent barging in on an adolescent's space can shut him up. Sometimes, he'll prefer to talk in *your* bedroom. Within limits, parents need to be flexible in cooperating with their teenager's conversation—wherever it breaks out. Once it does, make a mental note of the time and place, and use that to your advantage the next time you'd like to have a chat with your adolescent.

Use the Nonjudgmental Reply

Because we parents still vainly believe our grand speeches affect immediate change in our adolescents, we tend to fall into the trap of responding to what they say with either wholesale endorsement or outright condemnation. We become vending machines of opinion: Put in a few words on a topic, and out comes a full-blown lesson.

> "After he got it out of the lake, Jayden had to open his phone and put it in the sun to dry it out."
>
> "You know, Josh, if you crack open your phone, it voids the warranty and can do serious damage to the case."
>
> "Yeah, I know, so I told him he should make Ethan's dad pay for a new phone since it was his boat and Ethan shouldn't have told all of us to get in."
>
> "No, I don't agree that Ethan's dad has any responsibility here. No one made you or Jayden get into the boat. You see, Josh, individual liability is all about taking responsibility for your actions. When your uncle sold insurance, he used to always say . . ."

For many parents, continual teaching just seems like what we're supposed to do. Some may notice their teenager's eyes glazing over during the entire lecture, but the parent forges ahead so he can do his job. When we remember adolescents are no longer at the stage where they're open to teaching, some parents are left not knowing what to say to their kids.

An alternative solution to this problem is to develop the art of the nonjudgmental reply. These are statements or questions that do not seek to teach. Instead, they attempt only to identify, recognize, or acknowledge what the adolescent is saying. Learning to talk nonjudgmentally to a teenager can be the key to regular and open communication.

The art of the nonjudgmental reply begins with permitting yourself to let entire conversations go by without teaching. This will be infinitely more difficult for some parents than others. But remember, adolescents are no longer children. By eleven, they *already* know virtually all your opinions and beliefs. If you hear an opinion that's different from yours, it's not because your teen forgot yours; it's because he's thinking on his own.

> Learning to talk nonjudgmentally to a teenager can be the key to regular and open communication.

"After he got out of the lake, Jayden had to open his phone and put it in the sun to dry it out."

"I'm surprised he knew how to get it open."

"Me too. I think he kinda cracked it, though."

"Ouch."

"I know, so I told him he should make Ethan's dad pay for a new phone since it was his boat and Ethan shouldn't have told all of us to get in."

"You mean his dad should share some of the responsibility since it was his son and his boat?"

"Yeah. Ethan doesn't have any money, that's for sure."

"What did Jayden say?"

"He said he'd think about it, but I doubt he'll really do it. Ethan's dad is kind of intimidating."

"Yeah, I might be a little intimidating, too, if someone called and said I should pay for some guy's phone just because my son encouraged him to get in my boat—when I wasn't even there."

"That's true. I couldn't believe Jayden had his phone with him!"

To understand nonjudgmental conversation, think of a conversation you might have with an adult friend or a family member who is younger than you but still an adult. In conversing with your teen, you would use similar approaches, such as asking interested questions about your teen's views or interests on the topic at hand or reiterating what you just heard to make sure you're understanding him correctly. You can throw in your own opinion but don't overdo it. (You'll know they know when you're overdoing it, because their eyes may begin making that well-worn upward trek.) Make sure you own it as *your* opinion too. Remember, you're talking to adolescents, not children. You don't have to correct everything you hear that you don't agree with.

Nonjudgmental conversation is interested in and respectful of the person with whom you're talking. In my experience, mothers are better at this than fathers, and that may relate to the fact that so many American men have few close friends. Maybe we guys just don't practice talking with other adults except our wives or coworkers. Whatever the reason, dads may need to practice nonjudgmental conversation with their spouses or close friends by keeping the conversation going with neutral questions and statements.

Invite Your Adolescents to Solve Their Own Problems

Another important time to cultivate good communication is when your teenager is having a big problem. Most of the time we don't think of problems as communication-building events; to us, they're emergencies. But they're not. Even significant problems, such as failing a class, disciplinary action at school, or being mistreated by a coach, don't have to be solved immediately. These are serious issues, but they don't constitute emergencies. We too often try to come to sudden solutions as a means of curtailing our worry, not because the situation has to be resolved overnight.

When we jump in too quickly to fix our adolescents' problems, we miss an important opportunity to allow them to develop responsibility and problem-solving skills. Plus, an adolescent who was not consulted about a solution to his or her problem often feels resentment and resists a parent trying to help. The teenager is not invested in the outcome. Remember, adolescence is a stage for developing skills in self-reliance. Your job is to train your teenagers to handle problems themselves—not for you to make sure you always keep them safe.

When a problem arises, a parent should ask, "What are you going to do?" Many times, teenagers are stunned that they're even being asked. Because they've always had adults do their thinking for them, they may not have thought about how *they* might solve the problem on their own.

If your teenager answers, "I don't know" or "There's nothing I can do," it's best to leave the issue in her lap for a day or two. Tell her, "Why don't you think about it and tell me tomorrow what you think is the best way to handle this?"

Sometimes, adolescents surprise their parents with creative and appropriate solutions, yet many times they don't. Either way, adolescents should come to expect that you will ask their opinion about their problems. This demonstrates that, at this stage, you expect them to begin to figure things out for themselves. Awaiting their answer for some time further proves you're interested in their solutions and that it's *their* problem, not yours.

If your teenager suggests a solution within reasonable limits, try to go with his suggestion, at least for a while. If he insists (as teenagers often do) there's "nothing I can do about it," don't try to fix the problem yourself. Parents who are quick to agree with their teenager's hopeless assessment of a situation may find more reasons to come to their kid's rescue, but this doesn't allow their adolescent's problem-solving skills to stretch and grow.

Don't attempt to motivate your teenager's problem-solving by convincing him or her that the problem isn't that big. Even worse, don't fall into the trap of offering some explanation for something you know nothing about—for example, "I'm sure that's not what your coach meant"—when you have no idea what the coach said *or* meant.

Instead, use your teenager's problem as an opportunity to encourage her to figure out her own response, no matter how complicated the problem may seem to both of you.

> "I told you, there's nothing I can do. She hates me, and she only gives good grades to her favorites!"
>
> "So is everyone who isn't one of her favorites failing?"
>
> "Probably. Even Mason said she doesn't like him either."
>
> "That sounds pretty unfair. Have you talked to the teacher about this?"
>
> "No, I already told you she hates me!"
>
> "Is there someone else at the school you can take this to?"
>
> "I don't know."
>
> "Well, that sounds complicated to me. Why don't you think about it some more and see if you can come up with some ideas? We'll talk again tomorrow."
>
> "It won't do any good. There's nothing I can do!"
>
> "Look, Jacob, if you were six years old, I'd probably agree with you, but you're fifteen years old and smart enough to figure something out to bring this grade up. If you can't come up with anything, then I'll have to, but it's your grade, not mine. I'd rather you make a plan yourself. Anyway, nothing has to happen right now, so let's wait and talk tomorrow."

Provide Effective Praise

The operative word here is *effective*. The praise you give your teenager should not be the praise you gave to your child. Ever wonder why your adolescent sometimes reacts negatively even when you're trying to say something nice about her?

"Look at what a nice job you did on your poster. It looks great!"

"Not really. You should see Sophia's. Hers always looks like it was done by a professional."

"Well, I'm sure your teacher doesn't care if it looks professional or not."

"Oh yes, he does. He's always going on and on about making our projects 'look professional.' I'm just not good at this stuff."

"Well . . . I think you're very talented."

"Yeah, you're my mom. You have to say that."

When a parent points out something positive about an adolescent, the teenager may deny its accuracy and seem almost irritated. Parents sometimes worry too much about this, because they're still mentally referring to their books on parenting children and believe that praising a child is of the utmost importance to his or her self-esteem. But your teenager is not a child any longer. Treating them like a competent adult, rather than just a good boy or a nice girl, contributes to their self-esteem.

As with so many other adolescent issues, the desire for control underlies this problem. Although praise is a positive message, it's still a judgment from on high. The "praiser" sits in judgment over the "praisee." Adolescents don't like being in a one-down position—even if it involves positive feedback.

This doesn't mean adolescents don't want or need positive feedback. Of course they do. Their apathetic response signals that parents need to alter their methods of giving praise to their teenagers.

To effectively deal with this dilemma, share your own feelings rather than offering full character evaluations of your adolescent. This means you need to own your feelings about what or whom you're praising.

"I've got to admit I get a little jealous when I see your art projects. I could never do anything like that when I was in school."

"It's not that great. You should see Sophia's. Hers always looks like it was done by a professional."

"Maybe so, but if I could have drawn as well as you do, I probably would have considered design or advertising or something like that."

"Maybe. . . . Thanks, Mom."

By simply sharing how you feel, you can avoid the appearance of judging your teenager while still giving her needed encouragement. When you limit your feedback to your viewpoint, there's little for the teenager to argue. She can't very well say, "No, you're not jealous when you see my work!" The compliment is still there, but now it's confined to your perspective, with no larger judgment implied.

Another way to provide effective praise is to focus on a specific event rather than praising an entire personality trait.

"I knew when I told everybody to get their suitcases out to the car early that I could count on you to take care of your stuff. I wish your brothers were half as responsible as you are."

"It's just a suitcase. I couldn't sleep, so I just went ahead and threw some stuff in."

"But that's what I mean. You know how to make use of your time. That's what being responsible is all about."

"Whatever. When are we leaving?"

Adolescents tend to be put off by generalizations (unless they're the ones making them), but they will accept a response to a specific event. Again, this avoids the perception of giving compliments from a position of authority or expertise the adult claims for himself or herself and the adolescent doesn't have.

"Oh, good. Thanks for getting your stuff out here early. This helps me. You know how stressed I get when we're trying to get to the airport."

"No kidding. You should take a pill or something, Dad."

"I probably should, but in the meantime, getting your stuff together this morning helps. Seriously, thanks."

"Sure. I'll go check on Andrew."

"That'd be great."

Praise is best received if you just point out something he did and describe the good feelings you have about it.

By the way, if your teenager gets a haircut and looks better, tell him he *looks* older. Adolescent boys in particular are often not impressed by parents telling them they look more handsome or cuter, but they do take notice when told they look older. Between you and me, I don't even care if they actually look younger. If I think it looks better for one reason or another, I always go with *older*.

> Praise is best received if you just point out something [your teen] did and describe the good feelings you have about it.

This is one moment in your teenager's life when you can explicitly answer his question *When will you say I'm old enough?* You're telling him, "Well, today you're getting closer. You look older."

Now that you've started the process of Planned Emancipation and have done all you can do to establish and maintain good communication, you're ready to address the last major issue in managing your adolescent: limit setting.

CHAPTER 11

Limit Setting with Adolescents

If you want to recapture your youth, just cut off his allowance.
AL BERNSTEIN

Some of you may have skipped directly to this chapter. I understand the impulse. After all, I field dozens of questions from concerned parents who'd like a direct answer to the problems they face with their adolescents. However, as I've stated elsewhere, this book is not an encyclopedia. You can't look up your teenager's specific issue and get a specific answer. Rather, what you've learned up to now (if you've read the book straight from the beginning) sets a firm foundation for you to handle issues that arise. You can do this without a direct answer from me, or any other professional counselor, or well-meaning friends or family members.

For that reason, if you've jumped to this chapter, I implore you to stop reading now and go back to the beginning. Don't worry. You're not being graded. No one will know regardless. But to effectively implement Planned Emancipation and experience success in setting limits, you need to understand the process.

Does Planned Emancipation Mean No Discipline?

By this point, I hope you understand that granting your teenager more autonomy as he or she gets older doesn't mean parents become hands-off when it comes to discipline and setting proper limits. Like a foreign power that is systematically giving over territory, you can and must maintain effective control over those territories you haven't released yet. The question is how to discipline effectively.

"This is the last time I'm going to tell you, Emily. Stop texting and empty the dishwasher!"

"Okay, okay. Let me tell Alex that I'll talk to her later."

"You should have done that when I reminded you an hour ago. Don't make me come over there and take that phone."

"Okay, don't have a stroke," Emily says as she continues texting. "Just a second."

"Okay, that's it!" Emily's mom gets up from her chair and rushes toward her daughter.

"Mom, what are you doing?"

At this point, you can choose from an array of unhappy endings, from an embarrassing mother-daughter game of cell phone keep-away to a rather uncomfortable phone call from child protective services.

Time after time, I see parents who fail to set effective limits on their adolescents' behavior because they're still treating their teenagers as if they were children. Even when this doesn't lead to yelling or physical confrontations, this kind of discipline doesn't prepare teenagers for what lies ahead. I've even seen parents use the same childhood token economy charts ("Check the box for cleaning your room") with their fifteen-year-olds. While a compliant teenager may be willing to passively cooperate with this condescending form of discipline, I would argue this is ineffective because it doesn't fit the appropriate goals of limit setting for a young adult.

To begin transforming the way you think about disciplining your teenager, let's consider your ultimate goals.

The Difference between Disciplining Children and Teenagers

If you've been trying to discipline your adolescents as if they were still children, don't be too hard on yourself. You probably learned this from your parents, well-meaning friends, or other books. We also tend to rely on what's worked in the past—then we bang our heads against the wall when that fails to work now.

The contrast in disciplining children and adolescents goes deeper than just technique. The goals should be significantly different. The goal of disciplining a child is obedience. The goal of disciplining a teenager is responsibility. Consequently, getting from point A to point B in each of these situations will be quite different. I define the goal of disciplining children as follows:

Obedience = limited choice of action + coercion

When you tell your child how, when, and where to carry out a task, and he carries out that task to your liking, he has been obedient.

There's nothing wrong with expecting obedience from children. Because they must rely on their parents' care, children must develop obedience or possibly suffer grave consequences. When we tell a two-year-old not to touch the stove, we do so for her protection. Parents will often add coercion to this command to help the child learn a valuable lesson. When she reaches for the stove, we'll pull her hand away. If necessary, we'll also swat her hand to encourage obedience. It's entirely proper to tell the child what she must do or not do and add whatever action is appropriate for motivation. Obedient children do as they're told largely because they fear the consequences of disobedience.

Conversely, it's bad parenting to tell a two-year-old, "I wouldn't touch that stove if I were you, but do what you think best." A two-year-old cannot be expected to take responsibility for knowing how to handle a hot stove. He doesn't know the danger. So, in disciplining a child, the parent shoulders the responsibility for the child's actions. And because a child has only concrete thinking skills, fear of consequences can be helpful in teaching self-control.

However, parents forget that childhood ends after about age twelve. And obedience must not be the goal of disciplining adolescents.

To continue disciplining teenagers as if they were still children is to leave them ill prepared to handle adulthood. Adolescents who have never developed beyond the level of obedience will seek another strong-willed adult to obey as adults (a spouse, friend, or peer group). Parents may spend years expecting obedience from their adolescents, and then be surprised when their teenagers don't know how to take initiative and make choices in adulthood. These teens are easy prey for other, more charismatic influences, and are easily drawn away from the values they were raised with.

Obedience does not require that rules and limits be internalized. As soon as the rewards around an obedient adult change, he will gravitate toward any direction that rewards him most.

For limits to be internalized during and past adolescence, parents must aim for a different goal in limit setting: responsibility. We want our adolescents to become responsible adults, but what do we mean by that? If we're supposed to help this adult-in-training take responsibility for her actions, what kind of discipline works?

Developing Responsibility: The Goal of Limit Setting with Adolescents

Strictly speaking, when we say someone is being irresponsible, we're saying that person is not acting as if he or she is responsible. When someone comes upon a mess and asks, "Who's responsible here?" and someone answers, "I did it, but it was an accident," the one replying is admitting to making the mess while denying responsibility. He or she didn't choose to make the mess. If someone says, "I did it, but he told me to," that person is denying responsibility by blaming another person. To be responsible, someone must be able to choose his actions and be rightly held accountable for those actions.

Like my simple equation for obedience, responsibility can be broken into its components:

Responsibility = freedom to choose actions + accountability

You don't teach responsibility. Rather, you train people to be responsible by (surprise!) placing them in positions of responsibility. That is, for adolescents to learn to behave responsibly, they must experience situations where they have the freedom to make their own choices while also being held accountable for those choices. They (like anyone else) then have the option to behave responsibly or not. Even when parents are unable to hold their teenagers completely accountable, they should at least shift as much of the burden of responsibility onto the adolescent as possible.

When we see an adolescent speeding down the street while talking on her cell phone, we believe she's not being responsible. In most cases, however, the truth is that the adolescent isn't the one responsible for her driving behavior—her parents are! That teenager probably didn't purchase the car, pay for insurance, or even buy the gas. If something happens because of her poor driving, it will personally cost her little compared to what an accident will cost her parents. Installing speed-monitoring equipment or other fancy technology may be an understandable attempt to make a teenager obey her parents while driving around town. But to really begin driving responsibly, she must be required to take on more of the burden of accountability for her actions.

> There's no better teacher of responsibility than the burden of real-life consequences.

How did you develop into a responsible adult? Do you remember how you treated the first car you paid for yourself versus the one your parents may have provided for you? Remember when you started buying auto insurance and discovered what happened to the rates if you got a speeding ticket? There's no better teacher of responsibility than the burden of real-life consequences.

Too many parents want their adolescents to behave responsibly while they (the parents) still provide whatever their teenagers want and assume full responsibility for their behavior. These adolescents experience early adulthood like a Disneyland ride—thrilling, but unreal, and protected from imminent harm.

In *Postcards from the Edge*, the movie from the semi-autobiographical novel by Carrie Fisher about her relationship with her mother, Debbie Reynolds, the main character, Suzanne, is being chastised by a movie director for her irresponsible behavior:

> Lowell: "You're not going to get a lot of sympathy from anybody, you know that? You know how many people'd give their right arm . . . to lead the kind of life that you lead?"

> Suzanne: "I know, but the trouble is I can't feel my life. . . . I see it all around me, and I know that so much of it is good. But . . . it's like this thing with my, my mother. I know that she does all this stuff because she loves me, but I just can't believe it."[1]

Disciplining adolescents requires that parents recognize and allow their teenagers freedom of choice, while also being creative in holding them accountable for their choices.

It's surprising how few parents understand this type of limit setting. In our earlier example, a parent who repeatedly demands that a teenager go empty the dishwasher is seeking obedience. Threatening to "come over there and take the phone" is a pathetic attempt at coercion. By contrast, you can give your teenager the freedom to choose her actions by telling her, "Hey, I need you to take the job of emptying the dishwasher on weeknights. You can do it whenever it's convenient after supper, as long as it's done before breakfast the next day." Being careful to add,

"Oh, and if it's not emptied by breakfast the next day, I'll take a dollar from your allowance" holds her accountable for her choices.

The Four Laws of Disciplining Adolescents

Once you understand how proper limit setting encourages adolescent responsibility, you need to avoid a few common pitfalls. I call these the *four laws of disciplining adolescents* because if they're not heeded, your ability to effectively set limits will be seriously weakened.

1. A Parent Cannot *Make* an Adolescent Do Anything; You Are a Judge, Not a Police Officer

If you think about it, shifting your goal from obedience to responsibility should change how you see your role. As a parent of teenagers, you need to think and act, not like a police officer, but more like a judge.

Your job is not to make your teenager do or not do something, but to creatively hold him accountable for his choices. I put this down as the first law because parents can be surprised at how quickly arguments with teenagers escalate into yelling matches or even physical altercations. Some fathers spend much of their kids' childhoods benefiting from an intimidating physical presence that implies, *Don't mess with me or else.* Some dads even state such vague challenges aloud. They shouldn't be surprised when at least one of their adolescent children then decides to find out what "or else" is.

Getting drawn into a verbal or physical wrestling match with an adolescent is a surefire way to seriously weaken the validity of your authority. No teenager has ever said, "I thought there was nothing wrong with missing curfew until my dad got me in that headlock. Then I realized that curfews are good for me."

Getting physical with your teenager, or just behaving in a physically intimidating manner, reinforces his view that you're a bully. It doesn't matter how your dad used to parent. Our previous generation of parents didn't have all this figured out either. If you're counting on brute force and intimidation in today's world, you must also prepare for the distinct possibility of a social worker showing up at your door and wanting to ask you a few questions. Physical intimidation is the weakest form of influence you have in your arsenal. Avoid it at all costs.

If you find yourself edging toward physically or verbally abusing your teenager, it's time to recuse yourself from the situation for a while. Tell your son or daughter, "I don't like what I'm doing here. I'll talk to you later. Give me time to think about this." Remember that most emergencies aren't emergencies, and effective discipline doesn't have to happen in the immediate aftermath of a bad situation. After all, how quickly does the real world discipline adults who've messed up? Sometimes the best course is to press pause, regroup, and then confront the situation the following day. Plus, it may help your teenager to likewise calm down and consider the true consequences of her actions.

If a police officer hears of a possible carjacking, the officer must take action to try to stop it from happening. That's the officer's job. But if a judge hears of the same carjacking, the judge will likely think, *When that case comes across my desk, I'm going to have to decide what the consequences for the perpetrator's actions will be.* A cop tries to ensure that people obey the law. A judge must ensure proper consequences are given when the law has been broken.

If your teenager purposefully defies you—let's say he wants to go to a party you forbade him from attending—your first recourse is not barring the doorway and screaming, "Over my dead body!" Even if you succeed in keeping him from going that particular night, your actions only fan the flames of a control battle. For example, you might say, "As your parent, I can keep you from attending a party I don't approve of." But over time, you can't win the battle. Your teen might point out, "As my parent, you can't always know where I am and what I'm doing." Instead of demotivating your teenager to attend parties, you've probably only succeeded in increasing his motivation to choose his own actions.

Acting as a judge instead of a police officer means you clearly state your rule in this matter: "You may not attend any parties unless we've spoken to the parents who will be there." There's no need to bar the door or even stop sipping your coffee. But what happens when your teenager angrily proclaims, "I'm going if I want to, and there's nothing you can do about it!"?

Remember, you're a judge. You simply smile (trust me, a calm, smiling parent is very scary to teenagers), take another sip of coffee, and say, "Let me put it this way. If you do choose to attend this or any other party without our permission, I just hope it's worth it, because your

---
Your strength lies in one important fact your teenager often forgets: Everything he owns belongs to you.

---

grounding will be long and severe. I'm a little rattled right now, so I don't even know just how bad it will be, but let's just say, it will be bad."

It's essential that you understand your strength in intimidating an adolescent doesn't come from physical coercion. Your strength lies in one important fact your teenager often forgets: Everything he owns belongs to you. This kind of leverage is invaluable for two reasons: It provides you with an almost unending supply of disciplinary measures, and it doesn't take away the freedoms you've granted. We'll discuss this at length later in this chapter.

2. Adolescents Learn from Experience, Not Words

When kids are young, we often use words to help them avoid having to experience the negative consequences of their behavior. Children usually have a basic sense that their parents know things they don't. Remember when your five-year-old peppered you with questions about everything? "Why can't I cross the street yet?" "Why can't I have a big ice cream?" They didn't always like our answers, but they used to think we knew things.

Shifting your goal from obedience to responsibility also means you should focus less on teaching and more on training. That means fewer words and more action.

Parents of adolescents often continue to use lots of words to try to shield their teenagers from consequences. What they fail to take seriously is that adolescents are no longer asking for instruction, and they don't appreciate being protected from consequences.

SPEECHMAKING

Parents who don't understand that adolescents learn from experience often fall into the trap of speechmaking. Making speeches are Mom and Dad's way of offering discipline while keeping real consequences from occurring. But substituting speeches for real-life consequences prevents adolescents from learning responsibility.

Giving your teenager a fixed allowance to cover all social events can be a good training ground for budgeting. But what do you do when she tells you the church youth group is going to the amusement park, and she's already spent her allowance? Telling her, "Oh, wow. Sorry about that. Is there something you could sell on Craigslist?" may sound uncaring, but requiring her to find her own solution is the only way for her to learn responsibility. Making a speech about the importance of money management while you reach into your wallet and start peeling off twenty-dollar bills will ensure she learns nothing from the experience.

3. Anger and Yelling Make You *Weaker* as a Parent

When I was once pulled over for speeding, I remember feeling nervous as the officer calmly approached my car. He was very matter-of-fact: "Sir, I pulled you over because you were going over the speed limit. Please hand me your license and registration." So why was I nervous? (No, it wasn't the officer's gun!) I was nervous because he had this big pad of traffic citations in his hand (one of which he generously gave me). Later, I told my wife about the ticket.

But what if the officer had stormed up to my car, banged on my door, demanded my license and registration, and berated me with a loud voice and wild gesticulations, saying, "Did you see how fast you were going back there?" The story I would have told my wife would have been much different. Such a story would have wholly centered on the wild police officer. I probably wouldn't have even mentioned much about why I got the ticket.

If you're a parent prone to yelling matches with your adolescent, these are the kinds of stories your teenager is telling his or her friends. You become the center of the story, and the actual consequences of the situation fall by the wayside. Instead of taking responsibility and relating, "I was late for curfew and got grounded again," the story becomes "You should have seen my dad when I walked in. He was so mad he was shaking. I wasn't two steps inside the door before he unleashed nearly every cuss word I know. I think he even made up a few."

Anger and yelling don't help the situation for a host of reasons, but there's one main reason it's so counterproductive: Responding with anger doesn't help your teenager see himself. It only helps him see you in a very bad light.

If you're constantly wrestling with yourself not to respond in anger to your adolescent (and you don't often deal with anger in other areas of your life), you may be failing to pull the trigger on consequences. This is where it helps to be reminded of the second law of disciplining adolescents: Adolescents learn from experience, not words. You must allow consequences to fall on your teenager, or she will never mature into a full adult. Getting angry and yelling won't make these consequences happen any sooner, so it's best to reconsider your approach if this is an issue that tends to repeat itself in your parenting.

4. Lack of Parental Unity Undercuts Effective Limit Setting

When parents aren't on the same page concerning the discipline of their teenagers, their lack of unity will greatly undermine any limit setting. Remember, the need for individuation leaves teens naturally feeling that they don't need your limits, but they will follow them to avoid consequences. When one parent allows behavior that the other restricts, both parents lose credibility. Even worse, such disagreements significantly increase the teenager's resentment toward the parent who won't allow a particular behavior. It's better that your teenager thinks both of you are crazy for not allowing something, rather than think neither of you knows what you're talking about.

You and your spouse agreeing on a clear expectation—even if that means you have to grant more freedom than you'd like—is preferable to vague responses from both parents that lead to a confused teenager and upset parents. For example, if Dad says, "I know your mom said it's okay, but you have to come check with me first," mixed messages are being sent. Your adolescent shouldn't be held responsible for the communication problems you have with your spouse. That's not his job; it's yours.

Of course, this can be a huge challenge when an adolescent's parents are divorced, but I encourage such parents to still strive toward unity in their parenting. Divorced parents can tell their exes, "I still don't like you either, but this isn't about us. We both care about our daughter, but our parenting differences are keeping us from influencing her. How can we work toward agreeing on things so we don't keep running into these issues?"

Unfortunately, such an agreement is often not possible. If you're the more restrictive parent, you may need to consider lowering your expectations to help with your teenager's frustrations. Teenagers in these situations do not generally think things like *My mom doesn't let me spend the night with friends like my dad does, but I know she really knows what's best for me.*

Marriage and single-parent issues that affect parenting will be further discussed in chapters 30 and 31.

When parents agree on what they expect and what consequences their teenagers will face if those expectations aren't met, adolescents at least have a firm understanding of those expectations and consequences—which leads us to codify them.

CHAPTER 12

Implementing Limits: The Expectations and Consequences List

My mother refused to let me fail. So I insisted.
WALKER PERCY

Moms and dads cannot expect their adolescents to intuitively know their parental expectations. I've worked with more than one family who described their teenager's behavior as out of control. I remember sixteen-year-old Michael sitting in my office and staring at his shoes while his parents loudly exclaimed that he was out of control and never did what they told him to do. Surprisingly, he had no behavior difficulties in school or any other setting. I spent several minutes trying to pin down exactly what his parents meant by "out of control."

Dad: "And I told him I'm not going to take being treated like this!"

Me: "Can you give me an example of this behavior you won't stand for?"

Dad: "Just last weekend, he asked to go to his friend's house. I told him he couldn't until he finished mowing the lawn.

When I got home, he was gone, and the lawn hadn't been touched!"

Michael: "After you left, Mom said it was okay for me to wait until the next day because the grass was still wet!"

Mom: "Actually, I did tell him he could wait 'til the next day."

Dad: "Well . . . he should have called and told me that. He just doesn't care!"

Michael seemed pleased with my attempts to pin his parents down. Granted, he'd taken full advantage of their poor communication and lack of follow-through (teenagers are smart like that). However, in this case, Michael's perceived out-of-control behavior resulted from his parents' inability to define their expectations and follow through with clear consequences when he failed to meet them. If his parents had created a list of expectations and consequences, they would have been working from the same page—literally. And Michael would have been fully aware of what out-of-control behavior meant to his parents.

The Expectations and Consequences List You Already Have

Whether you've considered this parenting technique before or not, your household already has an Expectations and Consequences list. It may not be written, but it certainly exists. This list is what your teenager already believes you expect of her and what consequences she knows to expect if she fails to meet your expectations. But often this common-law list is not what you truly desire when it comes to setting limits on your teenager's behavior.

How could he know what was expected of him when the boundaries were so vague and the consequences so meager?

I remember one time when John, a fifteen-year-old from a chaotic family, complained that he never knew what to expect from his parents' discipline. I told John that I thought he knew his parents pretty well and, in fact had a history of playing them to his advantage. Together we wrote out his parents' Expectations and Consequences list, based on their past behavior. Here's a summary of our conversation during the process:

> "Let's look at a specific example. What time are you supposed to be home?"
> "That depends."
> "What do you mean?"
> "Well, my mom tells me to be home at a reasonable hour."
> "What's reasonable?"
> "I don't know."
> "What does your dad say?"
> "Ask your mom."
> "If you're not home at a reasonable hour, what happens?"
> "Mom mostly cries and says I'm ruining her life."
> "What does your dad do?"
> "He's usually asleep."

When I look back, this conversation sounds funny, but my heart went out to John. How could he know what was expected of him when the boundaries were so vague and the consequences so meager? His answers—which I hear often but with different specifics—revealed that a latent Expectations and Consequences list already existed, but a new one needed to be created.

Using the previous example, the Expectations and Consequences list that already existed included the following:

EXPECTATION	CONSEQUENCE
Be home at a reasonable hour.	You'll make your mother cry.

These types of chaotic, default Expectations and Consequences lists often lean heavily in favor of the teenager. In our current example, the adolescent decides what *reasonable* means, or he'll at least make an argument for his definition like a lawyer in a John Grisham novel. And he probably won't bat an eye toward making his mother cry; he knows she'll get over it. In other words, there's no consequence that costs the teenager something. For him, it's a win-win.

Isn't This Just a Behavioral Contract?

Many parenting books recommend "behavioral contracting." But there are important differences between an Expectations and Consequences list and a parent-teen contract.

First, behavioral contracts work best when used to link compliance with privileges: "I, Patty, agree to practice piano every day for thirty minutes in exchange for thirty extra minutes of phone time." Behavioral contracts also connect a lack of compliance with consequences: "I understand that if I fail to practice at least three times in a week, I'll lose my phone for the weekend." This is a fine technique for children, but as discussed earlier, teenagers are not motivated by privileges. They want freedoms, and those are posted on the Freedoms list.

Trying to add extra incentives by giving privileges runs the risk of seeming patronizing: "And you can have a nice pizza party with your seventeen-year-old friends if you turn in all your homework!" For adolescents, the main reward they want is freedom. Don't get me wrong. They'll take your giant wads of cash or shopping sprees for good grades if you offer them, but those things aren't appropriate motivators for teenagers. Since you've already astounded them with their Freedoms list, there's no need to beat around the bush when it comes to expectations and consequences.

Second, the term *contract* carries the nasty little implication that your teenager must agree to something. I can't tell you how many parents have complained to me, "We tried a behavioral contract, but he refused to sign it!" or "We reminded her that she agreed to this, but she didn't care!" Listen up: Your Expectations and Consequences list is *not* an agreement between you and your teenager! It's a promise from you that "If you do [blank behavior], I promise I'll give [blank consequence]." Don't ask him to sign it! After all, if he were honest with you, he'd say he didn't need any list of expectations and consequences because he feels he can handle everything on his own.

This doesn't mean your adolescent should have no input into this list, but we'll get to that later.

Three Goals Your Expectations and Consequences List Accomplishes

Recall what we discussed at the end of the last chapter: Teenagers need consistency. Following a clearly outlined Expectations and Consequences list keeps your parenting consistent. Clarifying this list is like posting speed limit signs, along with the fine that can be expected, so the driver knows the limit and the fine he can expect if he goes beyond the limit. It makes everything clear to everyone involved, while also accomplishing three distinct goals.

1. Reducing Conflict with Your Teen

Have you ever found yourself in an argument, not about your teenager's latest transgression, but about the fact that she didn't think what she did was wrong? Instead of dealing with the issue, you find yourself going around and around about *why* what she did was wrong. To use our previous example, "Be home at a reasonable hour" isn't helpful because each party will define it differently.

By establishing clear expectations and consequences before the teenager leaves the house, a parent stands to avoid unnecessary conflict later that night. Of course, your teenager may not like your expectations, but your clarity can reduce the need to revisit this issue.

2. Helping Your Teen Develop Responsibility

If your teenager doesn't understand your expectations, how will he ever know what you deem to be responsible behavior? This cuts to their deeper question: *When will you say I'm an adult?* If he has no way to measure his growth into adulthood—no milestones of responsibility to achieve—how will he know if he's maturing into an adult?

Setting expectations sets the bar for growth. Furthermore, outlining the consequences of negative behavior helps your teenager anticipate such consequences in advance of making particular choices. As in real life, she will learn to weigh the pros and cons of choosing a particular path.

Here's a tough one: Your teenager has a midnight curfew, but he calls you at eleven thirty and tells you, "My friend texted me and needs a ride home from a party because he's drunk." Your teenager knows that giving his friend a ride will make him late for his curfew, but he tells you he'll take the consequence because his friend needs him. Is this irresponsible behavior?

I would argue this shows responsible behavior, even though he's violating curfew. Remember, your goal is not getting him to obey your rules as much as it is for him to learn how to be held accountable for his choices.

Last question: Should you still give the consequence even if you're proud of your kid for being a good friend? It could go either way, but I would caution against automatically withholding the consequence. If he knows you won't hold him accountable, he's not acting responsibly. It's up to you. Just don't tell him, "No, you come home, and I'll call your friend's mom" or something like that.

3. Facilitating Independence for Your Teen

Today's expectations become tomorrow's freedoms, and the Expectations and Consequences list makes this progress visible. In other words, imagine your Expectations and Consequences list pinned right next to your teenager's Freedoms list (i.e., room, school, clothes, etc.). Under Expectations, it reads, "I will clean my room before I leave for school every day." Under Consequences, it reads, "$1 off allowance."

When you finally decide to allow your teenager the freedom to keep her room as clean or as dirty as she'd like, you can go back to that Expectations and Consequences list and in her full view strike out those sentences and write the freedom on the Freedoms list. Teenagers relish hearing, "Remember this expectation? We're taking it off. That's up to you now."

Nothing says, "I'm getting somewhere!" quite like an adolescent watching her parents drop a parental expectation.

Once your teenager experiences that for the first time, she'll start seeing your Expectations and Consequences list in a whole new light. Rather than forbidding her from fun, it's promising her future freedom. Over time, one list should transfer to the other, so that when your adolescent leaves your home, she'll have full autonomy and will answer only to real-world consequences for her choices.

How to Create an Expectations and Consequences List

A key purpose for this list is to clarify your expectations. Look at the following Behavioral Expectations worksheet. What you ultimately create for your teenager may be different, but this worksheet gives you a guideline that includes many of the common issues that arise in my office.

(EXAMPLE) EXPECTATION	Priority	Current Compliance
No items left on floor, and bed made by __:__ on [day(s)].		
No items left on bathroom floor; countertops and mirror wiped down by __:__ on [day].		
Lights out and in bed by __:__ on [day(s)].		
Assigned homework completed by __:__ on [day(s)].		
When going out, parents must be notified and agree to destination and time of return.		
Must be in the car and ready to leave for school by __:__ on [day(s)].		
All house trash emptied and cans at the curb by __:__ on [day(s)].		

(EXAMPLE) EXPECTATION	Priority	Current Compliance
Clothes and other personal items removed from the [shared house space (e.g., living room)] by __:__ on [day(s)].		
No cursing, name-calling, or giving direct orders to parents.		
Must be home on school nights by __:__.		
Must be home on weekend nights by __:__.		
No smoking tobacco, e-cigarettes, or other paraphernalia.		
No use of alcohol or any other intoxicating substance or being present when it is being consumed by minors.		
Other		
Other		

You'll notice that the example expectations are written a bit differently from what you'd expect. The key to creating an effective Expectations and Consequences list is to communicate your expectations in "video camera" terms. In other words, if you were recording a video of your teenage son or daughter fulfilling a particular expectation, how would you describe what you see? The point is to make your expectations as clear and visual as possible so that no one can plead ignorance. (They may plead ignorance anyway, but that won't be your problem.)

For example, an expectation that states, "You need to be responsible for taking out the trash" is not a good, written expectation. What would that look like on video? Plus, your teenager would likely argue, "I was responsible in July. And I'll be responsible again . . . in October." This expectation needs to be more clearly delineated: "You will take the trash to the curb every Tuesday and Friday before you leave for school." That's an expectation that could be filmed every Tuesday and Friday. (I don't recommend filming him, by the way. Putting it in these terms is a helpful way for parents to clarify their expectations.)

You'll also notice that the two questions at the top of the Behavioral Expectations Worksheet are about *priority* and *compliance*. Thinking those through can help you avoid looking ridiculous. I've talked with parents who were so frustrated that their teenager never took out the trash that they started threatening, "Next time you forget, you'll have no car for a month!" I had to remind them that it was only trash. (And let's get real: They weren't going to take his car for a month.) On the other hand, if the parents had shaken their fingers and threatened, "Next time you drive home drunk, I'm taking your phone for a day," the importance of this behavioral expectation would not have been conveyed.

Once you've written out your expectations, you'll want to take some time to think about how important each one is and how much trouble you're having getting your teenager to comply. You'll rate priority and compliance levels one through ten for each expectation. For instance, completing homework will likely be a high-priority expectation (e.g., nine), but cleaning the bathroom should be a low priority (e.g., two).

Adding together the scores for importance and compliance can help you decide which expectations (if any) need to be written out and clarified.

So what's the point of tracking priority and compliance? Over time, this system will help you and your teenager see what needs to be worked on. If your adolescent usually complies with cleaning the bathroom, his or her aggregate score will be low—one or two for priority, plus one or two for compliance. Low scores mean no issues. A low score indicates the expectation doesn't need to be put on the list because it's not a problematic issue.

Allow me a quick aside here: Just because I list certain behavioral expectations on the worksheet does not mean you should automatically work on that issue with your teenager.

Don't make a lack of problems into a problem. In other words, if your teenager already takes care of her homework with little to no nudging from you, there's no need for you to do anything. You're better off not even talking about the areas in her life in which she's already meeting your expectations.

If anything, her behavior should prompt you to consider putting that on the Freedoms list. If you condescendingly write it on the Expectations and Consequences list, you run the risk of creating rebellion. She might wonder, *Why would Mom make me do what I'm already doing? She must not think I'm adult enough to know that I already know to do that.* That's not what teenagers say, but that's what they're thinking. Don't make an issue of issues that aren't issues!

———————————

Don't make a lack of problems into a problem.

———————————

But if your teenager's aggregate priority and compliance scores are high, you have reason to be concerned. Or better put, you have reason to clearly define your consequences. For instance, if meeting curfew is a high priority and your teenager rarely gets home on time, the total score is twenty—ten for priority and ten for compliance. This reveals a problem area, which leads to the next—and maybe the most important—part of the Expectations and Consequences list.

Define the Consequences

Believe it or not, it's a very loving thing to stay up late into the night devising creative ways to help your teenager suffer appropriately—when necessary. Do you recall where your actual power over your teenager resides? It's not in your physical strength, your mental agility, or even your loud voice. Your actual power is much more basic, but much more personal to your teenager: Everything she owns is yours.

"But that's her stuff. I don't have a right to take her stuff away from her." Of course you do. Everything she owns is yours—the clothes she's wearing, the basketball hoop outside, that laptop her grandparents gave her for Christmas. You control it all.

Occasionally, I have to educate an entitled teenager who doesn't realize this. He'll pontificate in my office, "They can't take my Xbox! I bought that with my own money!" I'll answer by saying to him, "Let me put it this way: If they take it from you, who ya gonna call?"

("Hello, police? My father just took my Xbox from me! . . . Hello? . . . Hello?")

Now we come to the Consequences list. To begin, take a quick inventory of the stuff your teenager enjoys using—his cell phone, tablet, computer, WiFi, TV, video games, allowance, use of your car, and so on. You likely know your teenager better than anyone else, so you know what things he thinks he has to have every day.

And for heaven's sake, don't ask your teenager what he thinks! "Hey, Son, which things would hurt most if we used them in disciplining you?" Only an idiot teenager would answer, "Well, don't take my phone whatever you do, 'cause that would motivate me!" Smart teenagers will say the opposite of what's true: "I don't care if you take my Xbox!" If you've watched your teenager, you already know whether that's something he uses.

Some parents fall for this trick and complain that they can't find anything to take away from their adolescents. If you start watching and your teenager doesn't do anything—use the phone, play games, watch TV, or go out with friends—something is wrong (like depression), and you may want to consult with a therapist.

Now, I'm not suggesting you be vindictive. Where possible, I advocate that the punishment should fit the crime. What I *am* suggesting is that you create a list of things you could pull from your teenager as a consequence of not meeting your expectations. The best consequences for everyday expectations are those that last only about twenty-four hours.

One thing I hope is obvious by now is that you're not looking for the one big thing you can take when your teens mess up. Why? Because you can only do that once, and I hate to tell you, but they're going to mess up more than once, and you'll need multiple ideas on what to pull from them so that a consequence is truly a consequence. It's essential that you have at least a small list of things so you'll have more flexibility in your discipline options.

Also, you're not trying to devise coercive consequences. Remember the difference between disciplining children versus adolescents? You're not trying to make your adolescent "never do that again." Your goal is to make the road toward that behavior very bumpy so he will decide for himself to move over to the smooth side of the road. We learned the first law of disciplining adolescents in the previous chapter: You can't make an adolescent do anything. Dangerous behaviors may require pretty big bumps in that road—but they're still only bumps.

In other words, don't always look for the nuclear option. Learn to launch medium-range missiles. Find what may hurt for just a day. Ensure that the magnitude of the consequence matches the magnitude of the offense.

But you must still pull the trigger on minor offenses every time! *By far, the major cause of parents' blowing their tops with their teenagers is that they didn't pull the trigger on appropriate consequences earlier.* The longer unmet expectations go without proper consequences, the more likely your teenager will keep pushing the boundaries to discover whether you'll ever do anything about it.

Consequences

So once you've made your inventory of things your teenager enjoys using—things you might take away temporarily as a consequence for her failure to meet an expectation—rank each of them according to the following system. (*Note:* Do not consult your teenager about this.)

3 – Very important to my teenager
2 – Somewhat important to my teenager
1 – Not very important to my teenager

For example, if your teenager's weekend curfew is eleven o'clock, some sort of consequence *must* happen at 11:01. It doesn't have to be a big consequence, but it must be *something*. Otherwise, eleven o'clock is just a suggestion. Those of you who don't say anything until eleven fifteen because you don't want him racing home at the last minute are sanctioning him to race home at about eleven ten! If it's on the list, it must be accompanied by a consequence. I'll have some suggestions about this at the end of the chapter.

THING TEENAGER ENJOYS	IMPORTANCE
personal computer	
cell phone	
allowance	
video games	
TV/movie streaming	
use of car	
car ride to/from school (vs. school bus)	
going to a friend's house	
having friends over	

Create and Implement an Expectations and Consequences List

The list you'll make is just a plain page titled "Expectations and Consequences." Take a sheet of paper and draw a line down the middle. I recommend you keep this list simple and avoid pontificating introductions (e.g., "In order for us as a family to achieve a more perfect union . . ."). If your teenager won't listen to your speeches, do you think she'll read your written diatribes?

Pulling from your two worksheets, you'll be writing the expectations on the left side and the consequences on the right. The final Expectations and Consequences list can be constructed by following a few simple steps:

1. *Complete the Behavioral Expectations Worksheet by writing out your clear expectations for your teenager.* Take time to carefully consider what ought to be on the list. I've listed several common expectations that you're free to use or amend. Please note that some of my example expectations may already be on your teenager's Freedoms list, so just draw a line through those.

2. *Use your priority and compliance ratings to decide which expectations (if any) require written clarification.* Your final Expectations and Consequences list should include only those expectations that need to be clarified. An expectation that's not a big priority, and is one your teenager usually complies with, shouldn't be added to the list. Just keep doing what you're doing. Occasionally remind him about that expectation. Keep the Expectations and Consequences list to a minimum because you will be using consequences to enforce each expectation.

   > Remember to use language that a cinematographer could read and then film your teenager accomplishing.

   Remember to use language that a cinematographer could read and then film your teenager accomplishing. Instead of "Keep your room tidy," write "Clean your room by eight o'clock every Wednesday evening." *Tidy* means something quite different to your teenager from what it does to you. In being as clear as possible, you should significantly cut down on those arguments about an adolescent's understanding of a particular expectation.

3. *Write expectations requiring clarification on the left side of the list, accompanied by an appropriate consequence on the right side.* Every expectation must be accompanied by a consequence. If you don't write in the consequence, you may as well write, "Or I'll get mad and yell at you." See the following example list.

4. *Allow the adolescent the opportunity to give feedback about the Expectations and Consequences list.* It's important that you display

a real interest in hearing your adolescent's feedback when you first show her the Expectations and Consequences list. In most cases, your list should only be a written form of rules you already have. Telling her you've written these out because you fear there have been recent misunderstandings may not make your teenager happy, but you should strive for some feedback about which expectations are most objectionable and/or which consequences seem unfair. And if at all possible, you should try implementing her suggestions. Depending on the maturity of your teenager, this may not be possible. (Wadding up your list and throwing it on the floor isn't useful feedback.)

However, if she does reply negatively to a specific instance ("That's kind of a big consequence for not feeding the dog."), you can be flexible and discuss what may be a better course of action. Even if you're pretty sure her suggestion won't work, you can at least consider replying, "Let's try your option for two weeks and see if it makes any difference."

EXPECTATION	CONSEQUENCE
Must be in the car and ready for school by 8:00 a.m.	• If you're not already up, we'll wake you at 7:45 a.m. If we have to wake you, you'll have an early bed restriction of 10:00 p.m. • Fatigue will not be accepted as an excuse for disrespect, etc.
Empty the dishwasher on Mondays, Wednesdays, and Fridays by 8:00 p.m.	• After 8:00 p.m.: $2 fine • If not done by 9:00 p.m.: 24 hours without phone • If still not done by next morning: grounded for 24 hours
School: No more than 1 C on any 6-week report card.	• First time: no electronics (recreational computer use, video games, TV) on weekdays (Sunday at 6:00 p.m. until Friday after school) for 6 weeks • If not brought up by next report card: no electronics on weekdays and weekends for 6 weeks • If not brought up after that: grounded for 6 weeks

EXPECTATION	CONSEQUENCE
No disrespect: • No cussing. • No name-calling. • No giving direct orders (e.g., "Get out of here!"). • No threats.	• $1 fine (we may decide this should be higher)
Must be home by 11:00 p.m. on non-school nights.	• 1 to 15 minutes late: 10:00 p.m. curfew on next non-school night • 16 to 30 minutes late: grounded on next non-school night • 31 or more minutes late: grounded for more than 1 day depending on how late (we'll let you know)

Keep in mind that seeking your teenager's feedback is not the same as trying to come to a joint agreement. The list you're showing is a completed list, not suggestions awaiting your adolescent's approval. A normal teenager, no matter how compliant, doesn't think he needs any of your expectations and consequences.

1. Implement the Expectations and Consequences List with Consistency

The issue at stake is not getting your teenager to behave correctly (or to be unmerciful and unyielding because of a written contract). The issue is maintaining consistency in how you're going to respond to her transgressions. In being consistent, you draw clear lines for your teenager to follow. When she deviates outside those lines, she should already know what to expect from you before even talking to you.

2. Regularly Review the Expectations and Consequences List for Necessary Updates

Let's say that one of the consequences for your teenager is the loss of a dollar for every dirty plate or cup you see in his room. If he has lost fifteen dollars every week for the last month, that's a consequence that needs to change because it doesn't seem to have much effect. Either the cost needs to increase, or a different consequence needs to be written—for example, for every dirty plate found, he loses video games for twenty-four hours.

You should also regularly review the list to strike out the expectations and consequences that have moved onto her Freedoms list. For instance, if you're granting her autonomy to keep her room as clean or as dirty as she sees fit, call her over and cross out any consequence and expectation that concerns her room, and write the word *room* onto the Freedoms list. Do this in front of her so she can see that you truly, honest-to-goodness are no longer requiring her to keep her room clean. Adolescents love these updates!

Lastly, you may need to review the list for issues that once weren't a problem but have now reared their ugly little heads. For example, a significant drop in grades from a teenager who never had such issues before may require clarifying expectations and consequences for schoolwork. The addition of a boyfriend or girlfriend may require adding expectations and consequences for where and how often they can be together. You'll have to use your judgment and communication skills to learn what may be a new and problematic issue in your teenager's life. Don't hesitate to add new expectations and consequences to the list, but only do so when needed.

I recommend reviewing your Expectations and Consequences list every three months.

Common Issues with the Expectations and Consequences List

Lying

It can be unsettling when parents discover their adolescents have deceived them, whether directly or by omitting important information.

Even more disturbing, these same teenagers often express no regret and may even act as if their deception is justified. However, you may be surprised to learn that when parents list *lying* among their concerns, my first goal is to find out if this is normal teenage lying. That's right, there's a type of teenage lying so common that you shouldn't make too big of a deal about it.

What I call "normal teenage lying" are lies intended to thwart a parent's attempts to monitor and supervise teenage behavior. If a parent asks, "Did you finish your homework?" few teenagers have the guts to answer with the real truth, which would be "I'm not going to answer that question because I don't believe it's your business to be supervising my schoolwork!" It's easier just to answer, "Yep."

If you find out later that your teenager didn't finish his homework, don't expect a lot of guilt and remorse. I'm not saying this type of lying is okay. You just don't need to worry that this behavior is an early sign of a future life of crime.

These lies are essentially passive-aggressive responses from an individuating teenager who thinks his parents are nosy. This kind of lie should usually be taken as a sign for you to back away from giving help he obviously doesn't want. Instead of weakly chasing down every deception and punishing each lie, it's more effective to simply acknowledge, "I wish you'd had the guts to tell me if you didn't like my asking about homework."

After that, it's time to change your tactics. In the place of reminders, just let him know what the consequences will be if his grades drop below a minimum level. This same method should be used for any situation in which your teenager's lying displays resistance to your check-up questions.

Believe it or not, one other type of lying you shouldn't be too concerned about is the obstruction-of-justice lie. If a teenager is confronted with the question "Did you and Warren smoke marijuana at that concert?" it shouldn't be a real stunner if she says, "Uh, no. Of course not!" The problem here is that she used drugs, not that she lied about it. When adolescents blatantly violate your expectations, they should pay for it in the consequence you give for violating your rule, not just because they tried to cover their tracks.

Look at it this way. The next time you read of someone arrested for murder and obstruction of justice, this just means that he killed someone, and when the police asked him about it, he lied. No one reading that article says, "He lied to the police? Wow!"

Some parents have told me that a severe violation like getting drunk or sneaking out at night would not have been such a big deal "if she had been honest with us!" However, placing "honesty with parents" at the top of the behavioral priority list sends the infantilizing message to your teen that any irresponsible, or even dangerous, behavior will be okay as long as Mom and Dad know about it. Not only does this message exaggerate a parent's power to protect her adolescent, but it also suggests that openness with parents is the most important of all behaviors.

I don't mean to imply that lying isn't a bad thing. However, a good understanding of adolescents can help parents maintain a proper perspective on this behavior and avoid overreacting. If you want to add an extra consequence to a rule violation ("because you lied to us"), feel free. Just don't get too bent out of shape over it.

Disrespect

Parents are often concerned about their teenager being disrespectful toward them. While this probably should be addressed in your Expectations list, I recommend caution. You want to be careful about shutting down open communication about things that anger your teenager. This is covered in depth in appendix 2.

Belligerence

Some of you may need to consider adding a belligerence rule. When your teenager has asked to do something or go somewhere and your answer is no, it's important that he has the freedom to tell you why he thinks your answer is wrong and/or why this upsets him. You should listen and consider his objections.

But if the answer is still no, there's no more need for discussion.

Belligerence is when you've said no, and your teenager starts using words to hammer you into changing your mind. I've known of a few parents who found themselves locked in their bathroom to get away from an angry teenager who wouldn't stop arguing.

Most of the time, belligerent teenagers are the product of a parent-adolescent relationship that hasn't mastered agreeing to disagree. (See chapter 10 for how to improve communication with your adolescent.) After you've stated that the answer is still no, it's best to just remind your adolescent that you understand she disagrees and she's too old for parental explanations to change her mind. Many teenagers will keep repeating that they don't understand why their parents won't let them do something, but the issue isn't understanding—

> Many teenagers will keep repeating that they don't understand why their parents won't let them do something, but the issue isn't understanding— they just think you're wrong.

they just think you're wrong. This can usually be defused by clarifying, "I don't think the problem is understanding. I think you believe we're crazy for not letting you go. That's okay because we kinda think you're crazy for wanting to go. We just don't agree."

After you've clarified that this is an agree-to-disagree moment, your next step is to refuse to be drawn back into the debate. Extinguishing the hidden reward of hooking you back into the discussion should be enough to do the trick. Your teenager may go away angry, but at least she won't start pounding on your bathroom door.

Not getting hooked back in can be harder than it sounds. Many teenagers are quite good at saying that one precise and provocative line to rope you back in. One-liners like "You guys never really loved me anyway!" don't represent deep, lifelong resentments that just happened to have come out during a discussion about going to a party. These are well-chosen, well-timed darts you need to practice ignoring.

If this doesn't work after a couple of weeks, then—and only then— should you add a belligerence rule. Write out that you will give one reminder after your teen has voiced his objection and the answer remains no. After being warned, he cannot bring the issue up until the next day. If he brings it up tomorrow, you'll need to listen again to his restatement of why he doesn't like your decision. That's when you say, "Yep, that's what I thought your concerns were. The answer's still no, and no more talking about it 'til tomorrow." Two to three minutes each day won't kill you. Besides, he most likely won't bring it up again.

The consequence for belligerence would be small and easily repeatable, like a one-dollar fine or a half-hour off video games that day. When teenagers are worked up, they may find it hard not to argue, so be prepared for three or four consequences in a given day. The main thing, however, is to not get hooked back in. It may be worth a two- or three-dollar fine to him. This gives him a good twenty more minutes of arguing that starts all over when you turn and angrily restate what you've already made clear: "Now, look—we've always been fair with you, and just because we say no doesn't mean we don't love you, young man!"

Yes! He'll celebrate inwardly, *I've got 'em where I want 'em!*

Maximum Punishments and the Life Sentence

When a teenager does something surprisingly irresponsible or dangerous, like coming home drunk or getting suspended from school for stealing, parents are often stunned and start looking for ways to shut everything down until they can figure out what to do. It's perfectly appropriate, and may even be better, to take two or three days to decide what consequences you'll give. The first thing out of parents' mouths in these cases frequently has to be taken back anyway (e.g., "You're not going anywhere until you're thirty-five!"), so take your time. They're going to be grounded for a few days, so there's no rush. This is a serious situation, but nothing's on fire.

The trick is to discover how to maximize the effectiveness of your consequences without causing unnecessary battles with your teenager or increasing her panic. For example, you'll be tempted to take an approach that suggests your teenager is now a five-year-old and will have to slowly work her way back to adolescence. Telling a seventeen-year-old that she has to earn your trust back sounds logical, but it's too vague. Over time, this can exacerbate fear in an adolescent who, while guilty of a serious infraction, still needs to individuate. For the first few days, she'll lie low and sound like the compliant kid you want to see. However, two weeks later, she'll start souring and pushing your limits.

The better option here is to pick a maximum sentence with a clear endpoint, and (this is the hard part) then he should return to the same freedoms he had before the infraction occurred. It's like serving jail time, but he needs to know when his sentence is up. You should avoid the temptation to add a vague probationary period because this approach reverts back to treating him like a child.

Before you go arguing nonsense ("Well, if she acts like a child, she'll be treated like one!"), remember that no matter how shocking the infraction may be, the clock is still ticking. You must have her ready for full adulthood at least by the time she finishes high school. The only probationary exception to this rule may be when alcohol or drugs are involved. This is covered at length in chapter 22. For now, I'll just say that in these cases, you could release her from grounding while holding on to the right to random drug screens or Breathalyzer tests for a set number of weeks. Even these should be given with an end date, as long as there are no further infractions.

The question of maximum punishment is worth considering. I've found that a month of grounding (going out only to school or work and having no friends over) is about the maximum that's effective. More than a month too often feels like a life sentence and quickly starts to lose impact.

Don't take away all electronics, allowance, and so on during this grounding. You'll need that ammunition for smaller infractions that may occur during the extended grounding. Some parents try withholding things like getting a driver's license as a big consequence. I find that this technique often bogs down over many weeks, and too many teenagers just stop caring if they ever get their license. It has more impact if you let them get their license but restrict whether they ever get to use your car.

My point is that you want to maximize your impact in discouraging any such major infractions from ever recurring. Giving a strong, lengthy period of grounding is usually very effective. Don't give in to the temptation to make exceptions to this grounding, but you don't have to be vindictive either.

I realize you may want to show some flexibility on occasion. On the one hand, if your son is grounded on the date of that big concert he's been looking forward to, you can say that's just too bad—a real-life consequence of his real-life decisions. Suggest he sell his ticket. It's not your problem. On the other hand, if your son's grounded but already has a date and plans for homecoming, you might consider bargaining with extra grounding time. For example, "You can go to homecoming if you choose, but we'll tack on another weekend to the length we already told you." The goal of responding to big infractions is to make sure your teenager pays dearly in restricted freedoms for a set period of time, but you must bring him or her back to full freedom once the time is up. This is the only way your adolescent can get back to the important business of learning to take responsibility for his or her actions.

What about More Complicated Issues?

Implementing a Freedoms list and an Expectations and Consequences list can significantly increase communication, reduce conflicts, and improve your overall influence in the life of your adolescent. But what about more complicated topics?

Issues like alcohol and drugs, dating and sex, managing school, video games, and pornography require a careful balance of clearly outlined expectations and good communication. We'll cover these and many other topics in the remaining chapters.

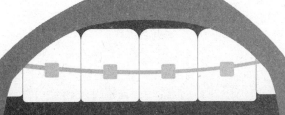

PART FOUR

Planned Emancipation and Adolescent Life Activities

How to Maximize Parental
Effectiveness When Guiding
Your Teenager

CHAPTER 13

School

You can lead a boy to college,
but you cannot make him think.

ELBERT HUBBARD

I remember seeing a billboard years ago featuring a report card with a big, red F on it. The giant headline above the report card read, "What if it's more than just bad grades?" It was an advertisement for a psychiatric hospital! You have to give credit to the sinister advertisers who came up with that. They knew how to play on parents' fears.

By far, grades and school-related issues are the most common problems that bring teenagers into my office. That's not surprising since teenagers spend so much time in school, and academics are essentially a teenager's main job. And while I won't try to cover all things related to adolescents and school in this chapter, I will review issues that relate to successful implementation of Planned Emancipation.

Parents naturally want to help their adolescents do their best in school, but they often end up fighting with their teenagers from September to May. Constant, bitter arguments over homework can cast a gloom over entire families every week. Exhausted parents end up happier about weekends and holidays than their teenagers are.

But academic issues during adolescence are more complicated than whether a teenager understands that school is important. Too many parents fall into the trap of treating every bad grade as a discipline problem and an opportunity to pull out their "Do you want to end up working as a fast-food cook your whole life?" speech. Helping an adolescent through school requires a careful combination of communication and limit setting that does more than try to ensure the best GPA possible. Adolescents must increasingly be given the freedom to manage their own school choices. We want them to do their best in school, but they must also gain insight into their own learning needs, directions, and interests.

Control Issues with Schoolwork

I'm always on the alert when a parent says *we* in describing a teenager's problems in school. "We started the year well, but we kind of started slacking off after fall break, right, honey?" Since the teenager will *always* refuse to answer such a patronizing question, I like to jump in with "So you're enrolled in his school too?" (Teenagers like this question.) Adolescents need to know that it's *their* academic career we're talking about.

To have the most influence on your teenager's school performance, you must address the issue of control. This means making a realistic assessment of what you can and can't control in her schoolwork, as well as seeking a path toward completely handing over freedom for your adolescent to make her own choices about school.

You can start addressing the issue of control by having conversations that attempt to assess what your teenager's own goals are. Instead of being upset about a bad report card (*don't* call the psych hospital), ask your teenager,

- "How do you feel about your grades?"
- "What were you aiming for?"
- "What do you think happened?"

These aren't rhetorical questions either. You need to listen to what he says and whether he has any idea of what the problems are. If he tells you he doesn't know, you can respectfully remind him that you're finished with high school, so it's not your problem, but you'd like to know what or whether he plans to do anything different next time. If there's no response or he needs more time to consider his answer, wait a couple of days and ask again.

No matter how school goes, in almost every case you should cease trying to exert any control over how your teenager handles it by her senior year. You should also start announcing this as soon as possible. Tell her you'd like to see her report cards, but how she handles her classes (whether passing or failing) is up to her.

Remember, after her senior year in high school, your role in her life will be as a benevolent bank. Your only interest at that point is whether you're going to spend even a nickel on helping her with college (with freedom always comes responsibility). If your high school senior still needs you to monitor her schoolwork, she has a more serious problem than a few bad grades. It would be better for her to discover and address this shortcoming while still living at home. If she doesn't, you might drag her through graduation and send her to college two hundred miles away and then months later find out she's wasting her time and your money—not to mention compiling a lousy academic record—texting her friends all day.

Limit Setting with Schoolwork

As your teenager moves through middle school and high school (up to his senior year), you'll need to set limits on his management of school. Homework is a common, early-control battleground in young adolescents. Parents who are used to happily working with their children to churn out homework suddenly find themselves in constant arguments with their young teenagers, who go to great efforts to keep their parents in the dark about what's been assigned and when it's due.

There comes a point when you realize the effectiveness of your efforts to help your teenager is outweighed by the cost of control battles. At that point, it's best to clearly state the problem: "I think, *now that you're older*, that my trying to help you with homework is just frustrating you." Try not to sound accusatory. As a matter of fact, the "now that you're older" part is a good thing. Remember, you are *for* his eventual independence.

A proactive response would be to add "How you manage homework and studying" to the Freedoms list.

> There comes a point when you realize the effectiveness of your efforts to help your teenager is outweighed by the cost of control battles.

However, with freedom always comes responsibility, so you will also be adding "Maintaining minimum grades" to the Expectations and Consequences list. In this example, the addition to the Freedoms list would look something like the following:

FREEDOM	BOUNDARY
Use your own judgment in handling homework and studies.	Must maintain minimum grades in all classes.

The addition to the Expectations and Consequences list might be something similar to what I've added here:

EXPECTATION	CONSEQUENCE
Must maintain grades with no more than 1 C at every 3-week progress report and 6-week report card period.	• 1st time: no electronics from Sundays at 6:00 p.m. until Fridays after school for 3 weeks • If not brought up by next progress report: no electronics at all for 3 weeks • If not brought up by next report card: no electronics and grounded until grades are brought up

This is a likely example for a middle schooler. The freedom granted to this teenager means you will stop checking, reminding, having secret communications with teachers, and so on. You are no longer taking responsibility for how her schoolwork is being managed. If done properly (and most parents struggle with keeping their mouths shut), *all* arguments about schoolwork can and should stop immediately.

Isn't that great? There's nothing more to argue about! It's up to the teenager now. You can just hear the crickets! What will you talk about then? After some time without policing her, you should be able to develop useful dialogue around other problems she may be having in school.

The mere fact that you aren't following your teenager around and nagging her doesn't mean she's not being held accountable for her choices. In the example above, there will be accountability every three weeks. Older teenagers should probably be given a longer period between accountability points. Much also depends on the report cycle of your teenager's particular school. But whatever the time period between accountability points, you should practice remaining silent about school management.

Emails from teachers should be forwarded to the teenager, and teachers should be informed of the arrangement you now have. Because of our confused culture, you may well get pushback, even from experienced teachers. That's okay. Their job is to get their kids to do well in class. They're likely used to dealing with parents who hold the teacher responsible for their helpless little seventeen-year-old.

The first thing you may have noticed in the example is the "No more than one C" expectation. I strongly recommend you set your grade expectations to the minimum acceptable grades. These are adolescents, not children. A limit like "No more than one C" gives them the flexibility to struggle without your involvement. It does *not* teach them that Cs are okay. I have never had a teenager come into my office and say, "Wow, I thought I needed to get As and Bs to get into college, but since my parents don't punish me for getting some Cs, I guess my grades are okay!"

The actual limit you set for minimum grades depends on your teenager. For a typical A/B student, you should consider allowing for one or two Cs per grading period. For a straight A student, you might set a maximum number of Bs. It's even reasonable to set a higher grade expectation for an expensive private school (as long as it's a school the teenager wants to attend). The point is that you want to set a grade level your adolescent would see as doable. The motivation for teenagers to succeed in school must increasingly shift from fearing their parents to looking to their future.

However, when the time for accountability rolls around, you must be ready. You gave them this freedom because they need to be respected as adults, and your consequences should reflect that same respect. Consider the following suggestions:

- Only grades coming from the school will be considered.
- "Amount of effort" is too ill-defined and will not be considered.
- Consequences do not apply during school holiday periods.

These kinds of considerations simply place the responsibility on the teenager. "The teacher said my grade is actually a B, but she hasn't put it into the grade book!" is not your problem. That's between your teenager and his teacher. Since you no longer monitor and badger him for apparently not trying, neither can you soften the consequences because he appears to be working hard. That's not the real world.

Lastly, your consequence is not set from a place of vindictiveness, but from a place of trying to reduce distractions that may be interfering with her schoolwork. So she should be able to entertain her little head off over spring break with her PlayStation, even if she got a bad grade on her last report card, but that distraction should be gone the Sunday night before school restarts.

I chose electronics in this example because that's often an appropriate distraction removal when it comes to homework. Also, I like the idea of progressive consequences because it displays restraint in interfering at all: "Look, I'm trying to leave you alone here, and I hate to see you not having anything to play with too, but why is it so hard to keep your grades up?"

Homeschool and Planned Emancipation

There has been a significant increase in the number of families opting to homeschool their children. Part of this has been due to the COVID-19 pandemic, but numbers were rising even before. In my practice, many Christian families are feeling a strong need to take control of what their children are learning. Most of the best stories you hear about homeschooling come from families with cute, little kids. Homeschooling adolescents is often not so cute.

The most common problems with homeschooled teenagers arise from control battles. There are great advantages to kids having their parents monitor their learning. Parents know their children best, and they can get creative with making home a good learning space. By adolescence, however, that same intimate knowledge of their kid's strengths and weaknesses can backfire. As the need for individuation increases, a parent's knowledge of her child's needs can be perceived as a threat to her teenager. Control battles ensue, and Planned Emancipation is a great way to resolve them.

Here's a case where that was exactly my prescription. "I just wanna go to regular school like everybody else!" the tall fifteen-year-old in my office half yelled at his parents. Jacob had been homeschooled since the first grade, along with his younger sister. Over the past four months, escalating arguments with his parents, along with spiraling grades, had brought this close family to my office. The flexibility with homeschooling had not only allowed Jacob to go on some amazing trips with his family, but it had also helped with his impulsivity and lack of organization. However, now that he was a young adult, this learning arrangement was causing problems.

Learning Problems

Success in school is much more than just a matter of motivation. But learning differences in adolescents often look like motivation problems.

When parents confidently tell me, "She could be a straight A student if she wanted to," I always ask, "How do you know that?" Or I ask, "How far back do you have to go to reach that conclusion?" I say this with the adolescent in the room. Teenagers like this question too.

Adolescents are not like eight-year-olds who need to have their self-esteem protected by leaving the room when the grown-ups talk about their learning problems. They chime in, "I've been trying to tell her that! I'm not as smart as she thinks!" They don't have their confidence boosted by parents constantly cheering them on. They need to take charge of their schooling. If your teenager sees real limits to his or her academic abilities, you should listen to that.

Most of the parents I work with are savvy when it comes to possible learning issues with their child. They have often already worked with the schools, had testing done, and have successfully implemented strategies that helped their kid do well through elementary school.

Then middle school hits!

One of the huge and often overlooked changes between elementary and middle school is the vast increase in *organizational complexity*. An elementary school teacher is equal parts teacher, secretary, and parent. If you forgot your worksheet, your teacher pinned a note on your jacket, reminding your parent to put it in your bag so you won't forget it next time. In middle school, your teacher barely remembers your name when he stops you after class to tell you that you have four zeros and may fail this semester! Okay, it's not usually that bad, but you know what I mean. Middle school and high school are vastly different from elementary school, not only because they teach more advanced material, but also because organizational management is both more complicated and falls almost completely on the student.

Learning differences in adolescents often look like motivation problems.

This kind of school environment for teenagers often exacerbates learning problems that once seemed fixed, and it exposes learning issues that have not been seen before. Problems like slow processing speed, auditory processing difficulties, or the inattentive type of attention deficit disorder (ADD) can even go undetected in families and schools. This is unfortunate because often the school (and the family) could be providing a great deal of support to the child. However, with the onset of individuation needs, teenagers naturally pull away from these supports. The resulting struggles in school may look like laziness, but those struggles stem from hidden learning problems.

Far too often, parents apply many years' worth of extreme consequences to a teenager who appears unmotivated, only to discover he or she was suffering from a learning problem all along. Whether you've had educational testing done before, if you're locked in a long-standing battle and nothing seems to get through to him about getting his grades up, you ought to seriously consider academic testing. It can give you valuable insight into his academic potential, as well as what may be causing the problem.

In the debate over laziness versus learning problems, the answer is never either/or. For example, teenagers with ADD are also often lazy. The presence of learning problems shouldn't prevent you from holding your teenager accountable by applying appropriate consequences for poor grades. It may require a change in the minimum grades you expect, but learning problems are not a pass for responsibility. If you've given over the freedom of managing school to your adolescent, you should be able to have adult-to-adult communication about what helpful, school-related tools you may be able to provide (e.g., tutoring, organizing tools, therapy). Keep in mind, these tools would be to help your teenager succeed in his (not *your*) schooling.

Specific issues related to deficits in attention are covered in chapter 25.

College and Other Post–High School Training

By the time your adolescent has finished high school, your parenting is essentially finished—whether you want it to be or not. This allows for a very different kind of relationship with your college-aged child. By now, your adolescent is fully individuated and can take charge of her future, which often includes college. Unfortunately (as you now know), this kind of relationship is not the norm in the United States. A common parent-collegian relationship is what I call "college as thirteenth grade." You should avoid this at all costs.

I first encountered this problem when I was in graduate school and taught an undergraduate course called Individual Learning Skills. It was the course you had to take when you were placed on academic probation. Half the students were there because they had never experienced overseeing their education. College was their thirteenth grade.

Limit setting, as outlined in chapter 11, had not been exercised for these eighteen- and nineteen-year-old adults, who were incredibly irresponsible in their schoolwork because they hadn't been held responsible for their schooling in high school. Many of them had parents who bombarded me with phone calls and letters (this was the 1980s, by the way), busily trying to control their kids' lives from hundreds of miles away. Over the years, I've seen a dozen college kids who adeptly forged fake grade reports and at least two adults who photoshopped fake diplomas. They did all this to pacify parents who maintained the delusion that they could still control their kid's college success.

If your young-adult child wants to go to college and you have funding options to help her, you should think of your relationship with her schooling as something like the benevolent bank covered in chapter 7. Banks don't make kids go to a certain college. They don't force them to hold off before pledging a sorority or fraternity, or come down there and talk to their teachers. Banks clearly state their policies and limits regarding what they'll pay for and what they won't. Good advice about the best schools or how to handle social organizations should remain just that—advice. Trying to use your financial support to micromanage her choices at college is a weak intervention and doesn't foster developing responsibility.

The best way to clearly outline the limits of your financial support is to stick to business and avoid dramatic generalities. Banks don't have policies that state "If you go up there and flunk out, you'll have to come home." Instead, they may offer a deal: "We will cover the cost of any accredited classes that you receive at least a passing grade in. You must pay back the cost of any failed class before we will pay for another semester." Another option might be saying, "We will cover the cost of eight semesters at an accredited college. If you fail to receive a degree in that time, you will have to pay for any remaining classes." Whatever line you draw, stick to it if possible.

Such clarity about support should open up much more communication about what's going on at college and give you more influence as an adviser. Your teenager can talk to you about problems because you're not the one she fears.

I should also mention that college is not for everyone. Most of the parents I work with went to college and hope for the same for their kids, but that doesn't mean college is best for everyone. Going to college doesn't even have to happen right after high school. I'm not talking about a gap year, either. Although it can be useful for some adolescents, no gap year should even be suggested that involves your having to pay for that year's expenses. To be blunt, there are few situations more developmentally stunted than the young-adult children of wealthy parents (sometimes called "trustafarians") globe-hopping like overgrown fourteen-year-olds.

When young adults feel the freedom to take charge of their education, parents need to be ready to discuss all options. Some very capable, intelligent people just aren't terribly academic in their skill sets. Further, in recent years, the cost of a college education has risen such that it's reasonable to weigh the benefit of some degrees against the burden of student loans and other financial considerations. However, many of these cost-benefit analyses continue to uphold the value of a college degree when the cumulative wage-earning power of college graduates is compared to that of high school graduates. My point here is that you can and should have the kind of relationship with your individuated adult child where all options for his future are openly discussed and your advice will mean something to him.

A Final Word about School

Having worked for decades with families and seen so many teenagers and parents wrestle over the frustrations of school, I have one big take-away point to emphasize: Always remember, it's only school!

That may sound controversial to some educators, but I want to make this point clear. There's no question that education is valuable, but when success in school overshadows family relationships, happiness, or even physical and mental health, you're doing it wrong.

I'm telling you this because it's a hole that's easier to fall into than you may think, and many families don't see it coming. One day you're a normal human being, and the next thing you know, you're a crazed, notebook-checking, teacher-hounding, tie-'em-to-their-desk prison warden.

School is a territory that can be difficult to hand over to your teenager. Progressively handing over control invites your teen to grow up and take charge of his education. It places him as the chairman of a committee of parents and teachers who are watching and asking him, "What are you gonna do now?" Consequences are there to ensure he won't be able to "crash" in school without suffering the proper deprivations that accompany failure. But giving more freedom encourages him to figure out what problems he may be having and teaches him to evaluate the effectiveness of any solutions that are being attempted.

After all, you've already finished high school! Now it's his turn.

CHAPTER 14

Sports and Other Extracurricular Activities

*This ability to conquer oneself is no doubt the most
precious of all things sports bestows.*
OLGA KORBUT

"Dr. Wilgus, Justin is a gifted athlete." The sixteen-year-old squirmed a bit in his chair as his father spoke. "He could be an all-star if he would just apply himself."

"He used to love baseball so much, but now he seems more interested in going out with friends," Justin's mother chimed in.

"He just doesn't seem to understand," continued his dad, "that if you want to succeed at something, you have to put in the work!" By now, Justin's gaze was firmly fixed out the window of my office.

Most parents know the advantages that come from involving their children in sports and other activities. Parents work hard to establish guidelines for their family, such as "Should we let them play more than one sport at a time?" A unique set of problems arises, however, when parents continue these same guidelines from childhood well into adolescence. Like all topics related to parenting teenagers, you should pay careful attention not only to *what* activities your adolescent is involved in, but also to *who is in charge of* these activities. This should be important to you because it's definitely important to your teenager.

Justin was a common example of this shift in priority. As with many kids who have been involved in an activity most of their lives, Justin's parents hadn't noticed an important change that occurred in him once he became an adolescent. His parents were still using their understanding of children to make sense of his lack of enthusiasm for baseball. When Justin's motivation waned, they redoubled their usual efforts to teach and remind their son of the importance of hard work and commitment to the team. What they failed to understand was that Justin already knew all that. His lack of motivation stemmed from his drive toward individuation. He wanted to know the answer to the question "When will my parents say it's time for me to decide about baseball?"

Control Battles

By now, you're probably getting better at spotting potential control battles in conflicts that arise with your teen. In the case above with Justin and his parents, the issue could be resolved by simply adding "freedom to manage sports/activities" to his Freedoms list. Often, however, it's not that simple.

Parents who have already invested deposit money and other financial outlays will have good reason to object if their teenager suddenly decides to quit dance, sports, or other costly activities. If your child was nine years old, I would suggest you use this opportunity to teach her to follow through with commitments, and not allow her to drop out. She may object at first, but later she would most likely be grateful that you made her stick it out.

With adolescents, the outcome can be very different. It goes back to the basic need for individuation. Requiring teens to continue the activity after they've declared a desire to quit can backfire in a big way. I have known adolescents who reacted to parental overcontrol by deliberately blowing games, sneaking around and missing rehearsals—you name it. With teenagers, it's usually best to show respect for their age and desire to make their own decisions, while holding on to the realistic need for you to get your money back. Recognizing your adolescent's freedom to quit an activity while handing them a stiff bill for the money you've laid out can be a good motivator to finish at least the current season.

This amount shouldn't be punitive: "You have to pay me back for all these years we put into your soccer playing!" Young adults often have good reasons to reconsider activities in which they've succeeded in the past. Parents may not agree with their reasons, but you should realize you can't force them to participate when they no longer want to. Control battles over activities that are meant to enrich a teenager's life defeat the purpose of the activity.

What if They Don't Want to Do Any Activities?

Respecting a teenager's objection to parental control over his activities is not the same as supporting a teen's indolence. You can and should make allowances for your teen's preferred extracurricular activities, but "no activity" shouldn't be on the list of choices.

Particularly for young adolescents, it's reasonable to expect them to involve themselves in some activity that takes them out of the house, requires the involvement of others, and perhaps includes a certain amount of physical exercise. Since COVID-19, an alarming number of children and adolescents seem to have become used to not getting out of the house much. Allowing teenagers to choose the activities they want can reduce some of the control issues while still requiring them to participate in *something*.

This usually sounds like a parent saying, "I hear you want to quit basketball, and you're too old for me to make you keep playing. But you'll need to pick something else that involves being out of the house and being with other kids your age for at least [X] hours

> Allowing teenagers to choose the activities they want can reduce some of the control issues while still requiring them to participate in *something*.

a week." You'll probably need to give your teen a deadline for signing up for this other activity.

Let your teenager know that if she fails to pick another activity, you'll require her to go to one *you* think is best for her. Passive resistance is a common tactic with recalcitrant teenagers. Also, a teenager who digs her heels in and refuses to do any activity certainly doesn't need to be using electronic entertainment devices. Hopefully, it won't come to that level of battle, but it's best to be prepared.

Influencing Adolescents about Their Extracurricular Activities

When I was in high school, I played the French horn. I was among the few chosen for the all-state orchestra. I had offers to continue my music career after high school. But by late high school, I knew enough to consider the limited job opportunities and the stiff competition I would face as a professional musician. I knew I was good, but I also knew I wasn't *that* good. I quit playing at the end of high school and never looked back. My parents, wisely, left that up to me.

Adolescence is a time when young adults naturally reevaluate the activities that are important to them. This is a crucial part of young adults' developing insight into their own goals and abilities. By your teen's late adolescence, you *don't know* what activities are best for him to invest in. Your teenager, on the other hand, knows what you know about the value of certain sports or artistic endeavors, but only he knows where his heart is. Overall, it's best to remember that your goal is to have real input into decisions that truly are his to make, not to try to control those decisions for him.

CHAPTER 15

Friendships and Group Activities

One who has unreliable friends soon comes to ruin,
but there is a friend who sticks closer than a brother.
PROVERBS 18:24, NIV

"I just stay home and watch videos mostly." Maggie was seventeen and had seen me on and off since her parents' divorce when she was fourteen. Her depression had improved, and, I thought, so had her social life.

"Wait, what happened to Sierra? I thought she was your best friend." I always keep notes on the names of my patients' close friendships.

"Yeah, not so much anymore. We just kinda drifted apart."

"Maggie, she was your best friend!" I said, a little frustrated. "You're not even going to find out what happened?"

One of the biggest changes to adolescent life over the past decade has been the massive decrease in social interaction. In the past, parents of teenagers spent a great deal of time corralling and trying to keep tabs on their kids' social lives. Today, an increasing percentage of adolescents have little or no real social connections at all. As so-called social technologies reach further into our lives, adolescents often define friendships by those who see their social media pages more than by those with whom they have real-life interactions.

The result is that parents feel out of touch with their teenagers' social circles, or they wonder if their adolescents even have a circle of friends. It's tricky for parents to have any kind of effectiveness in the social lives of teenagers, but that doesn't mean there's nothing to be done.

Giving Freedom to Choose Friends

Trying to control who their teenager can be friends with has always been problematic for parents. Usually, this battle centers on the adolescent's desire to exercise his judgment in who he chooses to be friends with. A teenager will even argue in support of friends who have not treated him well just to maintain his right to choose for himself. Giving your adolescent the freedom to choose his friends should go on the Freedoms list right from the beginning.

Always remember that giving over control of something you can't control anyway doesn't decrease your effectiveness. Freedom usually allows a teenager to communicate more freely about specific areas of her life. Strong communication is a much better way to guide your adolescent through the sometimes rough waters of friendships.

But what about teenagers who seem to have no friendships? These are adolescents who rarely leave the house on weekends and never get calls to go out and socialize with groups. What good does "freedom of friendships" do in these cases?

One thing to note is that even teenagers with little or no visible social life often remain defensive. You would think that an adolescent suffering from a lack of social success would welcome feedback or help from a well-meaning parent. But of course, that's not usually the case. Even if your teenager doesn't seem to have any friends, it's still worthwhile to put "choice of friends" on the Freedoms list. I've talked to many teens who were struggling socially and quite confused as to why, but they still managed to muster up resentment that their parents "never let me do stuff with my friends." As in all areas of freedom, you want to take the issue of control off the table.

The Complicated World of Shallow Relationships

Friendships are difficult in today's culture, and that's not your child's fault. It's not yours, either. Human social relationships, for millennia, were based on large family structures that resembled clans. Most people lived in small towns and interacted with the same people their whole lives. Shared experiences laid a foundation for most relationships. Everyone knew each other and each other's family. Even if someone wasn't necessarily liked by many people, everyone still knew who he or she was.

Today, families move far more readily, and few adults feel any obligation to set up their households near other family members, or even near their hometown (if they ever had one). Skyrocketing divorce rates mean that many kids juggle social lives between two households. When parents' houses are even a fifteen-minute car ride apart, children's and adolescents' social lives are impacted.

In addition, screened technologies that demand teens' attention seem to suck out the small amount of downtime remaining for kids to interact and build friendships. Even if you're able to minimize these influences, they have a major effect on your kids' peers, the ones they need to connect with.

This means that social problems don't always reflect failure in your teen's social skills. True, there are always teenagers who navigate these turbulent times well and have good groups of friends, but they represent a smaller percentage than ever before.

Church and Other Religious Youth Groups

For Christian parents as well as Jewish and other religious parents, churches and other religious communities can provide a much-needed remedy for teens lacking meaningful social connections. I have worked with many churches, and the majority make significant efforts to provide spiritual and social connections for their adolescents.

Finding a faith community where your teen can make friends is important, but that shouldn't be your first goal when he or she is struggling. Growing up in the 1960s, I experienced the early days of church youth groups. As teenagers, we had our own minister, Kenny, who had longish hair and was considered to be cool. However, keeping adolescents involved in church by simply adding guitars and a youthful vibe seems to have run its course. The needs of teenagers today are far deeper. For Christians, this is where adversity becomes an advantage.

Social isolation and loneliness are the kinds of struggles that lead adolescents to long for deeper connections with God. Instead of wondering if that cute girl will be at youth group (like I did as an adolescent!), more and more teenagers seek and long for real truth that can help them get through each day. The prophet Isaiah told us, "But now, thus says the LORD, who created you, O Jacob, and He who formed you, O Israel: 'Fear not, for I have redeemed you; I have called you by your name; you are Mine'" (Isaiah 43:1, NKJV). These words have comforted me over and over in my own life. They are words of deepest connection and identity. Those who truly know God are never alone.

> Social isolation and loneliness are the kinds of struggles that lead adolescents to long for deeper connections with God.

Adolescents are young adults ready to be challenged about the reality of their faith and how it can and should apply to their social and emotional struggles. I have been personally encouraged by the faith of many of my teenage patients. Their experiences of social rejection have been transformed into periods of spiritual growth. Finding a church that encourages deepening discipleship for adolescent believers should be one of your top priorities.

Churches can be a huge support for teens seeking friendships. My wife and I were both very involved in the public high school we attended, but our closest friendships were among those we went to church with. In a world that's growing increasingly hostile toward the Christian faith, it's more important than ever to become deeply involved in a thriving Christian community.

Note, however, *if you want your teenager to find the support of a church community, you must attend that church regularly and often.* It seems odd to point that out, but there has been a startling decrease in church attendance by professing Christians. Many pastors tell me their regular church attenders now come about twice a month. Since the COVID-19 pandemic, many have been substituting watching an online service for real church attendance.[1]

Real friendships require time in the same room together. Virtual church attendance cannot provide the needed intimacy. Even in church settings, however, social connection can still be tricky. This is where student ministers can be helpful. I call them "professional cool" people.

In middle school, our daughter was having trouble fitting in with the other girls. We were new to our church, and our daughter was shy. We spoke to a student minister, and she took charge of the situation. She had a great relationship with these kids and was able to confront some of the girls about not being open to new people. That helped a lot. Weeks later, this same leader confronted our daughter when she didn't think she was doing her part in participating with others. That's the beauty of a strong church community.

No matter how much you try to help your teenagers' social lives, there will always be complications that are out of your control. These are the times you can use the power of Planned Emancipation to provide much-needed advice that doesn't feel so pushy to your teenager. Once you've silenced the control battle ("Hey, who you're friends with is up to you, remember?"), you can offer helpful advice.

I've worked with countless teenagers experiencing bitter failure in their social lives. The following are some of the things I point out and strategies I recommend. Remember, I'm talking freely with these teenagers partly because I'm not their parent, so you'll need to be careful to present these things as suggestions only and not requirements.

You Can't Be Friends with a Group

It's common for adolescents, especially young teenagers, to feel rejected by a group of friends. Social media can make this worse when kids see pictures of their friends having fun together without them. This apparent rejection can cause teenagers to feel almost panicked about being left behind. Sometimes parents are involved in these group dramas and may feel the same fears.

It's hard for adolescents (and some parents) to avoid the false belief that there's some sort of group mind that's making detailed decisions about who's in and who's out. Group dynamics do not foster careful consideration and often don't represent the opinion of each group member. Instead, the actions of groups tend to be the lowest common denominator of the individuals within the group. I've known many groups that failed to invite this or that person to a gathering, but never did a group spontaneously invite a social wallflower out of sheer compassion.

Then there's always the mean guy or girl who seems to be the center of the group, and who, for some reason, doesn't want your teen around. Many teenagers tell resentful stories of jerks. This is usually a popular guy or girl who seems to hold sway over the whole friend group, but who is mean to them specifically.

I always ask the adolescent to think about what skill this jerk may have that gives him so much connectedness and control. Mostly, teenagers don't want to think about this; they'd rather stew in their resentment. But when they do think about it, if this kid is truly mean, the influence and connection he wields is from things the teenager I'm talking to doesn't value for himself. She'll say, "Everyone likes her because her family's rich" or "No one will stand up to him because he's the coach's favorite on the team." The skills or characteristics that make certain teens popular in a group aren't usually skills that help a person get and keep close friendships.

Focus Instead on One or Two Close Friendships

Instead of trying to please a fickle crowd, children should be encouraged to develop their closest friendships throughout their lives. You can't set up playdates for a teenager, and you must be careful about how much you push this topic with your teen. Offering advice is usually good, but offering constant, increasingly intense advice begins to feel like pushing.

When I meet with an adolescent in therapy, I have the names of her closest friends written on her intake form. I regularly ask about the one or two same-sex friends whom she feels closest to. When we talk about social events in her life, I'm careful to ask, "So, what happened with _____?" I want to maintain a focus on these closest friendships over the course of time.

I suggest you do something similar with your teen. But note this: Ask about the friends who have been important to your teenager, not the ones you *wish* he would be friends with. One or two solid, long-standing friendships are a cornerstone for his life, particularly as he heads into independent adulthood.

CHAPTER 16

Dating and Sex

High school isn't about finding your husband.
It's about finding your bridesmaids.

INTERNET MEME

Pop quiz: You're watching TV with your kid. It's a show you've never seen called *The Big Bang Theory*, which looks funny until the following scene:

> Amy (the nerdy girl): "So how's everything going with you and Leonard?"
>
> Penny (the pretty blonde girl): "Uh, I don't know, it's still kind of weird. We haven't really recovered since he proposed to me in the middle of sex."
>
> Amy: "Oh, boo-hoo. If Sheldon proposed to me during sex, my ovaries would grab onto him and never let go."[1]

Choose your parental response from the following options:

a. Cover your kid's ears while you grab the remote and change the channel.
b. Wait until the end of the scene and ask your kid what he or she thinks of the conversation depicted.
c. Ask me *at our next session*, "Shouldn't that depend on how old my kid is?"

The right answer is *c*. Your response should be different if the kid in this scenario is a child or an adolescent. If this kid is an eight-year-old, then this example is how you learn that *The Big Bang Theory* isn't a good show for him to watch. However, if you're with a teenager, option *b* becomes a good answer. This could be one of many essential opportunities to talk about sex and relationships, and I don't mean to simply remind your adolescent of the dangers of casual sex. It's an opportunity to find out what he or she thinks about the topic. This kind of communication is aided immensely when you have initiated Planned Emancipation.

> Planned Emancipation can significantly increase your influence on your teenager's dating and sexual behavior.

Planned Emancipation can significantly increase your influence on your teenager's dating and sexual behavior. It's important to keep this in mind when considering such a scary topic. Even the thought of our kids becoming sexual beings can freak parents out. Then we start looking at our messed-up world and get even more concerned. The next thing you know, we're installing locks on every door. But parents who have established their support of an adolescent's eventual sovereignty over dating and sexual choices save a lot of money on security devices. They use their influence to train their teenager to keep himself or herself safe.

Exposure to sexual material takes away innocence, thus being primarily harmful to children. It's right and proper to keep sexual images and similar material away from children. I'll never forget the day my sweet, innocent, six-year-old son and I were walking into the grocery store together. He looked up and asked, "Daddy, what does [sexual obscenity] mean?" After I speed-walked him back to the car, he told me that he and a friend had read the word on the bathroom wall at school and then used their phonics skills to try to sound it out, but they didn't know what it meant. I still remember imagining what I'd do if I found the punk kid who had wrecked some of my son's innocence.

But when your child becomes an adolescent, you need to rethink your role. Maintaining innocence is *not* a possible or even useful goal then. As within every other aspect of your teenager's life, you need to plan for a reasonable transition from being a gatekeeper trying to fend off harmful cultural influences to a co-adult advising and influencing your young adult's choices. When you simply say no to anything you deem to be an inappropriate sexual influence without regard for your teen's age, you become an increasingly irrelevant voice to an adolescent who intentionally keeps her parents in the dark about her sexual choices.

Some parents may object here and pontificate, "It's always a parent's job to uphold appropriate standards." In my experience, these parents don't take their jobs more seriously than others. They're just more *scared* than others. If that's you, let me remind you that you certainly have the right to maintain standards in your home by vigilantly monitoring (as best you can) what is or isn't watched when you're around. But when your kids become teenagers, maintaining this right means you will sacrifice a huge amount of influence in one of the most confusing areas of their lives.

Intimacy and Security in Relationships

Adolescent romantic relationships have always been complicated, but now they're downright confusing—for teenagers *and* parents. When my parents dated in high school, they were "going steady." When I had a girlfriend in high school, we were "going together." Do you know what the exclusive dating relationship is called now? It's called "going out." Apparently "going" is still okay, but "steady" or even "together" is too confining for today's teenagers. Even the DTR ("define the relationship") talk has come and gone. Today's adolescents have real problems knowing how to define their relationships, and most have simply stopped trying.

No matter how dating relationships are labeled, they always involve two important elements: intimacy and security. Intimacy is the experience of knowing and being known by another. Romance is exciting and perilous because it involves sharing more and more about yourself with another person who, hopefully, continues to find you as attractive as you find him or her. Security comes from commitment, an understanding that we won't be intimate with anyone else. The risks of deeper intimacy naturally create a strong need for the security of commitment. This all goes along fine until deep levels of intimacy outstrip the security of commitment. High school dating stories are fraught with cheating and awkward breakup stories.

But dating relationships are only one type of intimate relationship. Adolescent friendships have always been an important source of intimacy and support. Close friendships provide desperately needed intellectual, emotional, spiritual, and experiential intimacy without the complications of sexual intimacy. Security is fostered in long-term friendships.

However, more and more adolescents today are isolated due to the mobility and mutability of families. The explosion of technology has created a generation of teenagers who don't truly know the difference between electronic and face-to-face human interaction. Even long-term friendship among adolescent girls—historically a foundational element to any group of teenagers—appears to be weakening. Teenagers often count members of the opposite sex among their closest or even best friends without reference to the complications that often occur. Yet close, supportive, same-sex friendships are critical in an adolescent's ability to handle dating relationships.

An internet meme I often quote to teenage girls says, "High school isn't about finding your husband. It's about finding your bridesmaids." Girls who try to make a boyfriend also fill the role of best friend put far too much pressure on the dating relationship. At best, they run the risk of dating someone long after they've lost interest. At worst, they may feel sexually obligated in order to maintain emotional intimacy.

Boys whose emotional openness with their girlfriends far outpaces their intimacy with other guys are often insecure, possessive, and even controlling in their dating relationships. When boys have close friends who share the same goals and beliefs and with whom they have shared important life experiences, they have the needed time and space to learn about themselves without the pressure and complications of romantic attachments.

Your first step in knowing how to best help your teenager navigate dating and sex is to take stock of what sources of intimacy are currently available to him or her. Does he have close, stable friends? Though she spends a lot of time with her group, is she very close to one or two particular girls? When teenagers tell me about their social lives, I remind them, "You can't be close friends with a group." Having five or six best friends means she isn't close to any of them. If his best friend is a girl, how does that work? We don't need to have seen every romantic comedy to know that guy-girl best friendships are frequently made up of someone (usually the guy) who's secretly attracted to the other (usually the girl).

> Your first step in knowing how to best help your teenager navigate dating and sex is to take stock of what sources of intimacy are currently available to him or her.

Teenagers who get into trouble with painful dating relationships and promiscuous sexual behavior are trying to fill a strong need for intimacy. Intense relationships that quickly involve high levels of emotional and sexual intimacy are like junior marriages. Parents who try to have an impact only by ratcheting up control and limit setting end up playing the judgmental parents in modern-day versions of *Romeo and Juliet*.

You must do all you can to encourage every type of healthy intimacy available to your teen. You can't set up playdates, but you can offer to drive her to the movies or the fair or a game to meet up with friends. If you've tried to set up your house as the go-to house for your kids' friends to hang out and that's working, great! If your place has become unpopular for some reason, don't keep hounding your teen by asking, "What's wrong with coming over here?" The issue isn't about you. It's about finding ways to help your adolescent meet his needs for connection and sharing. This includes doing all you can to increase your connection with him so he feels comfortable talking to you about his relationships.

Talking about Dating and Sex

Nicholas, a big, athletic sixteen-year-old, sat down heavily on the couch in my office. I had just checked in with his mother, who had said that his grades were a bit better and he was getting out with friends more but he wasn't dating yet.

"I thought you were still going out with Ashley," I said.

"Yeah, and that's what I need to talk to you about," he answered, sitting up, now more interested.

"Still haven't told your mom about her, eh?" I leaned back, slightly frustrated with this all-too-common scenario.

Nicholas answered as if I had asked something ridiculously irrelevant. "What? Nah," he said, waving his hand as if he were brushing off a gnat. "She'd just ask a lot of questions. Listen, yesterday she texted and said . . ." and off he went.

Nicholas was dealing with important issues in the first dating relationship of his life, and he couldn't even conceive of talking to his parents about it.

Teenagers need guidance in managing dating relationships, yet having the kind of parent-teenager relationship that allows for such openness is rare. As with most teenagers, Nicholas's issue was control. He hadn't received a clear message from his parents that they would respect his choices and decisions about dating, so he heard any questions from them as interrogation. If dating had been placed on a Freedoms list, he would begin to respond differently.

Everything we've covered in this book so far, especially on

appropriately giving freedoms and how to increase communication, is essential if you ever hope to talk effectively with your adolescent about dating.

The Christian Ideal of Marriage

For parents who are Christians, I have one note to insert here: Talk to your children and teenagers about marriage! It surprises me how little is said in Christian households about the goal of eventual marriage. Remember, the morals the Bible teaches about sex are centered on the sacredness of marriage. Warning your teenagers about the dangers of pregnancy and STDs is fine, but that's not the primary reason Christian young people should aim for some level of sexual restraint.

For Christians, you are dating either your future spouse or someone else's future spouse. Christian singleness is completely unlike secular singleness. When your teenager is getting interested in dating, ask whether the prospective date is someone she would ever consider marrying. If she's stunned by your question, that's more reason to talk further.

Inserting the topic of eventual marriage is difficult to do today. Virtually no one in popular culture is interested in the topic of marriage. That's why it's imperative that Christian parents loudly and regularly repeat the freedom their teenager has or will have to make his own choices in dating. Dating and marriage are at the top of the list of topics that most adolescents think their parents only want to lecture about. You'll have a tough time proving that you're only talking out of respect as a fellow adult. But if you win his trust and he believes you respect his freedom, you can have some important discussions that can help your teenager think through this important topic.

Talking about Sex Is Probably Trickiest of All

First, you must initiate any talk about sex. Review the section in chapter 10 on initiating communication. If you wait to answer whatever questions your teenager spontaneously brings to you, you will wait a long time. I hope you've already had discussions about what sex is before your child has reached adolescence. Teenagers don't usually have questions about the mechanics of sexual behavior. Although some may be misinformed about certain things, they're often too ashamed to admit it.

Initiating conversations about sex depends heavily on your comfort level. Children of any age have an internal monitor about what topics their parents can and can't handle. Your embarrassment will embarrass them. Kids don't like seeing their parents off balance. This may mean that you need to practice talking about sex (as weird as that sounds). Practice with your spouse or a friend. If you're married, you should already be very used to talking about sex with your spouse. If you're married and still find it hard to talk about sex, you have a marriage problem, not a parenting problem.

You must initiate any talk about sex.

Questions like "So, you and Hudson have been dating for a while now. How's it going physically?" may seem hard to ask, and you run the risk of the old "Ew, Mom! What's wrong with you?" response, but the question should still be asked. Remember that these are *not* forced conversations. If she doesn't want to talk about it, you should respect that, but you should also bring it up again after some time has passed. Each time you do, you're reinforcing that you can handle discussing this topic but that you also won't force her to discuss it if she's not ready.

Parents who didn't enter marriage as virgins may worry about how to answer their teen when asked, "What did you do before you married Mom/Dad?" The best answer is usually something matter-of-fact: "If I thought telling you everything I did would help you, I would, but I don't think that would help you. Just know that I didn't handle this perfectly myself, so I know it can be tricky."

That may sound evasive, but I would say it appropriately frames the conversation. You're trying to encourage an adult-to-adult conversation. Keeping a score of "who handled things better" just makes that harder. Usually, parents need to be clear that they're not coming into the discussion as some sort of sexual saint—teenagers don't like to think of parents as sexual beings at all. At the same time, details of your sexual history are too burdensome for teenagers. Giving details always runs the risk of either shaming a teenager who's struggling or implying permission to a teenager with less experience than you had.

Fathers and Daughters, Mothers and Sons

An adolescent's relationship with his or her opposite-sex parent is possibly the strongest influence over teenage dating relationships. Girls who have a close, supportive relationship with their fathers are less likely to get involved in inappropriate or risky relationships with guys. For guys, Janette Rallison's quote is almost an axiom: "You can always tell how a man will treat his wife by the way he treats his mother."[2] You may speak positive words and have developed a supportive relationship with your teenager, but when it comes to dating and sex, it makes a noticeable difference whether these words come from a mother or a father. These roles are not interchangeable. Planned Emancipation and your efforts at increasing communication should be helping these relationships along, but there's more you can be doing for your opposite-sex adolescent.

FATHERS AND DAUGHTERS

Father-daughter relationships commonly change significantly when a girl reaches puberty. Teenage girls are naturally self-conscious about their bodies as they develop, and dads are often unsure how to approach daughters who are now appearing more womanly. These discomforts often result in reduced physical affection at the exact time a teenage girl needs real reassurance and support from a man. Some dads respond by either ignoring her development altogether ("Daddy's little girl") or only referencing these physical changes as dangerous or slutty. Countless teenage girls have told me the same story of feeling closer to their fathers before they reached adolescence. They're always a little confused and sad about the distance that was created just because they grew up. Instead of trying to ignore or vilify a girl's adolescent development, a father must appropriately acknowledge the changes and take the lead in helping her feel good about them.

In her memoir *Bossypants*, Tina Fey recounts a workshop she attended where women were asked, "When did you first feel like a grown woman and not a girl?" She writes, "Almost everyone first realized they were becoming a grown woman when some dude did something nasty to them. . . . It was mostly men yelling [things] from cars. Are they a patrol sent out to let girls know they've crossed into puberty? If so, it's working."[3]

This is exactly what I hear from girls and women in therapy, and it should break any man's heart. When a girl begins transitioning to womanhood, she needs to know if men find her attractive, interesting, smart, or funny. The first man in line to answer these questions is her dad. If he's not there to respond, plenty of other men will line up to answer, but they'll want something in return.

Fathers need to prepare their daughters for womanhood by modeling how they should expect to be treated by a man. This should start at least by early adolescence but can begin at any age. A father should regularly ask his daughter to do something with him without her mother or any other kids. If this sounds like a date, that's exactly what it *should* sound like. He should consider activities she likes and make sure there is time just to talk together. A dad who asks his daughter relevant questions about her life and remembers what she answers teaches her that what she thinks and feels is important and valued. Fathers need to be vocal about their daughters' beauty both inside and out. (See the section in chapter 10 on giving compliments.)

> Fathers need to prepare their daughters for womanhood by modeling how they should expect to be treated by a man.

It should go without saying that a teenage girl also learns how women are to be treated, in part, by watching her father's relationship with her mother. We'll discuss this more in a subsequent chapter on parents' issues. For now, it's enough to remind dads that they cannot afford to put off working on any problems in the marriage until after the kids are grown. Teenage girls are very aware of how their mother feels in her marriage and are greatly influenced by their parents' marriage relationship. To oversimplify here: Dates with your daughter should be far outnumbered by real dates with her mother!

Finally, fathers can be very influential in a girl's choice of boys to date. Men love to pontificate on how they're going to talk to "any boy that comes for my daughter." They compare their daughters to a fine automobile or fragile piece of china and add various threats if a boy should damage this priceless treasure. By now, you should know that speeches are only as effective as the relationship you have with your daughter.

If a father wants to intimidate his daughter's date, he should start his speech by saying, "You know, my daughter and I are very close. I just want you guys to have a great time, and *I can't wait to hear all about it* when she gets home because *she tells me everything* that goes on in her life." If that's true, that's all the scary you need.

MOTHERS AND SONS

A mother's influence on a teenage boy's dating behavior is not as clear-cut as it is with fathers and daughters. The most common problem I see in this area is teenage boys who feel infantilized by over-nurturing mothers. I remember talking to Vic, an angry, good-looking seventeen-year-old who came to a session with two things on his agenda:

1. Complaints about his mother, who treated him like a five-year-old but who had such a temper that he could never stand up to her.
2. How many girls he was planning to pull (i.e., get as much sex from as the girl would allow before dumping her) over his summer internship at his church. He had a bet with a friend about who would get more hookups.

With all you've read in this book, it should come as no surprise that many young men feel their mothers will never see them as adults. While all adolescents dislike being treated this way, it becomes a particular problem for boys in romantic relationships. Mothers are a boy's first relationship with the world of women, and as he approaches adulthood, if he receives the strong message that he's inadequate ("You'll always be my boy!"), his sense of shame and inadequacy will haunt him in seeking intimacy with girls. This is usually manifested in two ways: (1) he becomes passive and expects or needs the girl to direct him in romance or (2) he seeks to overcome his sense of shame by using girls to bolster his flagging sense of competence.

The foundation for mothers to avoid this negative influence is already laid in Planned Emancipation. While both parents (when present) need to display their support for a teenage boy's eventual autonomy, a mother must display her wholehearted faith in her son's eventually succeeding to full adult status. Ironically, this message of support is particularly difficult for mothers, since they tend to be wired for nurturance. A mother's nurturing tendencies make it hard for her to express respect for her son's autonomy without feeling like she is withholding love.

Moms can most influence their teenage sons' dating behavior by showing them the positive impact they can have on a woman. While it doesn't quite work the same way for a mom to ask her son on a date as a father would his daughter, a mom can look for opportunities to ask her son to pay the bill at a restaurant ("Would you mind going up to the cashier this time?") or notice if he holds the door and tell him how good that makes her feel. A mother should avoid coming across as a teacher: "You see, when you pull out the chair for a girl . . ." Teaching is best done before your son becomes an adolescent. (Again, see the section on giving compliments/praise in chapter 10.)

The respect a teenage boy feels when he's given freedoms can be significantly augmented by a mom who isn't afraid to ask for her son's help with things she can't do. These requests should not be delivered as a mom telling her child what to do but from a woman asking a young man to help with things he can do for her: "Jake, could you get the bag of dog food out of the car? It's so heavy, and you're much stronger than me." To a teenage boy, that sounds different from "Jake, get the dog food out of the car and then start your homework."

Most importantly, a mom should never forget to thank her son for his help. If adolescent girls fear they're unattractive to men, adolescent boys fear they're incompetent and consequently unable to have a noticeable impact on women. A teenage boy's mom can greatly build his confidence and therefore teach him how to care for a woman.

The help a mother seeks from her son should be appropriate. She shouldn't burden him with things he can't handle. Asking for and thanking him for feedback on how she looks can build his confidence. But adding, "Your father never gives me compliments!" implies that he must carry the responsibility for her feeling unfulfilled in her marriage, a weight that's much too heavy for a teenage boy. Again, that's a marriage problem, not a parenting problem.

A mom can also teach her teenage son about women by appropriately letting him see when he has hurt her feelings. A surly teenage boy rudely rejecting his mother's well-intentioned efforts to help is an all-too-common sight. These mothers often ignore their son's rude behavior or patronizingly remind him, "That's not how we talk." This response may be appropriate for a six-year-old boy, but it teaches a young man that it's okay to disrespect women if you don't like what they say. If his response violates your rules about respect (e.g., cursing or name-calling), then a consequence should obviously be given. Most of the time, this rude behavior doesn't rise to the level of violating the Expectations and Consequences list.

Regardless, a mom with a teenage son should not shy away from letting him know his words and actions hurt her feelings. Again, this should not be delivered in a condescending, teaching manner ("When boys talk to their mothers like that . . ."), but as vulnerable, adult-to-adult feedback ("This may not matter to you, but I just want to tell you that when you _____, it made me feel foolish and unimportant"). If he shrugs this off, you'll have to let it go and say nothing more. If he makes some sort of apology, which most boys will at least attempt to do, he must be thanked and shown that his words have made a difference.

Lastly, a mom should be careful how she relates to a girl her son is dating. A mother should be welcoming and friendly with her son's girlfriend (whether she likes her or not). But she should be careful not to get *too* close to her too quickly. When moms insert themselves into their sons' dating relationships, they can add unnecessary complications and even interfere with the natural flow of the relationship. There's nothing more awkward than a mom who maintains a close relationship with her son's ex-girlfriend. Be warm and friendly, but remember that it's his girlfriend, not yours.

Freedoms and Limit Setting with Dating

With sex and dating, the first decision to make is choosing when your teenager will be allowed to date. There's a great deal of data outlining the dangers of early dating, but waiting too long can invite unnecessary rebellion. The most common age is sixteen, the same age as driving. When your teen reaches the age you specify, dating should be added to the Freedoms list with appropriate boundaries.

The freedom to date means your adolescent can make his or her own decisions about when, how, and with whom to pursue dating relationships. This may seem like a big step, but in many ways it only codifies a freedom your teenager already has. Adolescents who are old enough to drive and spend significant time away from home are certainly able to have a great deal of interaction with the opposite sex, whether parents want them to or not. Rules like *You can't have a boyfriend* are easily ignored and hard to enforce. In such cases, parents are reduced to the status of inquisitors trying to ferret out the truth from an adolescent who insists, "We're just friends."

Parents' fears about dating are more clearly dealt with in the boundaries that come with this freedom. These boundaries are unapologetically trying to help adolescents deal with the temptations of sexual intimacy. The following might be an example for a sixteen-year-old girl:

FREEDOM	BOUNDARIES
Use your own judgment in dating.	• Cannot date anyone older than high school age. • Planned activities or home with parents present. • Home common rooms only. No bedrooms.

If this teenager asks, "Why can't I have a boy in my bedroom?" she should be given a straightforward answer: "Time spent alone with a boyfriend—especially in a bedroom—tends to foster familiarity leading to eventual sexual behavior." There's no need to be vague about this goal. If she argues that they aren't planning to have sex, parents should point out that this limit is not because they're teenagers. Sexual temptation is tricky for adults of all ages. Married men and women don't plan on having sex with others, but they also know it's unwise to spend lots of time alone with someone of the opposite sex.

Remember that these boundaries don't ensure that your adolescent won't engage in sexual behavior, and you should tell him or her that. If your teenager wants to become sexually active, you can't stop it. These boundaries are only an effort to reduce the temptations that come when couples have a great deal of unsupervised time together. By combining such boundaries with continued efforts at open communication, you can do a better job of guiding your adolescent through some of the more trying aspects of dating.

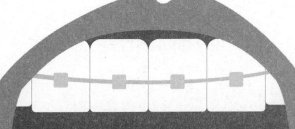

PART FIVE

"But What About…?"

How to Keep the Scary Stuff
from Derailing Planned Emancipation

CHAPTER 17

Fear and Planned Emancipation

God gave us a spirit not of fear
but of power and love and self-control.
2 TIMOTHY 1:7

In this section, I'll address some of the primary issues that tend to derail Planned Emancipation. Smartphones, pornography, alcohol, and other things tend to cause parents to pull back from the freedoms that are so important to adolescent development. While each of these can certainly be a threat to an adolescent's safe, healthy development, parents are simply not able to ensure their teenagers won't be affected by them. Each year, their teens gain more control over their own choices, whether parents like it or not. Planned Emancipation offers a path for parents to consult with and influence adolescents to make their own, responsible choices.

The thing that most affects parents' management of these issues is fear. When parents continually burden themselves with complete responsibility for their teenagers' choices, freedoms can go by the wayside. When teenagers cross the line with intoxicating substances or inappropriate sexting, parents must respond with consequences. But once the consequence is finished, adolescents need to return to the level of freedom they had before.

Fearful parents may feel annoyed with any call for continued freedoms when risky behavior is observed. However, the orderly transference of freedoms to teenagers' control is still the oxygen necessary for their growth into autonomous adulthood. Fear tempts parents to pull that air hose away from their teens while trying to explain that it's too unsafe for them to breathe that air right now.

Most parents I help are from the Christian community. Many of the examples you'll read come from Christian and Jewish families. I often speak in churches and Christian schools as well. Do you know the command given most often throughout the Bible? "Fear not." We Christians have little excuse for panicky, fear-based parenting, and yet, often the most fearful parents I've known were those most devout in their faith.

> There is no reason to allow your fears to derail your teenager's eventual autonomy.

I encourage you to read carefully the following chapters on "scary stuff." There is no reason to allow your fears to derail your teenager's eventual autonomy. Maybe working through those fears can lead to deepening your faith in the process.

CHAPTER 18

Smartphones and Other Portable Screens

iPhone is like having your life in your pocket.
STEVE JOBS

No one could have predicted in 2007 the impact that Apple's iPhone would have on all our lives. Other smartphone devices quickly followed. These screen-based devices affect all of us, but they *dominate* the lives of teenagers. If we had only known then what we know now. Someone should have stood up in the audience and shouted back at Steve Jobs, "But I don't want my life in my pocket, and I sure don't want my kids' lives in their pockets!"

Smartphones are by far the subject parents ask me about the most in dealing with their adolescents. For so many teenagers, taking away a smartphone is like cutting off their oxygen. As a good *Feeding the Mouth* parent, you should choose a point when you will leave phone use up to your teenager. The time of giving this complete freedom, however, should probably wait until his senior year, or maybe even spring of his senior year. Giving over freedoms in many other areas can help with his resentment about phone restrictions, but it won't go away completely. Most teenagers rely *a lot* on their phones.

Many good resources and ideas exist for dealing with electronics and kids. This chapter only suggests important things related to Planned Emancipation.

Why Are Phones Such a Big Deal?

One of the primary challenges of adolescence is navigating social relationships. Far too many teenagers perceive a smartphone as their primary connection to the social world. As we will discuss in the next chapter, social relationships that are primarily conducted through screened devices are fraught with complications and dangers. It's tempting for teenagers to feel as if screen-based interactions with peers are the same as real life.

Most teenagers hate when parents restrict phone usage, but teens with insecure or nonexistent social connections can become particularly desperate when separated from their phones. You can strengthen your resolve to set phone limits by reminding yourself that real social relationships take place in real time and are three-dimensional. Relationships are not enhanced greatly by typing or looking at video clips on a screen. Even talking over the phone is at least closer to real-life social interaction. Many teenagers have forgotten completely that their phones have this real-time talk feature.

There are some great things about smartphones and our social lives. They can, for example, facilitate meeting together or help connect people separated by distance. But when you take away your teenager's phone and she screams that you've cut her off from her boyfriend, whom she has never met personally and who lives hundreds of miles away, there's something wrong with how that phone is being used.

Phones and Planned Emancipation

Technically speaking, teenagers can't have complete freedom over phone use until they're able to legally obtain their own phone contract (eighteen years old in the US). Since phones are a kind of "life utility," parents usually feel obligated to provide a phone for their kids, often into early adulthood. This creates tension in parents, who are paying for the phone yet need to provide their adolescent kids a sense of growing freedom over phone use. Not to mention that parents are constantly tempted to snoop on their teens' communications.

You certainly have the right to try to control every aspect of your teen's phone use. If you understand the power of Planned Emancipation, however, you'll understand the need to use this control sparingly and in a manner that doesn't provoke unnecessary conflict with your adolescent's need for increasing autonomy.

What to Do about Phones

To intervene effectively with social media, pornography, games, and so on, you must first pay attention to the devices themselves. Research has traced significant, harmful effects on a generation of teens who have access to some sort of screen all the time. We're talking about the harmful effects of the screens themselves before we even begin to discuss what kids are seeing on these screens.

Take Inventory of All Screened Devices

How many screens are in your family's possession right now? Include in that number all the now-outdated devices that still power up. Do you even know? When I was a kid, we had one screen. It was a big picture tube thing in a furniture-type box that sat (for some unknown reason) on four spindly furniture legs. I recently met with a teenager whose parents had grounded him from his phone for two weeks. He wasn't upset. His friends had provided him with *four* older phones he was using with WiFi.

Taking inventory of all screened devices is essential for you to manage the impact these have on your teen's life. Old devices should probably be sent to recycling centers. When grounded from devices, teenagers sometimes start desperately looking for screens the way a reformed smoker looks for cigarettes.

Make Screen Rules for Your Entire Household

If you haven't already, you should make at least some screen-based device rules for your entire household. Research shows that carrying screened devices has significant effects on our general attention to the world and people around us. We seem to automatically assign a small part of our focus to monitoring what may come through on our phones.

> If you haven't already, you should make at least some screen-based device rules for your entire household.

This distractibility has different effects depending on whether a phone is near us, far from us, or even whether it's turned on or off. To focus on your life, you must have your phone turned off and in a different room.

You should consider banning phones from family gatherings. Having a phone in your pocket during family meals will sap a bit of your attention away from the people around you. Years ago, I was interviewed by a therapist in California who told me that the standard practice for teen gatherings was a parent at the door with a basket for everyone to put their phone in. I told her we hadn't gotten that memo yet in Texas.

Reconsider Your Use of Screen-Based Devices

You probably know smartphones aren't just a problem for children and teenagers. It's surprising how often a preoccupation with the phone comes up in marriage therapy. Where we focus our attention is becoming a major complication for all of us. If you haven't already, you would likely benefit from reevaluating your relationship with screened devices.

One reason I encourage this is my own experience. Now in my sixties and having been diagnosed with ADHD, I assure you that I am not good at managing distractions. Even though I've always been good with computers and cell phones, I don't regularly carry a smartphone. Instead, I'm among a growing group of adults who carry intentionally distraction-free devices. We're way past the "you just gotta discipline yourself" stage when it comes to screen use. Smartphones are designed by smart people to draw us in and keep us focused on them. I for one want to encourage others to use moderation, not from a position of strength but of happily confessed weakness.

It can be helpful for your adolescent children to see you setting limits for yourself. This is especially true if you're enacting phone limits for the first time or needing to pull back from how much you've already been allowing. Telling your fifteen-year-old that he can't have his phone in his room overnight anymore, even though he's always had that privilege, is tough. It can be moderated a bit if you can honestly add that you and his dad are also keeping your phones put away at night.

On the other hand, I'm not saying you need to bargain with your teenager. The answer to "How come you keep your phone at night, but I can't?" is that your phone *and* your teenager's phone belong to you. While limiting your screen use is good for you and may provide a good example, that's not the same as saying you *must* match the limits you set for your kids. That's a slippery slope you do not want to go down.

Screens at Night

Perhaps the most important rule parents must make about screened devices is having set limits at night. A great deal of research connects sleep deprivation with the blue light emitted by screens. Screen use at night disrupts the body's production of melatonin, which is essential in sleep regulation. That's in addition to the obvious sleep disruption for teens who are watching their phones for many hours at night.

It's usually best to have a base, or charging station, where all devices must be returned before bed. Again, it doesn't hurt if you put your device there too.

Not surprisingly, nighttime screen rules are the most disobeyed, argued about, and manipulated limits in most households with teenagers. Try not to be surprised by this, just stick with it. When you wake up one day and realize you haven't been consistently enforcing your phone limits, just make a quick announcement that limits are back in place.

There isn't another area of limit setting quite like phone limits. It's like the Ring of Power in Tolkien's Lord of the Rings. Phones call to their owners, seeking to be found and used. But these are the hardest rules to maintain consistently, so it's best to be patient with yourself.

Grounding Teenagers from Their Phones

Realistically, it can be difficult to take away your teenager's phone use completely for a long time. Schools, sports teams, and other activity groups often rely on communicating through texting and other communication apps. Often kids just need to coordinate with a study group or their manager at work.

The result of this dependency sometimes requires parents to adjust the definition of *grounded* in relation to their teen's phone. You can try keeping full control over the phone and being the gatekeeper for whatever specific use your teenager needs her phone for. The main problem with this approach in Planned Emancipation is that phone grounding can feel patronizing ("Now you're a ten-year-old and have to ask me for everything.").

An alternative can be to adjust the definition of *grounded* to mean that the phone must be turned in early, say seven in the evening. Your teen will hate this, but less monitoring is required if you simply leave it up to your kid to figure out how to complete all phone communications before a specific time.

Another option may be to provide a "grounded phone." This should not be a phone for kids but perhaps a cheap phone with very limited functions. This could be provided during a long grounding from a regular phone. Again, the goal is to retain the effectiveness of taking away an adolescent's phone without saddling you with constant demands for exceptions to the consequences or a sense of guilt that you've ruined your child's social life.

Portable screened devices did not exist when I started working with parents of teenagers. It's hard to overstate the complications these devices have added to the process of Planned Emancipation. I often find it tempting to lead some sort of "Let's ban all these devices!" movement.

But this can't be done. Your teenagers must be prepared for a world saturated with these devices. As with all other aspects of their lives, your job is to find an orderly path of retreat from controlling *and* protecting your adolescent from the harm these may cause. Remember that as control leaves, real communication can take over. It's the most effective means of training your teenager to manage these devices for himself or herself.

CHAPTER 19

Social Media

For every action, there's an equal and opposite reaction
plus a social media overreaction.
ANONYMOUS

You need to be an integral—though not interfering—part of your adolescent's social media usage, and you need to set proper, progressive limits so your teenager can be a responsible internet citizen while he's in your house, and especially when he's not.

How Much Do You (Not) Know about Your Teenager's Social Media Usage?

If you asked your adolescent how many friends she has, what would she answer? It's conceivable she'd say, "I dunno. Maybe three hundred?" Her answer would shock you because you've only ever seen her hang out with a few people. But for teenagers, the most attractive part of using social media is connecting with each other.

Most adolescents don't place too many barriers between their real-world and online friends. For them, friends are friends no matter where they first met. As digital natives, this is the world they were born into, so it can be challenging for parents to fully understand their worldview, especially when it comes to how they live their lives online. This is a good reason to become a better student of technology, particularly the ever-changing trends that attract teenagers, though these trends often last only for a season. For instance, how many social media accounts does your teenager have? And which social media apps are currently trending?

When it comes to the real risks of social media usage, parents tend to fret most about online predators and harmful social gaffes that can follow teenagers for the rest of their lives. Though there are legitimate risks regarding predatory presences, allow me to allay your fears.

Start by being wise in how you monitor your teenager's accounts for predators. I once met the mother of a seventeen-year-old, six-foot-four-inch offensive lineman who kept announcing that she needed to monitor his accounts because she was afraid of online child predators. I would think he'd be able to take care of himself if he ever found himself in a predatory situation. Plus, what does his mom's overprotectiveness tell him about whether he's truly a man who can take care of himself?

Parents of daughters are often much more concerned about online predators and with good reason. However, research suggests that teenage girls who are lured to meet predators often have major family and social issues that make them more vulnerable to sick advances.[1] While there remain good reasons for parents to monitor social networks, especially with young teenagers, there's no need for unreasonable fears that "anything can happen" when adolescents use the internet. Maintaining your relationship with your teenager is easily the most important element in providing safety online.

But as you know by now, implementing Planned Emancipation and earning transparent communication in return should help ensure that your daughter (or son) doesn't have to seek a replacement for your love and affection. You doing your job is far more effective than any program, so don't let software be the parent you need to be.

The more prevalent risk to your teenager with social media is its persistence. You and I had the blessed fortune to live in a world where video cameras were not ubiquitous and when a social gaffe at school was laughed about for a day and then just as quickly forgotten. Today, major faux pas (a.k.a. epic fails) take on a near-eternal life of their own once they're posted online. And when screenshots can be taken of anything and quickly published to the world, your teenager's heat-of-the-moment private text message to one friend *about* another friend could turn into an embarrassing and long-lasting relational nightmare.

Despite their technological prowess, most teenagers don't fully understand the ramifications of their online choices. To them, it's just a text message or a tweet. But as with many other aspects of their still-developing lives, they don't grasp how a momentary lack of discretion may affect their real life in dramatic ways.

Why Social Media Are So Important to Your Adolescent

As with video games, you shouldn't make your teenager go cold turkey on social media. Why? Because engaging in social media often comes from her intrinsic need for real-world relationships. Danah Boyd says it well in *It's Complicated: The Social Lives of Networked Teens*:

> Social media plays a crucial role in the lives of networked teens. Although the specific technologies change, they collectively provide teens with a space to hang out and connect with friends. Teens' mediated interactions sometimes complement or supplement their face-to-face encounters. . . . Teens simply have far fewer places to be together in public than they once did. And the success of social media must be understood partly in relation to this shrinking social landscape.[2]

According to "Friendship 2.0: Adolescents' Experiences of Belonging and Self-Disclosure Online" in the *Journal of Adolescence*, teenagers have more casual conversations than intimate ones online.[3] The casual exchanges include the following:

- instrumental conversations (e.g., going over homework, making plans for hanging out, and so on)
- maintaining a sense of connection (e.g., checking in about the day's events, sharing jokes, complaining about mutual issues, etc.)
- defining friendship groups (e.g., tagging close friends in pictures, sharing affection, forming different text groups with certain friends, etc.), but also connecting with casual acquaintances or peers who are not part of one's close friendship group[4]

But don't be naïve: Intimate conversations still happen too, but they take the form of self-disclosing personal conversations that share feelings and struggles. According to an observer of this study, "Girls and younger adolescents engage in [intimate online conversations] more often than boys and older adolescents."[5] Girls and younger teenagers who identify as shy or quiet often use online services or texting because they feel more comfortable doing so rather than risking vulnerability in the real world. Plus, teenagers who share more personal information online feel a "sense of more control over self-expression and opinion online relative to offline."[6]

So how can you implement Planned Emancipation in ways that teach your teenager how to use social media responsibly?

How to Set Limits on Social Media

1. *Join the social media site(s) your teenager uses.* You don't necessarily have to "friend" your son or daughter (if he or she would even accept your request). Rather, join the sites you know your teenager uses so you can understand how they work and what their benefits

and drawbacks are. You can't have a frank discussion with your teenager about social media if he or she keeps using words that have no meaning to you.

2. *Inform yourself about the dangers of social media, but don't obsess.* For all the ills I've already outlined, there's much good to be gleaned from proper social media usage. Landing a job these days seems to require at least a working knowledge of it. Social media options are not going to die; rather, they're going to transform and likely become even more ingrained into our culture. Take the time to read about the newest fads.

3. *Talk about social media with your teenager.* Don't make a grand speech about getting abducted or how other kids have suffered greatly because of one incident that went viral. Rather, have an honest conversation with your teenager about how he uses social media. Ask why he likes a particular social media site or app over another. Use news stories about online bullying or the newest social media trend as a launching pad to discover more about what he's doing online. Don't pry—discuss.

4. *Set clear, progressive freedoms.* Because I like to keep freedoms simple, I encourage my clients to approach social media in three tiers. These middle- and late-adolescent freedoms could be added to the Freedoms list when appropriate:

- An early adolescent may not have any social media accounts.
- A middle adolescent may have approved social media accounts so long as parents have the password.
- A late adolescent may have social media accounts without parents knowing the passwords.

You'll notice that I didn't specify ages. It's up to you to decide when the proper time is to allow your son or daughter to join a social media site. As with video games, the time may come sooner if

---

Join the sites you know your teenager uses so you can understand how they work and what their benefits and drawbacks are.

---

an adolescent's friends are all hopping on to a new site. Use your discretion to know when the time is right and be sure to communicate often what you expect from your teenager regarding how (and how often) he uses social media. If your adolescent shows signs of internet or social media addiction, consider using the same consequences as outlined in the next chapter.

CHAPTER 20

Video Games

*Video games are a waste of time for men with nothing
else to do. Real brains don't do that.*

RAY BRADBURY

"After I got behind in my classes, I just kinda stayed in my room the rest of the semester."

Eric, a tall, thin eighteen-year-old, squirmed a bit in one of my office chairs. He was living with his parents again after failing every class during the one semester he had attended a large state university. Eric came from a strong family that kept a close eye on how he managed his time and computer use. It didn't help that his older sister was about to graduate cum laude from that same school.

"What did you do in your room for two months?" I asked.

"I played *Call of Duty*," he said, staring straight at the floor.

"What else did you do?"

"Well, I went to the café for food," he added.

"Wait," I asked hesitantly, "are you saying you spent eight weeks in your dorm room playing a game on your computer?"

"Well, no." Eric sighed. "I also looked at a lot of porn."

A Whole New Electronic World

I would love to tell you that Eric's story is unique. It isn't. In just the last five years, I've seen a significant increase in the number of college kids who've gone through much the same thing. What's changed is not that this *didn't* happen as much a few years ago; this *couldn't* have happened a few years ago. I've heard it said that marijuana today is ten times more potent than it was thirty years ago. The same can be said when comparing current video games to those from even a decade ago. (Porn as well, but we'll discuss that in depth in the next chapter.)

You probably had some experience with video games growing up. Perhaps you spent too much time on games as a kid. But there are constant and sometimes drastic improvements to games and gaming systems. The power of newer video games to immerse players into a compelling, unreal world creates a control battle that many parents have with their teenagers.

The Consuming Power of Video Games

Many parents worry that their kids are addicted to video games. However, the overuse of video games as a diagnostic category remains a bit in flux. The World Health Organization's International Classification of Diseases (ICD-11) includes a diagnosis of Gaming Disorder but cautions, "Studies suggest that gaming disorder affects only a small proportion of people who engage in digital- or video-gaming activities."[1] The most recent edition of the *Diagnostic and Statistical Manual of Mental Disorders* (the DSM-5, a.k.a. the bible of psychiatric diagnosis) lists internet gaming disorder as "a condition warranting more clinical research and experience before it might be considered for inclusion in the main book as a formal disorder." The DSM-5's condensed summary of internet gaming disorder goes on to say,

> "Gamers" play compulsively, to the exclusion of other interests, and their persistent and recurrent online activity results in

clinically significant impairment or distress. People with this condition endanger their academic or job functioning because of the amount of time they spend playing. They experience symptoms of withdrawal when pulled away from gaming.[2]

Before you start to panic, there's good reason for gaming addiction to remain in the consideration-for-inclusion category for now. Millions of people play video games, even at levels many of us would consider excessive, without suffering life-threatening consequences. What we *can* say is that an addiction to video games is probably real and, if not taken seriously, can have serious repercussions.

As for the real-world cases I most often see and hear about in my office, my conversation with Eric in this chapter's opening is typical. If a parent has been strict about video games with a teenager who's always wanted to play them, that teenager may waste his college years because he finally has the freedom to choose between playing *any* game available to him or doing homework.

> If a parent has been strict about video games with a teenager who's always wanted to play them, that teenager may waste his college years because he finally has the freedom to choose between playing *any* game available to him or doing homework.

I use *he* on purpose as well. In a large survey from 2010 to 2020, boys from the age of fourteen use video games up to five times more than girls.[3] I'm not naïve enough to believe gaming addiction doesn't strike girls as well, but there's a particular skewing toward the teenage male demographic when it comes to games—and porn. My guess is that this happens because these two specific "entertainment" media are very visual and very nonintimate. But according to the same survey, girls are more likely to use social media, which brings a different set of troublesome issues into the mix of adolescence.[4]

As I said before, today's games are nothing like what you likely grew up with. Yesterday's games were more of a distraction or even a novelty.

But today's games—because of their immersive worlds, realistic visuals, social connections, and heightened presence in the culture at large—can become an addictive substance.

One could argue that mobile games in particular are now developed as if every player were a dog in a grand Pavlovian experiment: "If you complete this action, we'll grant you this reward." Massively multiplayer online role-playing games (MMORPGs) are immensely popular. Gamers in these immersive worlds often join guilds of other players to complete quests. These are the types of games that reward long hours of play. And these games are most often played by those who suffer health problems while playing.

When Should You Be Concerned about Your Teenager's Video Game Use?

Some parents understand the risks of video game addiction. They've heard news reports or have watched their teenager play a violent game. Other parents may see no problem in letting their teenager play "harmless" games so long as the adolescent's grades don't suffer. After all, isn't it better to have him playing games within the house than doing who-knows-what with who-knows-who outside the house? Then there are the parents who have no qualms about playing video games right beside their teenagers: "No, Son. Don't use your sniper rifle, use the grenade launcher! Lemme show you."

Note that I'm not suggesting *all* video game playing is bad. As with every other issue we've discussed so far, the key is to plan for your teen's emancipation. (Did you see that one coming?) But to do that, you have to take stock of where your adolescent lies on the spectrum of video game usage.

The following list is provided as a framework to help you gauge your teenager's interest in video games:

- *Negligible.* If your teenager shows no interest in video games or plays less than a few hours per month, consider yourself blessed and highly favored. If it's not a problem, don't worry about it.

- *Under one hour per day.* In a 2014 survey of ten- to fifteen-year-olds, teenagers who spent an hour or less per day playing video games "showed higher levels of prosocial behavior and life satisfaction and lower levels of conduct problems, hyperactivity, peer problems, and emotional symptoms."[5] In other words, your teenager isn't likely to be addicted to video games, even if he plays an hour per day. He may even have a little more going for him than those who don't play at all.

- *One to three hours per day.* That same survey revealed that of those adolescents who played one to three hours per day, "no effects were observed for moderate play levels when compared with non-players."[6] Video game play spiked during the COVID-19 pandemic for fifteen- to nineteen-year-olds, but average daily usage in the US never reached two hours.[7] This just means that this level of video game use may or may not be a problem for your teenager. Two or three hours per day certainly seems like a lot of wasted time, but it's not necessarily a problem.

- *Three hours or more per day.* Not so shockingly, the survey also revealed, "Children who spend more than half their daily free time showed more negative adjustment."[8] This suggests a large share of time devoted to games may crowd out engagement in other enriching activities and risk exposure to content meant for mature audiences. While an adolescent who plays this much may not necessarily be addicted, spending such a large amount of time daily on nearly any type of entertainment would likely cause you concern.

The best way to determine if playing video games is a problem for your teenager is to assess what impact his playing has on important areas of his life. How much time spent playing video games is taking away from time spent in other—and more worthwhile—spheres of life?

Most parents tend to let their teenagers play video games so long as it doesn't negatively affect their schoolwork. That's a fantastic idea, but parents shouldn't always place schoolwork as the counterbalance to gaming. If your teenager shirks chores, fails to socialize with friends (in real life), or keeps missing family outings because he can't peel himself away from his gaming devices, that should carry as much weight as schoolwork. So long as an adolescent can effectively balance his time between the many spheres of his life, video gaming can still reside in one of those spheres. If it doesn't, when he goes to college he *will* spend at least the first semester earning a degree in first-person shooters and online trash-talking.

How to Set Limits on Video Games

For all the issues we've already discussed, there's a central reason you should set limits on your teenager's video game playing: It's hard to pull out of that virtual reality. Your son or daughter can sit down in front of a game with full intentions to play for only an hour and then get to doing homework, only to find himself scrambling to get homework done three hours later. And let's be honest, if a teenager doesn't like schoolwork, he'll find nearly anything else to occupy his time.

Most addictive behaviors are slow to develop and begin innocently enough, so it's essential that you're proactive about limit setting. While limits should be set when your son or daughter first shows an interest in video games, particular concern should be paid to boys in early to mid-adolescence (thirteen to fifteen years old).

Before setting the limit, consider these six issues:

1. *Know what kinds of games your teenager plays.* Sports games can be addictive, but not nearly as much as immersive games like MMORPGs. Strategy games aren't as violent as first-person shooters. In other words, you have valid reasons to distinguish between different types of games and may even consider setting different limits for those different types.

2. *Seriously consider the importance of games in her world.* Whether you like it or not, your teenager may want to play video games because *all* her friends are also playing them. Simply taking a moral stance against all gaming may risk seriously alienating you from your teenager and alienating your teenager from her friends.

When my son was in elementary school, we kept a hard line against all video games because they were such a waste of time. However, we had to reconsider when he came home and confided, "Look, I know you think video games are bad, but that's all my friends talk about at lunch, and I can't join in." So in setting limits on his gaming time, we had to consider the effects these were having on our teenager's real-world friendships.

This willingness to compromise demands communication. Otherwise, how would you know if your limit setting is significantly hindering your teenager's real-world social growth?

3. *Communicate, communicate, communicate.* Because Planned Emancipation will lead to better communication, you should have no qualms about having direct conversations with your son or daughter about your feelings on game playing. As you know by now, don't make a grand speech. Just say how you feel about how your teen chooses to spend her time, and be sure to allow her to make a rebuttal.

4. *Hold true to other areas of Planned Emancipation.* This should help in setting limits on video games. Because you've granted your teenager progressive freedoms in other areas of life, he should be able to trust you more easily when you say, "We're going to set some limits on your gaming now, but as you show us you can be trusted with how you use your time, those limits will become wider and wider until you only have limits of your own choosing."

5. *Hand over more control by mid-to-late adolescence (sophomore or junior year).* An hour of game playing per day is not unreasonable.

By the time your teenager is fifteen or sixteen, you should grant them more freedom to choose their games and how long they play—as long as their grades, friendships, family life, and so on don't suffer because of it.

6. *Drop the reins completely by the spring of the senior year.* By this time, you'll want to hand over complete control of his video gaming while he's still in your house. Otherwise, you may wind up with a collegian who's finally free of his parents' rules and spends more time gaming than studying. Plus, while your teenager is still in your house, you can use that time to better communicate the cons of too much gaming.

Enforcing limits on video game use can be tricky, especially if he's playing an MMORPG. The immersive aspect of these games can create a high potential for conflict at the moment your teenager needs to turn off and reenter the real world. So let me offer a few guidelines that can save you a world of trouble:

- *Never pull the plug.* You may want to review the four laws of disciplining adolescents in chapter 11 on limit setting. You're not trying to *make him* turn off the game. Getting sucked into a cheap control battle over a power cord just makes you look silly.

- *Don't give reminders when the time is almost up.* You should know this one by now. Following the guidelines you've set for using your video games (remember that!) is your teenager's responsibility, not yours. The one who reminds is the one who is responsible.

- *Set progressive consequences for going overtime.* This would be similar to the curfew example in the limit-setting chapter. Once your teen has gone even one minute past the time you've set, something should happen, but keep in mind that one minute over isn't that big of a deal.

A video game addition to your Expectations and Consequences list might look like this table:

EXPECTATION	CONSEQUENCE
No more than 1 hour of computer games on weeknights (unless restricted due to unsatisfactory grades). Set kitchen timer when starting.	• 1-5 minutes over: lose 30 minutes next weeknight • 6-10 minutes over: no game playing next weeknight • 11+ minutes over: consequence to be determined

This kind of system provides an answer to the teen's crisis ("Wait just a minute, I have to back this up [or finish this level, complete this round, etc.] or I'll lose everything!"). Remember, failure to plan is not your problem. When the teenager plays for ten minutes or longer beyond the expected hour time frame, don't pull the plug. The better maneuver is to simply say (in a quiet voice so as not to disturb their all-important game play),

Getting sucked into a cheap control battle over a power cord just makes you look silly.

"You're past ten minutes over. I'll let you know how bad the consequence is going to be in the morning." Then be sure to enforce that consequence the next day—which may very well be several days without games.

By consistently enforcing outlined expectations and avoiding unnecessary control battles (no yelling or speechmaking), you may be able to get some communication going. Don't get drawn into repeated arguments about "Why can't I play my games more?" Remember, you just need to agree to disagree. Remind your teenager that the time will come when the choice will be up to him. However, at some point (and *not* after delivering consequences), he should be able to respond to honest questions, such as "Why do you think it's so hard for you to track time when you're playing games?"

As you can see, the motivation for setting limits on video games is not to completely remove games from teenagers' lives. Rather, it's to ensure that they can pull themselves out of these unreal worlds and begin to understand how to use their time more effectively.

CHAPTER 21

The Shame-Based Power of Pornography

Porn trains the mind to regard sex as a spectator sport, to be enjoyed alone and in front of a screen. It removes love and mutuality from sex.
LOUISE PERRY

What's more challenging than talking to your child about sex? Talking to her about whether she watches pornography! But the consequences—both for her and for you—are much worse than the awkward, red-faced, stilted conversations you might have with your teenager. Nobody wants to talk about pornography, and that's precisely why it's so insidious.

Because of our hyper-connected, instant-gratification world, access to pornography has never been higher. Teenagers can even view porn when they don't mean to, whether it's an errant click on a website, a video a friend shows them, or even a scene in a movie. If you didn't already know that pornography is pervasive and easily accessible, well, now you do. Pornography's greatest appeal lies in the fact that it's everywhere, and yet no one wants to talk about it. But using pornography is based on shame and secrets, and this is a vital aspect to consider when talking with your teenager about the issue.

Pornography is not just a guy's problem. While men do wrestle with pornography more often than women, women battle the issue too. The

Fifty Shades of Grey series has sold more than one hundred million books and given rise to a new genre label: mommy porn.

A quick side note: If you or your spouse view (or read) pornographic material regularly, I urge you to seek whatever level of help you deem appropriate, whether that's through counseling, a church group, or trusted friends. Pornography kills marriages, and divorce is one of the *least* effective ways to parent a teenager. Plus, I can think of few better examples for curious teenagers than a parent who makes visible strides toward removing pornography from his or her life.

When it comes to discussing pornography with your teenage son or daughter, I always advocate for man-to-man or woman-to-woman conversations. If a single father or mother needs help talking to his or her opposite-gender adolescent, get a trusted family member, friend, or church youth worker to speak with the teen. Sons won't want to talk about pornography with their dads, but you can be certain that it's much harder to discuss the issue with their moms. The same thing can be said for daughters and their dads.

> Pornography kills marriages, and divorce is one of the *least* effective ways to parent a teenager.

In *Childhood and Society*, notable developmental psychologist Erik Erikson said, "Too much shaming does not lead to genuine propriety but to a secret determination to try to get away with things, unseen."[1] That's why it's so important to address the issue of pornography without adding to your teenager's shame. So how can you do that?

Setting Limits on Pornography

Read that subtitle again. It doesn't make sense, does it? You wouldn't want to tell your thirteen-year-old, "At your age, you're not allowed to look at porn, but when you're older and have shown us we can trust you, we'll let you look at some." That's ridiculous!

Ultimately, you don't want him to fight an addiction to pornography, or to consider it even remotely as a replacement for actual intimacy. If that strikes you as strange, thousands of books and online resources outline why using porn is so detrimental to a person's emotional and relational well-being.

But here's the hard truth: Your teenager, if he or she hasn't already, will very likely be exposed to pornography. So, while there are some steps you can take, the most important step is likely the hardest: communication.

"But Dr. Ken, we use monitoring software."

Good! All families who understand the negative impact of pornography should have monitoring software installed on their home computers and tablets. For those unfamiliar with these applications, they constantly run in the background and send usage reports to whomever the end user chooses. In other words, you can keep tabs on your teenager's internet activity whenever she's online. Just remember to *tell* your teenager that such software is installed. If you install it without telling her and make her endure a gotcha moment after she's accessed pornography, you're setting yourself up for more problems than just the porn problem. Plus, this will only add to her shame.

I don't recommend relying on filtering software with teenagers. Filtering software is good for children because it blocks accidental or naïve access to inappropriate sites. But for adolescents, filtering software can feel infantilizing ("Mom, can you come enter the password again so I can finish my report on breast cancer?"). Besides, most teenagers are more tech-savvy than their parents, so they get around filters fairly easily. Monitoring software is a bit harder to get around and fits better with teenagers' individuation needs.

The best way to influence your adolescent about pornography is through communication, not limit setting. You cannot and will not succeed in restricting him from using pornography by setting absurdly strong, stringent, and frightening limits and consequences. In doing so, you will amplify both the badness and the shame of it, which will likely cause your teenager to engage with it more often, both to rebel against your desires and to console his shame in one of the few ways he knows how.

Additionally, I've heard of parents who drag their teenagers to seminars about pornography use, hoping that a weekend of paid-for speechmaking will somehow fix their children. But without honest discussion with their parents about the seminar, no change occurs. As with every other aspect of Planned Emancipation, conversation always trumps making speeches—whether yours or anyone else's.

Setting expectations and consequences for porn can't just be a rule from on high. It must be discussed with your teenager in a frank conversation with the same-gender parent. A father ought to be able to openly discuss the negative ramifications of using porn with his son. Parents should approach the issue as helping the teenager maintain his or her boundaries.

Now, I'm not saying there should be *no* consequences for a teenager who uses pornography. Here's what I often suggest to my clients:

1. *A first-time offense* should be used as an opportunity to discuss the issue and not a time for you to react through some harsh punishment. Trust me, having to talk about it will be deterrent enough for your teenager. Still, you should be firm in warning that there will be consequences for a second transgression.
2. *A second-time offense* may carry weighty consequences, like no electronics for a week. Remember, try to make the punishment match the crime. There's no need to throw in grounding or take away her allowance. Without access to electronics, your teenager will likely have a difficult time using pornography.
3. If your son or daughter displays a continual pattern of porn use (despite your best efforts), seek professional help through a counselor or trusted religious leader. It's never a good idea to pretend that if it's not necessarily hurting anyone, it must be okay. Prolonged pornography usage can have highly detrimental effects on your son's or daughter's future relationships.

As I've said before and will reiterate because of its importance, overdoing the consequences will lead to your teenager feeling more ashamed and, consequently, turning back to pornography. It's a vicious spiral, and he'll need your help to escape. And be wary of cranking up the consequences for each offense. Instead, increase the frequency of communication about the subject. Your ability and willingness to talk about this painful topic can be the most effective way to influence your teenager's porn use.

CHAPTER 22

Alcohol and Other Intoxicants

I would not put a thief in my mouth to steal my brains.
ATTRIBUTED TO WILLIAM SHAKESPEARE

I speak fairly often at a local church where I once taught a class called Communicating with Your Teenager. We had a group of about fifty parents there for the class. A few months later, I came back and offered a class titled Alcohol, Drugs, and Teenagers. *Three hundred parents* crammed into the room, ready to take notes! Figuring out how to deal with teenagers' potential alcohol and drug use is kind of a big deal.

As with all the topics we've covered so far, the goal of this chapter is to maximize your effectiveness in influencing your adolescent's choices regarding alcohol and drugs. Since we're focusing on your parenting, I won't bore you with statistics on teenage substance use. It's a problem, but if you don't believe me, a quick internet search for "teenage alcohol statistics" will sober you up quickly.

Alcohol and drug use scares parents for what it can do to their teens, but also because it's a difficult behavior for parents to control. But you're different! You've been reading this book (without skipping ahead, right?) and already know the elements needed to manage this tricky aspect of many teenagers' lives. Simply stated, adolescents who regularly receive appropriate freedoms from their parents, who can talk openly with their parents, and who know the significant consequences they can expect if they're caught, are at an extremely low risk of having trouble when making choices about alcohol and drugs.

The Real Problem Is Intoxication

I've listened for more than thirty years to parents and teenagers talking or arguing about alcohol and drug use. What stands out most is just how muddleheaded these arguments get—on both sides. Parents get easily stumped by ridiculous arguments from their adolescents:

- "But we're always careful to have a designated driver!"
- "You guys drank in high school!"
- "But marijuana is legal in [fill in current number of] states!"
- "Everyone drinks at my school!"

Trust me, these are not good points. The trick to maintaining sanity in your thinking and talking about the use of alcohol or drugs is to keep your eye on the ball. The issue is *not* drinking alcohol or using drugs. The issue is *intoxication*.

Intoxication is what should clarify a parent's stance on alcohol and drug use. Once you've grounded yourself in this obvious but often missing piece of reality, the line you must draw becomes clear, whether your teenager agrees with it or not.

Here's how I would combat adolescents' arguments when it comes to drugs and alcohol:

1. Intoxication is why alcohol is illegal for anyone under twenty-one years old in the US. When drinking was legal for eighteen- to twenty-year-olds, they had a bad habit of getting intoxicated and causing accidents, so they lost that privilege—and so did your teenager.

2. Intoxication is why marijuana remains controversial (in this country, at least), because you're talking about adults responsibly managing varying levels of intoxication. No one has "one hit" of marijuana with dinner. Besides, no state is considering legalizing recreational-use marijuana for anyone under twenty-one, so why are we even talking about this?

3. Intoxication is why *any* sort of other drugs, whether prescription or esoteric (like various forms of K2, a synthetic marijuana), should remain completely off-limits. All these substances are attractive because of their ability to produce various forms of intoxication.

4. Intoxication on any kind of regular basis (i.e., four or five drinks three to four times per month) has been shown to cause damage to adolescent brain development. Intoxication makes people stupider.

5. Having a designated driver is a method for managing levels of intoxication and is encouraged for people twenty-one and older.

6. Whether a parent became intoxicated while in high school does not affect the present dangers surrounding his or her teenager's becoming intoxicated. Parent status is not earned by appropriately handling your own adolescence.

If anyone (adult or adolescent) has a drinking problem, it's an intoxication problem. An alcoholic refuses even one drink because he cannot trust himself not to succumb to the temptation to become intoxicated.

Recognizing the central issue of intoxication also requires that you take stock of *your* relationship with it. Children and teenagers always remember if they've seen a parent visibly intoxicated. Whether the parent

> Trust me, teens almost always know when a parent is using drugs or abusing alcohol. They just never tell the parent that they know.

was moderately intoxicated (glassy-eyed, laughing out of context, etc.) or heavily intoxicated (passed out, slurring speech, etc.), they *always* remember. It scares them to see their parent out of control, even if just a little. It's reasonable to expect your teenager to abstain from using alcohol even if you occasionally have a beer or one or two glasses of wine. But it's very different to expect her to respect your limits when you display a lack of self-control in that same area.

I mention alcohol use here because if you're using any kind of drug for intoxication, you're likely already a bit of a joke to your teenager. And trust me, teens almost always know when a parent is using drugs or abusing alcohol. They just never tell the parent that they know. If you're unsure whether this applies to you, you should talk to someone who's educated about alcoholism.

Drinking to Feel Grown-Up

It's hard for studies to narrow down the causes of alcohol and drug use in teenagers. One major influence reported by teenagers is that they drink to feel grown-up. Since adolescents' primary need is individuation, this should come as no surprise. Other influences like peer pressure and the examples given by society fall under the same category of drinking to feel grown-up. Teenage peer pressure never seems to cause outbreaks of bowling mania or math club craze.

Adolescents are all in the same developmental stage, so they feel pressured by that which appears adultlike. Society's example is a similar thing: an example of behavior from cool adults. Sadly, in our culture that is so confused about what constitutes adulthood, drinking alcohol is particularly attractive because it's considered to be something grown-ups do.

Can you guess where I'm going with this?

Planned Emancipation reduces adolescent motivation to use alcohol and drugs! By openly giving over sanctioned, adult freedoms, you reduce your teenager's need to feel grown-up. He already does feel grown-up! "I don't have to ask my parents what music to listen to." "I keep my room however I want." "They don't have to approve of who I date." These freedoms become anti-alcohol and drug-use weapons, so to speak.

My kids told me that when they were questioned about not drinking alcohol, they felt they were being accused of being a goody-goody, which has nothing to do with good versus bad behavior. Rather, it carries the awful connotation of a teenager who mindlessly carries out his or her parents' wishes. But being able to list several areas of freedom my wife and I had already handed over gave our kids confidence. They knew they were making their own choices about alcohol. They weren't just goody-goodies.

There are many reasons why kids get involved with alcohol and drugs; taking away the need to feel grown-up is not a surefire cure, but it can be a big help.

Parental Control of Teenage Drinking and Drug Use

Setting effective limits on teenage drinking or drug use requires understanding your role as a judge and not a police officer. (See chapter 11, on limit setting.) Parents who only understand their role as police officers make dangerous, compromising stands like "Since you can't keep them from drinking, I just tell them to make sure they don't get behind the wheel when they're drunk."

The minimum legal drinking age was raised to twenty-one because adolescents have terrible judgment when managing alcohol use—not because no one thought to advise them *not* to drive drunk. This "parents must be police officers" fallacy is also behind the absurd line "I let them drink at my house so at least they'll be safe." This rule makes your house the first stop on a teenage pub crawl.

To set effective limits on adolescent alcohol and drug use, parents need to act as judges, ready to hand down significant consequences for violations. Only evidence of a pattern of alcohol or drug use (i.e., more than two violations) may require that a parent do a little detective work. Although it may seem contradictory, knowing you're a judge and not a police officer keeps you from compromising your stance on such dangerous behavior and allows for better communication with your adolescent. You want to know their true thoughts on alcohol and drug use.

As a judge, you should set limits on alcohol and drug use. You can add them to your Expectations and Consequences table. See this example:

EXPECTATION	CONSEQUENCE
No use of alcohol or any other intoxicating substance or being present when it is being consumed by minors.	• First offense: grounded for 2–4 weeks • Second offense: grounded for a minimum of 4 weeks • Third offense: maximum grounding plus assessment by drug and alcohol counselor

This is only an example, and yours may look different, but I want to point out some important elements here. Let's take a closer look at peer pressure and parental expectations.

Social Pressure and Parental Expectations

Your expectations should include consequences for alcohol and drug use, but consequences should also exist when your teenager is present when and where these substances are being consumed. One reason for this is that your behavioral expectation doesn't require that you prove your kid was drinking or using drugs. Parents are rarely confronted with smoking-gun evidence of substance use, such as a teen coming home staggering drunk or a bag of marijuana being discovered in his room. Teenagers are too old for you to be trusting their behavior just because you assume they would never do something as wrong as using substances.

If you have solid evidence your kid was at a party where minors were drinking, you'd be a fool to feel comforted because your little darling assured you that she didn't drink anything. You should honestly tell her you can't simply take her at her word. That's not a condemnation of her trustworthiness; it's a by-product of her getting older. Adults can't just "not use" illegal substances. They must *maintain the appearance* of not using illegal substances. All minors anywhere near alcohol or drugs are at risk of being arrested. Adults likewise, including young ones, should not be anywhere near where illegal substances are being used.

Another reason for adolescents to avoid being where other minors are consuming substances is peer pressure. Even a confident, strong-minded adolescent will be slowly worn down by well-meaning friends. Therapists like me who have talked to teenagers for years will tell you the same thing.

Peer pressure almost never looks like a bunch of teenagers standing in a circle around some geeky kid, all saying, "C'mon man, just try it." Friends of non-using teenagers at the party may say, "That's great. Good for you." However, an hour later, or at the next party, they will ask again and again. The pressure doesn't come so much from peers trying to get them to drink or use. It's more from the friends' complete inability to comprehend that "No thanks" doesn't mean "Ask me again later."

Alcohol and marijuana usage tend to have predictable effects on adolescent friend groups. They're very jealous and consuming recreational activities—they take in only one or two at first but then quickly take over the whole group. A friend group that gets together to drink beer once may go two months before doing the same thing again. But within a year, they will probably be drinking beer every time they get together. You never see this with other group social activities. I've never had a teenager tell me how his group used to go fishing once in a while, but now that's all they ever do.

All minors anywhere near alcohol or drugs are at risk of being arrested.

Because adolescents never get together to share a glass of wine with dinner, teenagers who attend beer parties or marijuana gatherings are always getting intoxicated. This means that even if your kid sincerely doesn't want to participate, he will be alone or among a very few who are sober, and that can feel quite lonely. Like a kid who's snorkeling at the surface while all his friends scuba dive below, eventually, he'll want to try a deep dive himself.

If your teenager regularly tries to involve you in arguments about how unreasonable your limits on substance use are, she may be displaying a problem already. Some teenagers loudly protest that not being allowed to be around minors who are consuming alcohol or drugs would ruin their social life. If they're right, that's all the more reason to stand your ground.

I often suggest to teenagers in substance-using friend groups that they simply ask their friends, "Hey, my parents are coming down hard on me about being near alcohol, so why don't we get together this weekend and just not have beer around, okay?" Then I ask, "What would your friends say to that?" Sometimes these adolescents are willing to admit these "friends" wouldn't sacrifice alcohol for friendship. I call this little discussion, "Who's your bud?"

Group intoxication creates false intimacy and stunts social growth. Teenagers can quickly develop a dependency on intoxication as the only means they know of connecting with others.

Strong, Progressive Consequences

You must have a clear statement of the response your teenager can expect if you receive evidence of alcohol or drug use. Remember, this includes if you have evidence of her presence where alcohol was being used by minors, or where illegal substances were being used by anyone. Evidence may be information received from a reliable source (e.g., a parent), a beer bottle cap in her car, telltale odors, and so on. Clear signs, however, are not the same as irrefutable evidence. If you've had a couple of signs you can't be sure of, tell her that because of these weird episodes, you may drug test her or use a Breathalyzer. Both are available at most drugstores or online.

A strong, logical consequence of substance use is grounding for a period of time. Grounding usually means the teen doesn't go anywhere except school, work, or any other essential activity you allow, and no one comes over. I would also remind you that grounding longer than one month quickly begins to lose its effectiveness. It's up to you, but two weeks is often a good minimum consequence. The goal is to have a strong consequence that's realistic for the first time you discover something. You want to make the point that this stuff is serious.

Some of you will ask, "But what about assuring them that they can call and I'll come pick them up, no questions asked?" That's a good idea, but "no questions asked" should mean no questions asked *that night* and should never imply "no consequences." Remember when we talked about teaching during a crisis? When an adolescent has made a serious mistake by drinking but is responsible enough to contact you and avoid hugely compounding his mistake, that's the time to drive up to the front of wherever he is, text "Here," patiently wait for him to get in, and say . . . nothing (except maybe, "Glad you called."). Giving out consequences can wait until the next day.

Speaking of calling, another plan you might offer your teenager is a signal (text or otherwise) she can send that tells you she wants you to "make her" come home. For example, a text message her friends can see may read, "All good here. Tell Uncle Charlie hello for me." That message can be prearranged to mean "Wait ten minutes, then call me like something serious has come up and you need me to come home now." Some adolescents will roll their eyes at the suggestion that they can't handle themselves, but many like the idea of a backup plan if they find themselves in an awkward spot.

A second goal is to clearly outline the serious consequences if this behavior is repeated. If an adolescent develops any sort of pattern of substance use, he's at great risk of having that behavior explode in adulthood, when parental restraints and legal age limits are removed. One or possibly two infractions are serious, but continued use of alcohol or drugs after lengthy grounding and knowing that worse consequences are coming suggests something more serious may be going on. If an adolescent displays a clear pattern of alcohol or drug use, it makes no sense to just continue to get tougher, since you've already displayed your willingness to give strong consequences. At that point, you need to investigate the possibility of a developing addiction pattern.

Addiction patterns in teenagers rarely reach some kind of gotta-have-it, physical need. After two or three violations that have had serious consequences, it's hard to understand why they wouldn't stop using alcohol or drugs. An evaluation with a drug counselor can help uncover underlying problems, such as a strong attachment to a substance-addicted friend group or even an attempt to manage the teenager's moods or stress.

Whatever the underlying cause, just be aware that the Expectations and Consequences list can be a strong deterrent for most adolescents. But when alcohol or drug use becomes a pattern, evaluation for addiction is in order, not a never-ending escalation of severe consequences.

Talking about Alcohol and Drugs

When it comes to risky behavior, cops are harder to talk to than judges. That may sound weird, but what I mean is that if you stay clear in your position as judge versus cop, communication is still possible. It's normal for adolescents to evaluate their parents' rules and decide whether they agree with them. With something as serious as alcohol and drug use, we want to encourage open dialogue whenever possible.

For example, picture a policeman and a guy who may or may not be a criminal talking together at a Starbucks in Texas. (I know it's a bit weird, but stick with me here.)

"So, why is it illegal to smoke marijuana in Texas but legal in Colorado?"

"Why? Are you planning on smoking a little marijuana?"

"Not necessarily. I'm just sayin' it doesn't make sense for something to be illegal here, but the same thing is fine just the other side of the Oklahoma Panhandle."

"You'd have to ask a cop in Colorado. Is there something in your pockets I should know about?"

That sounds like a bad cop movie, but here's my point: When you're a cop, this kind of communication is always tainted by tension. It's the tension between a police officer whose job is trying to keep people from breaking laws and someone who fears that what he says will incriminate him. This is not a great foundation for open communication.

Now let's take that same weird example and replace the police officer with a judge:

> "So, why is it illegal to smoke marijuana in Texas but legal in Colorado?"
>
> "That's a good question. Technically, even though the state says it's legal, Colorado is still violating federal law, which creates a bit of tension, as you can imagine."
>
> "It doesn't make sense for something to be illegal here, but the same thing is fine just a short distance from here."
>
> "That's true. Are you in favor of repealing our laws on marijuana?"
>
> "Definitely. When you consider the cost of enforcement to the benefit, it just doesn't make sense."

Do you see how different the conversation feels? This same guy may find himself in front of this judge for sentencing sometime in the future, but that's not a concern at the moment. Right now, they can talk and even disagree about what the laws and punishments are, but no one has to fear that something is going to happen just because they're talking.

This is what's possible when you see yourself mainly as a judge. When there's no case before you, that's the time to attempt dialogue. Begin having open discussion even if you don't have a concern about your teenager drinking alcohol or using drugs. Remember, don't make this an opportunity to start a speech about teenagers and drinking. You want to find out what your adolescent thinks about teenagers and drinking. If you have a compliant kid who starts in with a hearty, "I totally agree with you," take the risk of nudging her a little. "Why do you agree with me? What do you think is wrong with a teenager drinking a few beers occasionally?" Don't worry that your teenager will run off yelling, "Hey, Dad says it's okay!" Again, these are teenagers, not eight-year-olds.

One glance at your Expectations and Consequences list will remind your teen of where you stand. If you don't have this one written out (since it's never been an issue), this may be an opportunity to clarify your position verbally: "I mean, don't get me wrong, if we find out you've been drinking, there will be serious consequences. But you and I both know I can't ever be sure you're never gonna drink, so I'm just curious what your stance is on this." By clarifying what you'll act on (evidence of drinking), you can also remind him of things you're *not* trying to control (his opinion).

By applying a good balance of freedom, communication, and clear, uncompromising consequences, parents can maximize their influence over their adolescents' choices concerning alcohol and drug use. The seriousness of alcohol and drug use also requires that parents check their fears at the door and make efforts to come alongside their teenagers in navigating these issues.

PART SIX

The Inner Lives of Teenagers

Planned Emancipation in an
Increasingly Internal Culture

(In all the chapters in this section, I will not attempt a general discussion of deep emotional issues
but will only address them as they relate to the effective use of Planned Emancipation.)

CHAPTER 23

Pros and Cons of Self-Awareness

But you can't get away from yourself. You can't decide not to see yourself anymore. You can't decide to turn off the noise in your head.

JAY ASHER, *THIRTEEN REASONS WHY*

One of the major changes I have witnessed over thirty years of working with teenagers is their relationship with their emotions. Often in the past when parents brought their teenager to see me, they might include concern that their kid was depressed. So I would ask the teenager, "Do you think you're depressed?" It used to be that the answer was always, "No!"

Today, while adolescents continue to resist diagnoses suggested by their parents, many will announce to me their self-diagnoses: "My girlfriend has major anxiety, which makes it hard sometimes since I tend to get depressed." In many adolescent circles, it's no longer embarrassing to refer to a problematic, emotional diagnosis when describing oneself.

I often read articles that suggest our teenagers' increased awareness of emotional states is a good thing. As a psychologist, I agree, since greater emotional awareness is one of the main goals of psychotherapy. This increased focus on negative emotional states among teenagers does carry some problems, however. Removing the social stigma that burdened people with emotional struggles is a good thing, but developing an overly scrupulous self-focus that looks for every discomfort is not.

Self-Diagnosis by Internet

I remember in graduate school when I sat through my first psychopathology class. We spent an entire semester learning the names of all kinds of disorders of thinking, personality, emotion, and trauma. I recall my friend who sat next to me. With every new category, she would lean over and whisper, "I think I have that!" When we got to borderline personality disorder, she leaned over again, but this time I whispered, "I know, you think you have that."

"No," she said, "my mother has that!"

Adolescents who spend huge amounts of time flitting around the internet are more likely to come across random, authoritative-sounding sources that will confidently teach them about their internal states. Not surprisingly, these sources are often inaccurate and do not provide sufficient cautions about the "I have that" effect that happens to people (including psych students in psychopathology class!).

For example, what should you do when your teenager announces, "I've been depressed for a long time, and I just never told you"? I know few parents who would ignore such a statement. No parent should ever ignore a teenager's admission that he's in any kind of despair. My point is that in the age of the internet, it's reasonable for parents to respond with caution as well as concern.

Level of Functioning

When evaluating the significance of your adolescent's emotional state, it's important to consider whether he's able to fulfill the basic requirements of his life. As you probably recall from your own experience, adolescence is commonly filled with angst, melancholy, fears, and so on. These emotions, while painful at times, do not necessarily rise to the level of clinical concern. A teenager with a tendency toward shyness will find the beginning of a new school year difficult, but a teenager who misses half his classes due to crippling anxiety requires parental intervention.

There's no need to rush your teenager to a therapist every time she announces a negative emotional state. The first line of help should be her friends and parents.

When your teenager is displaying real struggles in normal, daily functioning, however, it's best to consult a psychologist or professional therapist. I recommend seeing a professional who has experience working with adolescents. A good therapist will conduct a careful evaluation before jumping into treatment. Sometimes a teenager doesn't need counseling, and a good therapist can tell the difference. Also, it's usually not a good idea to take your teenager to the same therapist you've been seeing. Your adolescent may have trouble trusting a therapist who's already heard your side of the story.

_____

When evaluating the significance of your adolescent's emotional state, it's important to consider whether he's able to fulfill the basic requirements of his life.

_____

If your adolescent is unhappy but still participating in school, outside activities, and social interactions, there's no need to panic. With this caution in mind, the following chapters discuss a few things you should know about the struggles adolescents have in their inner lives.

CHAPTER 24

Anxiety and Depression

I told my psychiatrist that everyone hates me. He said
I was being ridiculous—everyone hasn't met me yet.
RODNEY DANGERFIELD

"Your parents are worried that you're depressed. Do you think you're depressed?"

"No!"

Jessica, like most fourteen-year-olds brought to my office, didn't want to be there. Even though she had dropped out of sports and was struggling in school, she still didn't like it when her parents told her she might be depressed.

"Okay, so let me ask you, do you ever feel a kind of tired anger? Kind of flat, like 'If I had the energy I'd be pretty mad, but just . . . never mind'?"

"Well, yeah."

"That's usually what we call depression. Let me ask you this: Do you get bored easily? Not 'ho-hum' bored, but more of a [slapping my knees] 'Let's go! Let's get out of here!' sort of bored?"

"Yeah, I feel that a lot."

"That's what we call agitation. Maybe it's not as big a problem as your parents think, but it does sound like you often feel that flat, tired, angry kind of agitated boredom."

"That sounds about right."

When considering if your teenager is depressed, I recommend you look for that same kind of "tired anger." Even though tearfulness is often associated with depression, it's not the same as sadness. Sadness and grief are connected to events in our lives. A teenager who is crying for days after a bad breakup with her boyfriend isn't necessarily depressed. Time will help heal sadness. Depression is a different thing altogether.

Depression isn't an emotion in and of itself. It's more like the *absence* of emotion. Severe depression is when you're using your psychological resources just to "keep it together." It results in a narrowing of emotion—no real joy, but no huge letdowns, either. Depression looks like the following:

"Hey, you just won a million dollars!"
(In a bored voice) "Huh, that's great . . ."
"But you have to go to jail for a year."
(Same bored voice) "Oh, that's a drag . . ."

The emotion you see in depression looks more like fatigue. In adolescents, you often see a lot of anger as well. This occurs when their efforts at emotional control fail due to lack of sleep, poor eating, and so on. Depressed anger isn't directed and rational. It's a severe lack of patience with almost everything in life.

"Is That Why She's Mad at Me All the Time?"

I often talk with parents who have diagnosed their teenager as depressed strictly based on their kid's behavior when around them. But real depression is characteristic of an adolescent's general mood state, not just when he's with his parents. A teen who has good friendships, is involved in activities, and is well-behaved outside the home is not likely to be professionally diagnosed with depression.

Specific, directed anger toward parents, however—no matter how intense—should be taken seriously. This book should have already helped you see how our culture has normalized treating young adults like children. Adolescents commonly feel disrespected by well-meaning parents who are just trying to be helpful. This is by far the most common source of teenage anger toward parents and should not be misdiagnosed as depression. Labeling these intense, parent-specific frustrations as symptomatic of mental illness only adds to teens' sense of humiliation.

Anxiety, Fear, and Panic

Another common emotional discomfort teenagers express is anxiety. It isn't unusual for teenagers to say they are anxious about a test or an upcoming game. What they mean is that they're thinking about possible negative outcomes of this future event, and these thoughts light up their bodies' automatic response to threats. But what about teenagers who seem to be in a near-constant state of heightened, fight-or-flight arousal, or who can't order their food at a restaurant or make a phone call to schedule their doctor appointments? Is this the same thing as those who feel anxious about a test?

Top Down vs. Bottom Up

One helpful way to think about anxiety is to separate that experience from what is better called fear. When a teenager is anxious about the big game, she's technically describing *fear*. Fear is best thought of as coming from the top down. That is, fear is the experience of heightened arousal because of the thing she's thinking about (top down). It isn't unusual for an adolescent to fear tomorrow's final exam, but after she has finished the test and received her grade, her state of fight-or-flight arousal should diminish.

True anxiety begins in your body and is often unrelated to any specific thoughts. I remember in college when I first started drinking coffee. One morning I was sitting in an eight o'clock class and thinking, *Do we have a test today?* I had no reason to think that, but it felt like I was trying to figure out what was wrong. It took several minutes to recognize that I hadn't eaten breakfast but had drunk two cups of coffee. My body felt on high alert even though there wasn't an actual threat.

Most of the time, a true anxiety disorder comes from physiology and temperament. This is known as *endogenous anxiety*. I usually identify one or both parents with similar anxious temperaments. When treating teenagers with severe anxiety issues, I've often seen that they hadn't realized they have this problem. If your body has always been set to a state of high alertness, it takes a certain amount of cognitive awareness to understand that not everyone feels the same way.

Anxiety Is Not the Same as Fear

Anxiety originates in your body; fear originates in your thoughts. Trying to encourage an anxious teenager by correcting her thoughts is not only unhelpful, but it can also be quite annoying. An anxious teenager can often feel physically alerted in situations even when she knows there isn't a threat. One of the main reasons teenagers (and adults, for that matter) don't talk about their anxieties is that they know there's no logical reason to feel on high alert.

Think of it this way: A teenager whose adrenaline is pumping because he thinks there's a snake under the bed can be comforted by a trusted source assuring him that those fearful thoughts are unfounded.

I am particularly familiar with anxiety disorders not only through treating patients but also because anxiety runs in my family. I've had siblings, cousins, nephews, and nieces who all struggle with anxiety.

Our youngest daughter first displayed real problems with anxiety after a severe storm when she was seven years old. After a straight-line wind blew our barn into our house, it wasn't surprising that for months afterward all of us were pretty rattled whenever severe weather threatened. But it was different for her. She didn't seem to be getting better.

I finally took her to see my friend and colleague Dr. Paul Warren, a child psychiatrist. He was the first to point out that our daughter wasn't just fearful when storms came up. She was (secretly) obsessed with the weather all the time. What started as a realistic fear due to a traumatic experience had kicked off anxiety symptoms that far outlasted the effects of trauma.

Anxiety isn't something that people in my family *used* to have. These are temperamental challenges that must and can be successfully dealt with through different stages of life. When my daughter was an officer on the high school dance team, I remember being touched by hearing stories of support she received from friends whenever they practiced on the field in cloudy weather.

An anxious teenager may feel this same threat arousal simply because he's walking into a shopping mall. He already knows there's no real threat. When his parents try the same reassurance tactics that help alleviate fear, they don't seem to work. That's because Mom and Dad's helpful reassurances are piled on top of the teenager's own self-talk, which is relentlessly telling him to *cut it out* and *stop being so nervous all the time*. The result is often an anxious teenager who looks like he's angry with a parent who's trying to be helpful. To add one more layer of complication, if the "helpful" parent is also anxious and high-strung, that parent may start yelling back out of an unreasonable fear that her teenager "will never even be able to go into a mall!" The result may be one of those weird, viral videos you don't want to be the star of.

> Trying to encourage an anxious teenager by correcting her thoughts is not only unhelpful, but it can also be quite annoying.

Managing Anxiety

Teenagers with chronic, endogenous anxiety must learn to manage their anxieties, not keep trying to think their way out of them. Adolescents are too old for parents to be seeking a parenting trick that will eradicate their anxiety. Planned Emancipation parenting starts by recognizing the essential role your teenagers must play in dealing with their anxieties.

The first step in helping chronically anxious teenagers is usually to pull back from things that shield them from the real consequences of anxiety. Many parents, particularly nurturing mothers, just naturally fold themselves around their children's needs and instinctively help them. Without expecting it, these parents can wake up to the reality of a seventeen-year-old or older who relies on them to mitigate her social interactions so she doesn't feel the intensity of her anxieties. These often severely anxious teenagers don't even complain about anxiety. They complain about the parents they have grown dependent upon.

Adolescents are forming their own identities. It's difficult to incorporate limitations like chronic anxiety into a newly developing sense of self. Ironically, the anxious teenager's tendency to feel easily threatened and on high alert causes him to overreact to his own anxious tendencies. He would rather hide his anxieties in an unhealthy dependency on his parents than face them directly.

A parent's first step with an anxious adolescent, therefore, is to no longer allow your teen to demand that you take care of age-appropriate tasks that heighten his anxiety. He must feel the weight of his anxious temperament to learn how to manage it himself.

Second, talk openly about anxiety. Many anxious teenagers don't recognize that it's anxiety they're dealing with. A teenager can rarely verbalize that she would feel overwhelming anxiety if, say, she went to the back-to-school social event. Instead, she'll just say, "That's dumb, I'm not going."

In such situations, it can help if you cautiously start using the word *anxious* when your teenager complains. I say *cautiously* because you're not trying to convince her she's anxious. You are, however, letting her know the way it looks to you. Instead of saying, "All your friends will be there; you should go; you'll enjoy it if you just get it over with!" which is a remedy for *fear*, it's better to simply state, "I think these kinds of gatherings stir up your anxiety."

Whether your teenager acknowledges it or not, stick with identifying the anxiety when you see it and avoid jumping to quick-fix advice. This approach can help her avoid overreacting; instead, she can begin looking at ways to manage her chronic condition.

You can only offer advice on managing anxiety if your teenager has, on some level, acknowledged her struggle with it. Hold off on making doctor appointments or copying *Psychology Today* articles until she's open to them. Like anything else with teenagers, you must avoid control struggles. Many teenagers would rather struggle with anxiety and depression as long as it's their anxiety and depression and not yours!

Planned Emancipation and Anxiety and Depression

Significant struggles with anxiety and depression tend to affect Planned Emancipation in indirect ways. Chronic struggles with these issues may unconsciously signal parents to hold off before addressing issues of autonomy. Teenagers who feel periodically overwhelmed by anxiety or depression can get distracted from their drive toward individuation, but it's still there. Be careful that you don't mistake a teenager who remains at home more often because he doesn't feel like getting out for a teenager who no longer desires autonomy.

Adolescents must not be allowed to use the discomforts of anxiety or depression as reasons to remain stagnant. The goal of Planned Emancipation for these teens is to help them gain insight into these struggles and to cooperate with treatment. You mustn't attempt to fully manage the treatment of an adolescent's emotional struggles. A teenager who is actively participating in treatment may be granted some leeway when feeling emotionally overwhelmed. But a teen who uses complaints about depression or anxiety to avoid responsibilities, and who also refuses to pursue treatment, is not demonstrating the insight that is needed for autonomy.

CHAPTER 25

ADHD and Autism Spectrum Issues

I am different, not less.
TEMPLE GRANDIN

When my son entered middle school, he suddenly started racking up zeros on seemingly simple assignments. Being the sensitive, therapeutic parent that I am, I responded with angry lectures about the importance of school. I demanded to know why he didn't care. Later that year, when I was driving him to school, I saw him wince in a bit of pain. When I asked, he told me matter-of-factly that he always has stomachaches on test days.

It suddenly hit me: Why would a kid who doesn't care about school have painful stress on test days? When I consulted my close friend and colleague Dr. Paul Warren (yes, the same guy I took my daughter to see), he patiently walked me through my dawning awareness that my boy had ADHD. As a psychologist who has helped diagnose many adolescents with learning issues, I was reminded of the adage "The cobbler's children have no shoes."

Conditions You Can't *Feel*

In contrast to issues that involve self-awareness, adolescents who are impulsive, inattentive, or display autism traits struggle with a significant *lack* of self-awareness. It's difficult to have insightful conversations with these teenagers, specifically because they can't *feel* what the problem is. Despite the challenges, parents have generally increased their understanding of these diagnostic categories.

When these kids are young, parents are more able to obtain the educational and emotional support they need. When adolescence arrives, things get more complicated.

Attention Deficit Hyperactivity Disorder and Teenagers

The preeminent ADHD researcher Russell Barkley reminds us that "ADHD is not a disorder of knowing what to do, but of doing what one knows."[1] This is important to remember when interpreting a teenager's behavior. Receiving an email from a teacher because your fifteen-year-old has failed to turn in several assignments can trigger another wave of "school is important" speeches. But if this teenager has ADHD, this news probably doesn't signal a lack of motivation. ADHD significantly affects one's ability to organize his stuff, as well as his ability to manage time. This tends to have a significant impact on an ADHD teen's school performance.

Most of the obvious complications ADHD brings to adolescence involve school. For many kids with ADHD, school is a necessary evil. The confines of academic spaces are difficult for kids who are impulsive and energetic. ADHD girls tend to fare a bit better, but they must put great amounts of energy into keeping their grades up.

Parents will spend years supporting their child with ADHD; by the time the child reaches ten to twelve years old, the parents can relax a little, as they have found somewhat of a routine regarding school. Then adolescence hits, and it can feel as if all is undone.

By this point in the book, parents of kids with ADHD should have a better understanding of why teenagers with ADHD begin to push back against their parents' help. The need for autonomy is stronger than a desire for good grades. This creates a dilemma for parents who know they should be releasing control over school, but they fear the outcome of leaving it to their teen.

Parents of teenagers with ADHD must also keep in mind that someone who has difficulty staying focused *is not aware* when he's not focused. ADHD kids often complain they're unfairly targeted or that their teacher never told them when something was due, and so on. These are generally not lies. They are telling the truth about their own experience. They were likely distracted when the teacher made a particular announcement. Demanding your teenager "tell the truth" is of little use when he's telling the truth as he knows it. Remember, ADHD is not a problem of knowing what to do, it's a problem of doing what you know.

Another consequence of this lack of awareness is seen in social situations. ADHD kids tend to miss subtle social cues. This means they are often left out of social groups or even become targets for bullying. Again, ADHD kids don't know they're missing these subtleties. Parents with these kids know what I'm talking about. For years, they've watched cringy interactions among their ADHD kids and their peers. By adolescence, these kids are very aware that something isn't working in their social life, but they don't know what the problem is.

> By adolescence, these kids are very aware that something isn't working in their social life, but they don't know what the problem is.

This is particularly hard on ADHD girls. The social world of girls is more complex than for boys. If a small group of girls is discussing something vulnerable like how they feel unattractive, and the girl with ADHD cuts in and says, "Where are we gonna eat later?" that group of girls isn't going to hang with her next time. But they won't *tell her* that. To the girl with ADHD, it just seems like those other girls are mean.

Additionally, teenage boys like spending time with pretty girls. Many attractive teenage girls who have ADHD have told me, "I just like being friends with boys better." This gets complicated since most boys seek more than just friendship with attractive girls.

Planned Emancipation and Teenagers with ADHD

When it comes to ADHD and individuation with teens, the primary goal parents should have is simple to understand: The teen must gain insight into his own struggles. When parents continuously run interference to protect their teen from the consequences of his impulsivity and inattentiveness, the teen fails to gain needed insight. Many teenagers with ADHD don't think they have an ADHD problem. They think they have an over-involved-parent problem. When these parents remind their teen that they only stepped in because he was failing, they receive no gratitude. Adolescents with ADHD may not know how to fix their school problems, but they're surprisingly confident they don't want Mom or Dad's help.

Parents must back off appropriately so their teens can learn for themselves what accommodations they need. For schoolwork, this usually means giving teenagers the freedom to manage it themselves, as long as they maintain acceptable minimum grades. When they fail to meet those minimums (and they probably will), the consequences should center on removing distractions like electronics.

If parents go back to micromanaging, they never truly released school management as a freedom. It was a privilege their teen failed to retain. As I've said before, increased privilege with increasingly responsible behavior is a fine way to intervene with children, but it's not effective with teenagers. They *never* get the point when you insist that their bad grades forced you back to managing things. Teenagers are universally resentful when this happens.

It's better to stick to the consequences of the grade expectations. Like a judge following the law (rather than a cop trying to make this kid study), you have more flexibility to communicate about what may be going wrong. When your teenager complains that he never gets to play video games anymore, that's *not* your cue to say, "You need to understand that actions have consequences!" Instead, you should take a position that's firm but also understanding: "I know. I thought for sure you'd figure out how to bring your grades up after those last few weeks without games. What do you think makes it so hard?"

Good communication about ADHD is essential to make the invisible features of inattentiveness and impulsivity more visible. You can sincerely ask what your teenager has tried and what she plans to do differently. This is where it's good to mention (carefully) the tools you have probably provided. I don't recommend trying to force your teen to go to tutoring or even to take ADHD medication if she's against it. These are control battles you can't win, plus your teenager's resistance to these resources demonstrates her lack of insight. It's best to maintain the consequences of poor grades while offering advice about using resources (e.g., tutors, meds, etc.) you're willing to provide.

Autism Spectrum Issues with Adolescents

As Dr. Stephen Shore from Adelphi University said, "If you've met one person with autism, you've met one person with autism."[2] It's difficult to make general statements about anyone with autism spectrum disorder (ASD). My focus here will be to highlight the issues of ASD relevant to Planned Emancipation.

The first issue parents of ASD adolescents must deal with is diagnosis. Our understanding of autism has increased greatly in the past decades, and this is mostly a good thing. Autism used to evoke images of children rocking on the floor, unable to speak. Greater observation by Austrian pediatrician Hans Asperger and many others brought us to our current understanding of autism as it exists on a spectrum. More and more children, adolescents, and adults who are in many ways high-functioning are being diagnosed with ASD. This means the severity of ASD weighs more heavily on parents' interventions than the diagnosis itself.

Adolescents and adults with significant autism characteristics are not expected to live independently and so are not in view here. However, specific problems arise when teenagers are diagnosed with high-functioning autism. If an adolescent diagnosed with ASD is expected to be able to live independently, his parents must engage in some level of Planned Emancipation. High-functioning autism spectrum adolescents generally experience the same desire for autonomy as other teenagers. Unfortunately, depending on the impact of the disorder, ASD teenagers run a high risk of developing a hostile dependency on their parents. They know they need them, but they hate that they need them.

Planned Emancipation and Autism Spectrum Disorder

If your teenager has been diagnosed with ASD but functions at a level that won't interfere with achieving independent living, your goal is the same as with adolescents with ADHD. You need to help your teen gain greater insight into his ASD. Some parents express concerns about sharing an ASD diagnosis with their children. For kids twelve and under, I understand that caution, but for adolescents, such reticence can be harmful.

I usually recommend teenagers be invited to any meeting where assessment feedback is given. It's important to share with young adults the reality of their struggles. This often begins by giving these issues the proper name. Many of the ASD adolescents I work with are quite intelligent. While they may not comprehend interpersonal interactions, they can develop an awareness of this weakness

> It's important to share with young adults the reality of their struggles.

in themselves. There's relief in finding the right name for their experience. Saying the proper name can help these teens avoid labeling themselves as *stupid* or *someone no one likes*.

I diagnosed a particular client with high-functioning ASD while he was in high school. His parents were very involved and tended to clear the way for most of his academic and social needs. He didn't seem interested in knowing any more than what I told him about his ASD symptoms. He contacted me several years later, however, when he was working for a software company that sent him to major banks to coordinate the use of their product. For the first time, he experienced failure in his work due to his poor social skills. Without his parents as a safety net, he became very interested in ASD and wanted to develop skills to overcome his limitations. Although painful, his struggles were an important factor in his acquiring greater insight.

Adolescents with ASD need to be given the dual message that they're adults but have limitations. This is usually a balancing act, and it varies with each adolescent. Parents need to keep their eyes on the end-of–high school clock that hangs invisibly on their living room wall. There's a stark contrast between an eighteen- or nineteen-year-old high school graduate who can tell you about his ASD and the same-aged ASD adult who doesn't know what he struggles with and gets mad at his parents who keep hovering around, protecting him.

Developing Insight

For teens with ADHD or ASD to develop insight into their struggles, parents will have to watch them go through painful experiences as they interact with school settings and social settings in general. The parents I work with have done a remarkable job in providing good assessments and resources to help their kids get through childhood. Often, these parents don't realize how well they've done as they constantly scan the horizon for the next threat or misstep in their kids' lives.

It's more important than ever that parents feel a sense of completion when their kids reach the age of thirteen. This satisfaction isn't so these parents can sit back and leave their adolescents to fend for themselves. (I don't know any parents who have done that.) But a sense of "job done" is necessary so these parents can see more clearly the adults-in-training before them. Although it will be hard to watch their adolescents go through painful experiences, this is the only path to their teens' developing the all-important insights that will take them into independent adulthood.

CHAPTER 26

Brain Science, Trauma, and Other Rabbit Holes

*The dazzling real achievements of brain research are
routinely pressed into service for questions they were never
designed to answer. This is the plague of neuroscientism—
aka neurobabble, neurobollocks, or neurotrash—and it's everywhere.*

STEVEN POOLE

I've met parents who have done enough reading about child- and adolescent-related topics to earn at least two master's degrees. While this displays commendable passion, it often leads to overwhelming confusion about what's the best thing to do. An avalanche of books and articles now focus on the importance of understanding the teen brain. These may soon be buried under even more information on generational trauma and other seemingly crucial concepts parents must learn.

As we saw in the first chapters, *Feeding the Mouth That Bites You* focuses on a major cultural flaw that has led to our problems with teenagers and how you can make important corrections to this flaw in your family. "But what about a lot of other stuff I've read?" you might ask. There's a lot of good information out there about adolescence. This book doesn't discount the value of other information. The problem is knowing how and when to apply this information to parenting. My concern is always about *effective* parenting—what makes a difference in teenagers' lives and what increases parents' ability to influence their teenagers. New or even important information about teenagers that is misapplied is of no use.

Implications of Incompetence

The biggest problem with this ever-widening array of information is that it's almost always used to imply that teenagers are less capable or in greater need of supervision and control than previously thought. Articles about teen suicide or underdeveloped brains always seem to add to a parent's fear and end up implying a need to be more controlling and overprotective than ever. These are the topics that make up the user manuals I mentioned in chapter 1. Don't mistake the user manual for a map.

> Articles about teen suicide or underdeveloped brains always seem to add to a parent's fear and end up implying a need to be more controlling and overprotective than ever.

Remember, our culture isn't thinking about transitioning into adulthood. We've forgotten about that. But we *are* plowing ahead with new and sometimes genuinely exciting scientific data. The problem is not with the science data; the problem is with the implications we take from these new findings. With no road map toward adulthood, our culture always assumes that scientific data about adolescents means they are less competent and more in need of supervision.

I mean it. When was the last time you read a scientific article that concluded teenagers are *more* capable and in need of *less* supervision than previously thought? Whether the data are on teen brains, hormones, exposure to toxins—you name it, the implications increase parents' fears for their helpless teenagers.

Hormones

During the early decades of our new understanding of teenagers, hormones did most of the heavy lifting. Adolescence was often described as the result of raging hormones that seem to rip through a sweet child's body, rendering him angry and rebellious. It's true that in adolescence, gonadotropin-releasing hormone (GnRH) is released, and this stimulates growth and a series of physical changes that are almost as fast and body-altering as those seen in infancy. But are the changes the cause of problematic teenage behavior? How helpful is knowing about hormones to effective parenting?

The hormone-induced physical changes in adolescents are certainly stress-inducing. Teenagers need more sleep than ever (between eight and ten hours), and appetites can be voracious. This often leads to strong moods that can change quickly and energy bursts that can be difficult to control. It's easy to view puberty as a chemical storm that parents just need to ride out until normalcy returns.

The problem is that adolescents in all cultures undergo significant hormonal changes. Why don't they all behave like teenagers in the West? Puberty is a universal human stage of physical development, so why didn't these changes cause hormonal insanity throughout history? Hormones are helpful things to know about. It can be especially important for adolescents to be informed about these changes that might otherwise be scary. For parents, however, overfocusing on hormones as a cause of teenage rebellion is an oversimplified way of ignoring the data from history and other cultures.

Ever tried telling your teenager she's just being hormonal? This is much like when a husband stops in the middle of an argument to ask his wife if she's on her period. Hormones can increase the volume of emotions, but they don't create the conflicts that lead to these frustrations. This is where hormones join the ever-growing line of factors used to infantilize and dismiss the important issues adolescents need to deal with.

Brain Science

The latest giant pile of research parents feel they must master is all about the teenage brain. News articles, books, and social media posts now provide us with a constant flow of new research telling us the "real" causes of adolescent misbehavior and the fragile nature of their still-developing brains. Brain science is an exciting area of research. The implications we draw from this research, however, tend to be infantilizing adolescents' behavior and add to parents' fear and overcontrol.

To be clear, all of us in the field of behavioral science are excited about information coming from the new technologies in brain science. For me, this started with Dr. Daniel Amen and his work with brain SPECT (single photon emission computed tomography) imaging more than twenty years ago. The therapy group I worked with was in talks with Dr. Amen about opening a clinic in the Dallas area that would use this new technology to provide groundbreaking treatments for a variety of psychological disorders. Even though we didn't combine our practice with Dr. Amen, it seemed that new brain imaging would completely transform the practice of psychiatry and psychology.

Things haven't gone exactly as planned. The data are great, but the treatment implications that can be drawn from that data are trickier to interpret than we thought.

One example has been the discovery that brain development continues into our early to midtwenties. I remember specifically being taught that brain development finished around the age of five. This is a huge finding, but what do we do with that information?

By 2017, many media outlets were reporting on the implications of what now appeared to be an underdeveloped teen brain. Brain science experts were speculating on the fact that the amygdala—the part of the brain responsible for immediate, emotional responses like fear and aggression—develops earlier than the prefrontal cortex, the brain region thought to influence reasoning and impulse control. Articles reviewing this data quickly suggested this was the cause of many teenage problems, including getting into accidents of all kinds, getting involved with fights, and engaging in dangerous behavior.[1]

I knew these studies were in the news cycle because of how often parents came to my office with the latest headline connecting brain science to whatever negative behavior their teens were currently involved with. Finally, an extensive literature review done at the University of

Pennsylvania exploded this myth, stating, "We found that much of the risk behavior attributed to adolescents is not the result of an out-of-control brain."[2] It turns out that adolescents are necessarily involved with many new experiences, and their misjudgments in new situations aren't much different from older adults trying to manage new situations.

Why Did It Take So Long to Pull Back This Kind of Myth?

One reason for this seems to be that brain science currently holds first place in the public's view of what makes scientific discussion of human behavior valid. Several studies confirm this bias. If I tell you something surprising about teenagers, you might believe me since I'm a psychologist. But if I add something like "brain studies show that . . . ," you're significantly more likely to believe me. And if I add a picture of a brain scan to the page, there's an even higher likelihood you'll think I'm right.[3]

I'm not saying that brain science isn't providing important, scientific data. But the images you see of a brain scan are not photographs of the brain (although they kind of look like it). These are computer-generated maps of blood flow and oxygen levels in the brain put together with sophisticated computer software.

I'll never forget the time researchers at Dartmouth found what appeared to be brain activity in a dead salmon (causing neuroscientists to make important adjustments to their measurement systems).[4] It's important to remember that this is complicated science that's too often used to draw premature conclusions.

Another reason it took so long to rethink the myth of a dangerous teen brain is our cultural tendency to use information about teenagers as another excuse for infantilizing them. We now use brain science in much the same way we blamed hormones in decades past. Our culture always seems to be looking for some biological reason for problematic teen behavior. In her book *The Teenage Brain*, Frances Jensen, MD, tells a story of how her teenage son's strange behavior mystified her: "As his mother and a neurologist, I thought I knew everything there was to know about what was going on inside my teenager's head. Clearly

I did not. I certainly didn't know what was going on outside his head either! So as a mother and a scientist, I decided I needed to—I *had* to—find out."[5]

But her son's behavior needn't have seemed so mysterious. Careful research has shown that problematic adolescent behavior is tied directly to culture, not brain development. Jensen's research on the adolescent brain is certainly fascinating. (Maybe we could do brain scans on adolescents in the Inuit communities in the Canadian Arctic, except they don't have a word for adolescents.)

To be clear, the information in Jensen's book is very useful, especially regarding potential damage from drug and alcohol use. But these resources don't add much to how parents can respond more effectively to their teenagers. If anything, brain science seems to add to parents' fear of what now may seem like brain-damaged kids.

Trauma

The next wave of scientific data parents feel compelled to master seems to be trauma. Much like brain science, the scientific data coming in about the human experience of, and reaction to, trauma are providing important and sometimes groundbreaking information. My concern, again, is the real implications for parents and our cultural tendency to assume these data mean more fragility in adolescents and more need for parents to overcontrol.

Psychological focus on trauma traces its roots to war veterans. Beginning in the early twentieth century, soldiers' experiences of the horrors of war were studied more and more. By the end of the century, diagnosis and treatment of post-traumatic stress disorder were widely accepted in medicine and psychology. To connect an individual's symptoms to trauma required experiencing trauma that was outside the normal life experience of hardship. Trauma symptoms were limited to those who experienced a real threat of death or intense violation, such as physical and sexual abuse. Current psychological practice has expanded these criteria significantly.

Our current fascination with trauma started in the mid-1990s, when the major health insurer in the US Kaiser Permanente conducted the ACE (Adverse Childhood Experiences) study with a large database of their insured patients. The study was later repeated with a much larger database through the US Centers for Disease Control and Prevention.[6] This was a checklist that asked people to identify which adverse experiences they had experienced, such as parental divorce, imprisonment of family members, or physical and sexual abuse. These results were correlated with the individual's physical and mental health.

The results were compelling. Almost everyone had experienced at least one traumatic event, but those who had significantly more adverse experiences reported significant impairment in their health and wellbeing. The ACE study found a direct link between childhood trauma and adult onset of chronic disease, incarceration, and employment challenges. Intuition told us that adverse experiences in childhood had negative effects, but this had never been confirmed on such a wide scale. Researchers and clinicians turned their attention, more than ever, to studying, treating, and avoiding trauma.

In 1992, Judith Herman, a professor of psychiatry at Harvard Medical School, suggested the diagnosis of complex post-traumatic stress disorder. CPTSD results from a long period of stress that cannot be avoided rather than intense, short-term events. While not yet adopted by the American Psychiatric Association in the *Diagnostic and Statistical Manual of Mental Disorders*, CPTSD is increasingly cited as the cause of numerous symptoms, including emotional dysregulation, attention difficulties, anxiety, and depression.

Not surprisingly, this focus on trauma includes adolescents. Therapists now regularly treat adolescent struggles in the context of trauma. Some have proposed the term *developmental trauma disorder* as a childhood equivalent of CPTSD. This was popularized by the psychiatrist Bessel van der Kolk in his bestselling book *The Body Keeps the Score*. Complex trauma for children and adolescents has expanded to subjective experiences, such as abandonment and shame.

As a clinician, I find the research into the expanded effects of trauma exciting. But as with brain research, I'm concerned about the implications for parents. Parents who have read about expanding trauma understanding are still left with the question "So what should I do about this?" An increasing list of possibly traumatic experiences leaves parents unclear about whether their adolescent's negative experiences qualify as trauma. Even worse, the term *trauma* has entered the popular lexicon of self-diagnosis, even among teenagers.

Only a few years ago, it was difficult to get adolescents to even consider that they might fit into any psychological diagnostic category, such as depression, ADHD, or OCD. In recent years, however, this seems to have shifted significantly. Teenagers in my office often casually refer to themselves as bipolar or any number of previously off-limits categories. Unfortunately, like many young adults, these adolescents often use these diagnoses inaccurately. The popularization of these terms makes them vulnerable to *concept creep*, the tendency to use specific diagnoses for an ever-expanding list of symptoms.

> Teenagers in my office often casually refer to themselves as bipolar or any number of previously off-limits categories. Unfortunately, like many young adults, these adolescents often use these diagnoses inaccurately.

The popularization of the term *trauma* has suffered from this same effect of concept creep. Nick Haslam, professor of psychology at the University of Melbourne warns, "When we start to talk about ordinary adversities as 'traumas' there is a risk that we'll see them as harder to overcome and see ourselves as more damaged by them."[7]

When a teenager has endured significant trauma like physical or sexual abuse, parents should consider a good evaluation and treatment for the residual effects. But what about teenagers who experienced their parents' divorce or bullying at school? It's certainly wise to offer counseling to any teenager who is struggling and wants to talk to someone. I agree, however, with Dr. Haslam's caution. Naming difficult but ordinary events as trauma runs the risk of implying these are too difficult to overcome.

Implications for Planned Emancipation

Each of these categories has influenced parents I've worked with to reconsider Planned Emancipation, or at least to delay full autonomy. These tactics don't usually result in extending adolescence until they're ready. Most often, trying to hold a teenager back out of misplaced sympathy for trauma or an underdeveloped brain encourages these young adults to see themselves as defective. This results in the know-it-when-I-see-it autonomy standoff we talked about in chapter 5.

I encourage parents to be cautious when reading in-depth material on newly developing branches of behavioral science. Parents should keep a careful eye out for answers to questions like *What does this information say about how I should intervene with my teenager?* and *Have the implications offered by these discoveries been tested?* Careful discernment of this research is needed to avoid our culture's reflex to infantilize adolescents.

CHAPTER 27

Sexuality and Gender Identity

In the social jungle of human existence there is no feeling
of being alive without a sense of identity.

ERIK ERIKSON

It's hard to write a chapter I know will upset some readers. This, of course, is the nature of our current cultural debate on sexual and gender identity. A segment of Americans divides viewpoints on this issue as either pro-LGBTQ or phobic. For them, there's no such thing as thoughtful disagreement. For this reason, I will state that my religious views on sex and gender identity are aligned with the tradition of biblical, Christian faith. I use G. K. Chesterton's definition of *tradition* as "the democracy of the dead" that "refuses to submit to the small and arrogant oligarchy of those who merely happen to be walking about."[1]

As a psychologist, I know it's important that I join with others in my field to extend our understanding of human behavior through science. I have always been on the alert for Christian teachings that don't align with psychological research and clinical observation. But I have yet to find any valid research that clearly disproves the Christian understanding of human behavior and relationships, and LGBTQ data are no exception—not even close.

Parents in Despair

"Thank you so much for seeing us, Dr. Wilgus. We are just devastated and have no idea what to do!"

In the last five years, I've noticed a slight change in appearance that some parents have. This couple in their late forties was sitting in my office, and they had that look. It's a kind of soul-weary almost panic that I rarely saw in parent consults until recently. Unfortunately, I know what that look means: These parents had discovered that their child identified as gender diverse in some way (e.g., transgender, gender nonconforming, nonbinary).

"Our daughter has always been self-conscious about her looks, and we tried to be encouraging," her mother told me. "For a few years now she has refused to wear anything that looks too 'girlish.' Following your book, we didn't make her dress a certain way, but now we're worried that was a mistake."

Stories like the one above vary but have many common themes:

- The parents usually discovered their kid's trans identity indirectly. Rarely does a self-identified gender-diverse young adult directly inform his parents of this decision.
- This change in identity was not precipitated by a lengthy discussion of dysphoria about the teenager's biological sex, at least not that the parents knew of.
- Their teenager is almost always "out" to their friend group or at school before the parents know anything about it.

The following is perhaps the most important theme I see among families:

- The teenager who is coming out expresses great fear that their parents will reject them for who they are and doesn't seem to notice that their parents are doing everything they can to express that they still love and accept their teenager.

This last theme has been hard to watch. I'm sure there still exist some parents who react to their child's identifying as gay or trans with extreme anger or even by kicking their kid out of the house. I just don't know any of them. They don't come to my office, and I'm pretty sure they wouldn't be reading this book.

The parents I see are more like the people in that old *Twilight Zone* episode I always called "Billy and the Cornfield."[2] It's the one where an entire small town is terrorized and held hostage by a monster in the form of a six-year-old boy. This boy has the mental power to, when angry, destroy people with his thoughts by sending them to the cornfield, from which they never return. It's disturbing to watch terrified adults desperately trying to keep this kid happy, constantly telling him what a good boy he is.

Since LGBTQ identity sees only allies or enemies, Christian parents are often rendered mute, unable to voice their objections without the risk of being shouted down or emotionally cut off from their child. Many Christian parents have reversed their views about sexual purity and biological sex because of this pressure. They cannot believe that a loving God would reject their child for simply being authentic.

Many parents I see don't have a teen who has identified as LGBTQ, but the issue still causes problems. Most adolescents I see are not gay or trans, but they support anyone who is. It's hard for most young adults to see opposition to LGBTQ-identifying people as anything but discrimination against an oppressed minority. Even the most conservative Christian teenager is, at best, silent on the issue.

What You Need to Know

As with all the chapters in this book, I won't attempt anything close to a complete discussion on such a large topic. My goal is to offer a suggested strategy to increase your effectiveness as a parent, a strategy that takes advantage of the positive effects of Planned Emancipation. If you are pro-LGBTQ ideology, feel free to skip the rest of this chapter. The chapter on sex and dating may be more helpful to you.

Identity

I remember, some years ago, I was sitting with a sixteen-year-old boy and his mother in my office. I was doing a first interview, so I was asking basic questions: "How do you like your school?" "Do you have a best friend?" "Do you have a girlfriend?" To that last question, he answered no, but I noticed a slightly startled expression in his eyes. After his mom left, I asked him again the girlfriend question. He told me the reason for his reaction was that he was gay but his mom didn't know.

After apologizing for not just asking, "Are you dating someone?" I asked about the guy he was dating. My client told me the other guy was also sixteen and was named Andrea, but he went by Andy. I told him I was surprised his boyfriend's real name was Andrea, and he confidently stated that Andrea had been a girl when they started dating six months before but that Andrea had recently come out as a transgender boy and felt more comfortable with the name Andy. So, since my client found himself dating a transgender boy, he'd concluded that he was gay.

When I asked if his (previously girlfriend but now) boyfriend had started transitioning, my client said no. He said Andy wasn't ready to tell his parents and hadn't changed anything yet about his clothes or appearance. Finally, I asked to see a picture of my client and his boyfriend. He clicked around on his phone and finally showed me a homecoming shot of the two of them. In the photo, my client was wearing a black shirt and tie and standing next to an attractive teenage girl in a red-and-white satin homecoming dress. After my client and his mom left, I remember sitting at my desk, staring into the distance, and asking myself, *What just happened?*

I can tell you what *hadn't* happened. I had not just talked with a boy about sex. This kid's sexual behavior (fooling around with his girlfriend) hadn't changed at all from back when he was straight to now that he was supposedly gay and dating his boyfriend. That's important because a lot of people my age (older folks) think that their beliefs about sex are being questioned by younger people in their lives. Too many of us can't fathom why a twentysomething family member is upset because we think being gay or transgender is a sin. After all, hasn't the orthodox Christian view held that same standard for a couple thousand years?

What we need to understand is that my client, like all LGBTQ youth, was *not* struggling with sexual behavior; he was having a crisis of identity. An argument over appropriate sexual behavior is the *What do you think you're doing?* question. My client and many, many young people like him are struggling with the question *Who do you think you are?* And that is far more jolting.

> What we need to understand is that my client, like all LGBTQ youth, was *not* struggling with sexual behavior, he was having a crisis of identity.

LGBTQ ideology preaches that discomfort with your biological sex and same-sex attraction are fixed traits within each person and can be used as guideposts to your authentic individuality. Using language like *coming out* rather than *identifying as* suggests that an individual's sexual or gender identity was always there, waiting to be shown to the world. The fact that there is no scientific backing for this belief should only make you more respectful of its power. LGBTQ-identifying young people are searching for answers to deep questions about who they are. A quick "That's not biblical" answer will not have much impact.

Sexual Identity: The "LGB" and the "A"

The term *LGBTQ* is confusing and is still subject to change. This confusion arises from an attempt to make one entity out of a widely varying group of individualized micro groups. There are two main categories: (1) issues of sexual attraction (sexuality) and (2) issues of gender. These are not the same.

The *L* in *LGBTQ* stands for *lesbian*, the *G* stands for *gay*, the *B* stands for *bisexual*, and an *A* may be added that stands for *asexual*. These are all categories that describe one's inner experience of sexual attraction. The most common subcategory of those identifying as LGBTQ is bisexual. In a recent poll, however, most adults between the ages of eighteen and twenty-three identify as heterosexual.[3]

The term *asexual* refers to not having sexual attraction toward anyone. A lesser-known sexual identity category is *demisexual*, which refers to someone who only has sexual attraction to someone he or she is in love with. This used to be known as normal, human sexual attraction, but now it's among dozens of specific identities people are using.

You need to know that sexuality is not directly related to transgender issues. That is, don't expect someone who identifies as gay to start wearing dresses. If you have a teenager who has come out as gay, lesbian, or bisexual, the first issue to address is who they want to have sex with, not whether they're male or female.

In 2020, Democratic presidential candidate Pete Buttigieg held a rally in Denver. A nine-year-old boy stepped up to the microphone and asked, "Would you help me tell the world I'm gay too? I want to be brave like you." The crowd applauded and chanted, "Love is love!"[4] No one thought to ask what a prepubescent boy means when he identifies himself as gay.

It's also important to note that a teenager, especially a young teen, who has come out as gay has not necessarily acted out sexually. Remember, this is about finding identity, not necessarily planning sexual encounters. Parents must ask the question no one asked that nine-year-old: "What do you feel that draws you to identify as gay?"

Such scrupulous naming of inner experiences of sexual desire should give you some insight into the confusion going on here. The object of one's sexual interest is too variable to be used as an anchor for one's identity. To influence an adolescent who is busy trying to build her life on this foundation of sand, parents must be careful to focus on the real issue: From where do we get our identity? Just spouting, "Don't do sinful sexual stuff" is not helpful.

Gender Identity: The "TQ" and the "I"

Gender ideology is quite different from sexual identity ideology. If gay and lesbian voices are telling us there's nothing wrong with people of the same sex having sex, the gender diversity ideology is announcing that male and female aren't clear categories. The tension between these two communities is not publicized. These groups work together more as cobelligerents than as teams sharing an ideology.

The *T* is for *transgender*, the *Q* is for *queer* (also sometimes called *genderqueer*), and the *I* that may get added is for *intersex*. Again, I won't go into detail about these categories, but it's important that parents know the difference when seeking to have influence in the lives of their teenagers.

Gender diversity ideology stems from an increased focus on people's subjective experiences. There is now great interest in whether someone feels male, female, or something else, regardless of his or her biology. The popular term for male or female has now been changed to *gender*, a word borrowed from linguistics. English speakers may remember learning Spanish or French and being frustrated at what can appear to be arbitrary decisions about masculine or feminine nouns. This seeming arbitrariness is the point when using the term *gender* about humans.

Gender in humans refers to "socially constructed characteristics of women and men—such as norms, roles and relationships of and between groups of women and men."[5] When children are born, *male* and *female* are now described as their "gender assigned at birth." This language, again, is used to imply that *male* or *female* is an arbitrary assignment given out by the obstetrician in the delivery room rather than an obvious, biological sex identified at birth. I was present when all three of my children were born, and I assure you, my wife and I didn't look at the doctor for a judgment call on whether we had a boy or girl.

> I was present when all three of my children were born, and I assure you, my wife and I didn't look at the doctor for a judgment call on whether we had a boy or girl.

The term *intersex* is sort of a medical casualty of this new gender diversity ideology. To support the case that humans are not born male or female but on a spectrum, a bit of gerrymandering had to be done with the human body. There has always been a small percentage of people who are born with either a genetic or birth defect that affects genitalia and sex presentation. Genetic anomalies such as Klinefelter syndrome, XYY syndrome, hermaphroditism, and other conditions account for a small percentage of births each year. Combining these conditions does nothing to help these individuals' treatment and management of their conditions. The term *intersex* has been invented as biological confirmation of some people's subjective experience. Combining these very different biological anomalies allows for an artificially high number of people who are supposedly born neither male nor female.

Like sexual identity issues, gender identity struggles stem from an overly scrupulous self-examination of one's comfort with one's body. Horror stories about surgery and hormone therapy given to minors can cause parents to lose focus on the main issue: From where do we get our identity?

Current Gender Theory Is Bad Social Science

Teens who identify as transgender or some other gender-diverse category are saying they feel different from their body's biology. What most of them don't know is just how common serious discomfort with one's body is, especially among teenage girls. Instead, they're told this discomfort may indicate they are authentically a different gender from their biology, and it's their bodies that must be made to obey their subjective experience.

As a psychologist for more than thirty years, I'm quite familiar with the importance of accurately labeling one's inner experience. I agree with psychologist Jordan Peterson and others in my field who believe that what young people are being taught is a mislabeling of personality traits. Decades of research suggest that humans, across cultures, tend to display predictable clusters of personality characteristics that appear to be inherent and stable. Personality traits like conscientiousness, agreeableness, and extraversion have helped people to understand and communicate their own individual personality tendencies.

For many years, psychologists like me worked hard, particularly in the Christian community, to encourage greater diversity in what maleness and femaleness should look like. I have seen significant improvements in prejudices that would reject a boy as male simply because his interests and mannerisms didn't fit someone's narrow definition of *male*. The same progress has been made with girls. We've widened our overly narrow view of what it means to be female.

In my view, however, gender diversity ideology sets us back decades. Current gender theory suggests that individuals should look within and try to cluster their personality traits into clumsy and ill-defined gender categories. Instead of playground bullies taunting some poor boy, shouting, "You act like a girl!" we now have ignorant but well-meaning voices supporting the same claim as the bully. Boys and girls who feel like they don't fit the definition of their sex should be encouraged to expand their narrow view of gender. But instead, they're being encouraged to begin the impossible task of changing their sex.

This also explains the alarmingly high rate (as much as six times as many) of young people with autism spectrum disorder who identify as transgender or gender diverse.[6] Individuals with social vulnerabilities are more susceptible to gender ideology and the popularity that often goes along with it. Added to this social pressure, teenagers with ASD lack insight and are often the least capable of accurately identifying their inner experiences or personality traits. In other words, vulnerable adolescents are the most likely to get caught up in the confusion.

The Myth of Suicidality in Gender-Conflicted Youth

The pressure felt by parents has been ratcheted up even higher by a now commonly repeated myth that young people who are unable to receive hormone blockers and/or surgeries are at an extremely high risk for suicide. During a debate on the floor of the Georgia House of Representatives, Rep. Karla Drenner passionately declared, "To all the children in our state who are going to be negatively impacted [by a proposed law restricting sex change therapy for kids], please don't lose hope. Please don't give up. Please don't kill yourself!"[7] This argument furthers the extremities of this debate with the fictional choice *Would you rather have a live transgender kid or a dead one?*

This argument is not only wrong but also disrespectful to those who struggle with gender dysphoria. Compared to the average adolescent rates of suicide attempts or ideation, transgender teens do have higher rates. But when the rate of LGBTQ teens' suicidality is compared to that of adolescents who are experiencing other mental-health struggles, there is little difference.[8] Several LGBTQ advocacy groups have called for this kind of hyperbole to stop. Such arguments imply that LGBTQ teens are weaker than other struggling adolescent groups. There is also concern that these claims could normalize or encourage suicidal behavior in LGBTQ youth:

> Linking suicide directly to external factors like bullying, discrimination or anti-LGBT laws can normalize suicide by suggesting that it is a natural reaction to such experiences or laws. It can also increase suicide risk by leading at-risk individuals to identify with the experiences of those who have died by suicide.[9]

To be clear, mental-health struggles of any kind can contribute to an adolescent's increased suicidal ideation or action. Any and all discussion of suicide from anyone should be taken seriously. An adolescent's declaration of LGBTQ identification alone, however, does not constitute an automatically increased risk of suicide. Parents of teens who are struggling with sexuality and gender issues have enough to deal with; they don't need to carry the false guilt that their adolescents' lives are in their hands.

Responding to Gender and Sexuality Issues

You already know you can't control your teenager's thoughts. You know that making speeches is ineffective. Following the *Feeding the Mouth* pattern, the following sections offer suggestions that may increase your effectiveness with your teenager struggling with LGBTQ issues.

LGBTQ and Control Battles

Like all other *Feeding the Mouth* issues, a critical aspect in dealing with sexuality and gender identity is control. Adolescents' power to declare their own identity is another area where parents must begin to recognize freedoms. Establishing control is not the only motive LGBTQ-identifying teenagers have, but when it is, it's hard to have an impact on their decisions.

I've known teenagers who seemed to be good kids; they never pushed back against controlling parents. Then suddenly they declared that they were gay or trans and seemed to enjoy the spectacle of their parents' helplessness to do anything about it. When an adolescent uses LGBTQ identity as a means of planting a flag of control over his life, it tends to be planted very deeply.

> When an adolescent uses LGBTQ identity as a means of planting a flag of control over his life, it tends to be planted very deeply.

LGBTQ issues are a cultural hot button that can provide a teenager with a ready army of well-meaning people who will consider any opposition to her recently chosen identity as oppressive. Parents must tread carefully. Mom and Dad's fears can easily result in strong, even threatening statements that they have no power to back up. Their ability to remove an adolescent from toxic cultural influences is limited. The first line of intervention for parents is healthy communication with their teenagers.

By now, you know you can't make your adolescent change his mind, but does your teenager know that you know? One important step in trying to talk to your teenager about LGBTQ issues is for you to say and repeat, "I know I can't make you change your mind about this, but . . ." Remember that, paradoxically, avoiding this "You can't make me" battle is a good way to increase the influence your words can have.

Identify the Basis of Your Objections

The parents I work with who are devastated by their adolescent's identifying as LGBTQ are all Christian. This means that the basis of their objections is not their preferences but their understanding of the will of God. Orthodox teachings of Christians, Jews, and Muslims have historically all asserted that variance from heterosexuality or denying your biological sex is sin. It's notable how this obvious historical fact is being frantically researched and altered.

I have also talked to many churchgoing parents who don't base their objections on their faith. These parents try to base their argument on the social consequences of coming out or how their kids won't be able to have their own children and so on. I've never seen such objections have any impact. Most LGBTQ teenagers have already come out to their friends or to their school in general. Rather than being ostracized, LGBTQ teens often gain some amount of social currency. Also, since a high number of adolescents now state that they have no desire to have children, reminding them about your desire for grandchildren has no effect.

I strongly encourage Christian parents to be clear that they're more heartbroken that their LGBTQ teenager may not be a Christian than they are concerned over any aspect of sexuality or gender. While no one knows the heart of another and sincere Christians can be deceived, the notion of fulfilling one's self-chosen identity is antithetical to the Christian foundation of finding one's identity in Christ. When parents share their concerns about their adolescent's faith, we hope this is offensive on some level. Taking offense may indicate that he is actively trying to reconcile his LGBTQ identification with a true faith. In my experience, however, this is most often not the case.

The majority of LGBTQ teenagers and young adults I've worked with are not professing Christians. Their opening up about this identification provides an important clarification for parents to know about their teenagers' faith. It is more useful to continue discussions about their faith, or lack of faith, than to focus on LGBTQ issues.

The Changing Landscape

Parents dealing with LGBTQ issues can find encouragement by observing the rapidly changing social landscape of these issues, especially regarding transgender identity. In England, where transgender identity ideology has been years ahead of where it's been in the US, there has been a massive rollback of support for hormonal and surgical experimental procedures performed on minors. The Tavistock Centre, the UK's only dedicated gender identity clinic for those seventeen and younger, was shut down by the National Health Service after lawsuits and questionable research foundations for the treatments being provided.[10]

Look over the news headlines and substitute the now-ubiquitous term *gender-affirming health care* for *experimental hormone and surgical procedures* and you'll find some encouraging state legislation being passed that seeks to protect children and teenagers from life-altering decisions made on very shaky ground.

LGBTQ ideology sprang up seemingly overnight. Even though it's losing some of its hold on the public imagination, ideologies like this should remind parents of the importance of giving their teenagers a clear path to adulthood and the respect that comes with it—not to mention the need for plenty of ongoing, open communication. Parents can't afford to accidentally push their adolescents toward LGBTQ identities by overcontrolling their every decision.

CHAPTER 28

Influencing an Adolescent's Faith

Until the thirteenth year I talk to my son about God;
after his bar mitzvah I talk to God about my son.
ANCIENT RABBI

Since *Feeding the Mouth That Bites You* is about effectively parenting teenagers, a complete discussion of how faith and parenting intersect is beyond the scope of this book. On the other hand, it's worthwhile to say a few words explicitly related to helping parents have a positive influence on their teenagers' faith. These same principles should apply to parents of any religious background.

Raising Kids Affects Parents' Faith

Having children is good for parents' spiritual growth. It's not unusual for adults raised in religious homes to fall away from active involvement until they have children of their own. Foundational spiritual truths that have sat on the back burner for years suddenly become important. Plus, faith looks different when viewed through a child's eyes.

Most parents have already felt the impact young children have on their faith. Sharing the essentials of faith with preschoolers is a far deeper process than just dumbing down the teachings of Scripture. There's something profound and often moving when you search for answers to basic questions, such as "Why did God make me?" Even today, I have a rock on my dresser that my youngest gave me; inscribed on it are the words *from Jesuse [sic] and frances*. It accompanies a cartoon drawing of a little girl and a guy with a beard (who I assume is "Jesuse"). As a Christian, I know the Spirit is with me, but somehow, seeing those words from my baby girl makes it more real.

Unfortunately, seeing your faith through a teenager's eyes is exactly the opposite of when they were little. Young children's questions and interests show us more about what we *already* know. Adolescents' questions and interests show us exactly how much we *don't* know.

Pop quiz: How can an adult find out if he or she is stuck at a childish stage of faith?

Answer: Have a teenager!

To influence your teenager's spiritual growth, you first need to focus on what impact your adolescent is having on your faith. Do your teenager's questions and arguments make you mad? Do you find yourself defensively resorting to the never-effective answer "Because I said so"?

> To influence your teenager's spiritual growth, you first need to focus on what impact your adolescent is having on your faith.

A father once confessed to me that he ended up in a fistfight with his fourteen-year-old son because the son said church was stupid.

On the other hand, do you find yourself hoping to see spiritual growth in your adolescent son or daughter, but you just can't find the words to talk about your faith? I know many parents who consider their faith more important than their politics. When politics come up, they have well-thought-through positions on many topics, yet when religion comes up, they're suddenly back to fifth grade.

It's surprising how many parents still approach their faith like it was a club that's good for you and provides a set of moral principles that will make you "healthy, wealthy, and wise." (That's Ben Franklin, by the way, not the Bible.) Religious principles may get you past the importance of honesty and kindness, but you're going to get stuck when asked deeper questions about sexual behavior and gender identity, or what's wrong with people of other faiths or those who aren't religious.

Again, without going too far beyond the scope of this book, let me encourage you to embrace the confusion (or even annoyance) that your teenager's challenges and questions may bring up in you. Don't be afraid to answer, "I'm not sure about that," if that's the case. It's even better if you go back later and apologize for a previous defensive reaction, and tell your adolescent, "Your questions kind of scared me." Christianity, like any major religion, claims only to offer a greater understanding of God and our relationship to Him. None suggest that God can be fully comprehended. Your willingness to admit this to a teenager is much more likely to *increase* her respect for you and your faith than to decrease it.

Also, remember that the best time for teaching faith and its importance is during childhood. Hopefully, you have made your faith an important part of family life for thirteen or so years before having to change tactics. For observant Jewish and Christian families, this is what is meant when Scripture tells us, "You shall teach [God's words] to your children, speaking of them when you sit in your house, when you walk by the way, when you lie down, and when you rise up" (Deuteronomy 11:19, NKJV).

If you haven't done the kind of teaching you think you should have, or if your family hasn't been consistent in attending services, adolescence is a tough time to start. Teenagers know hypocrisy when they see it. Again, that doesn't mean you can't make changes during your kids' adolescence. It just means you need to be honest about why you're making these changes. You may need to be extra sensitive, or even apologetic, about the contradictions present in your example as a parent.

Religious Faith and Control

Some years ago, I saw a precocious fifteen-year-old boy from a close Hindu family. His father was particularly angry because instead of offering *puja* (an act of showing reverence to a god or spirit) at the shrine in their home, his son made deliberate gestures of disrespect toward it. (I think the boy was flipping off the statue as he left the house.) From a teenager, this act is very much the same as the kids who sneak over to Starbucks during church, or the girl I counseled who deliberately answered her cell phone during Shabbat services. Such behaviors are obvious signs of a control battle.

Because faith is so important to many families, parents often make the mistake of trying to control this aspect of their teenagers' lives for as long as they can. Unfortunately, most of the devout Christian families I work with allow so little freedom for their adolescents to explore faith for themselves that they invite rebellion or passive cooperation until the teenager can get away. Research has recently shown that somewhere between 60 and 80 percent of active high school youth will fall away from church involvement in their college years. Planned Emancipation must be applied to faith, just like any other freedom. By now, I hope you understand that this is to increase your *influence*; it does not mean you are turning your back on your job as a Christian parent.

Giving over this freedom starts with acknowledging the fact that your teenager may not think the same way you do about God. As I've said, the freedom to think differently is a fact that exists in any post-formal-operational-thought teenager. It's not some sort of risky privilege you're allowing. Asking even a young teenager, "I liked today's sermon, but I was wondering, do you agree with what he said?" is a fairly benign question, but it signals to an adolescent that her parents know she may not believe the same way. Parents who don't understand adolescence may think this will

> Eventually, however, you must pick a point *before he leaves your house* when your teenager can completely use his judgment regarding faith.

give the teen bad ideas or encourage heretical thinking. But parents who understand adolescent development (like you do!) know this kind of statement means *I'm not going to get into a control struggle over this.*

Later stages of freedom may need to be made clearer. When young adolescents push back on having to attend church, temple, or synagogue, parents should show real interest in understanding why they don't want to go. You might (and probably should) still require that they attend with you, but the reason should be more in line with doing this activity as a family. You may even have to put "getting up and ready for church" on your Expectations and Consequences list (e.g., "or no video games the rest of the day"). If your teenager says, "This isn't gonna make me believe in God!" you can readily avoid that Waterloo by conceding, "Oh, I know that. This is only because it's a valuable part of our family life, and it's the most important thing in both your mother's life and mine. I'm truly sorry it's such a burden to you."

As they get older, you should look for ways to give over freedom in this area as much as you can while still maintaining appropriate influence. For example, you might allow an older adolescent the freedom to choose which church he wants to attend. That freedom might look like this:

FREEDOM	BOUNDARIES
Use your own judgment in choosing which church to attend.	• Must be a Christian church. • Must attend once per week. • Must arrange your own transportation.

This kind of freedom can help lift some of the unnecessary control battles surrounding your particular place of worship. It doesn't help with control issues if your teenager wants to explore other religions. The majority of devout Christians (like most sincere religious followers) do not believe their faith is one of many paths to God. Because of this, they can't, in good conscience, grant their fifteen-year-old freedom to attend just any religious service of her choosing.

Eventually, however, you must pick a point *before he leaves your house* when your teenager can completely use his judgment regarding faith. Again, like letting go of curfew, many parents find the idea of granting complete freedom over faith to be scary, as if their kid were almost ready to commit to the ministry, join the priesthood, or become a rabbi. ("If only I hadn't let him choose for himself those last few months of high school!") On the Freedoms list, it would look similar to the following:

FREEDOMS	BOUNDARIES
Use your own judgment in whether to attend church.	

Talking about Faith

Teenagers don't like to be taught stuff they're not asking about. Religion is no exception and may be one of the touchier subjects in which to engage them. Also, since adolescents are mostly just trying to get by with their day-to-day lives, issues of life, death, and God are rarely at the forefront of their minds. However, adolescents are at a stage where they can engage in deeper thought about the purpose of life and the ultimate meaning of things. The trick is trying to get the conversation started.

One good way to talk about faith is to talk about *your* faith. That is, your teenager may not want to hear some general truth you want to teach but may respond differently if you ask, "Can I tell you something that happened to me today? I was praying this morning, and just then the phone rang . . ." This is like our discussion on advice giving, but it's even gentler than that.

Don't finish your little talk with a summary statement (e.g., "You know, God is so . . ."). Just tell him or her the impact the event had on you. If you want to ensure your teenager is listening, you may want to finish with the old "You probably think that's dumb, but this stuff affects me." Again, this *increases* the impact of your communication by assuring your adolescent that this isn't a teaching conversation. And it lets them know that there will be no control battle involved.

Finally, don't forget to actively listen to your teenager and try to understand where he or she is, spiritually speaking. Having a parent who is truly interested in a teenager's spiritual life, who doesn't condemn and isn't always pushing, is the best way to give an adolescent the space needed to grow spiritually while still at home.

And remember, even when your teenager won't talk to you about God, you can and must always talk to God about your teenager. The freedom to do that should be a source of great comfort.

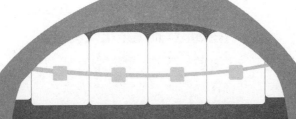

PART SEVEN

Let's Talk about You

Parent Issues That Affect
Planned Emancipation

CHAPTER 29

The Fire and the Knife: Lessons from Father Abraham

> "I and the boy go over there. We will worship
> and then we will come back to you."
>
> GENESIS 22:5, NIV

Brian was a big man and when the tears came, they came heavily despite his attempts to control them. He sat across from me in my office, and I pushed the box of Kleenex closer to him. I had seen this coming for a while. Brian had been seeing me about his relationship with his two teenage children. His daughter, now beginning her senior year in high school, barely spoke to him. She seemed to resent every word that came from Brian's mouth. He had always had a somewhat better relationship with his son, who was now a high school freshman.

Brian was a very concerned father who was often seen as overcontrolling. His hovering, teaching, and monitoring of all aspects of his kids' lives had also become a source of contention with his wife. Brian's parents had been uninvolved during his childhood, one of the main factors he saw contributing to the demise of his older sister. She had gotten heavily involved in drugs, became pregnant early in life, and seemed never to have fully recovered. Brian felt badly misunderstood for simply trying to avoid the mistakes his parents had made.

After attending one of my workshops on parenting adolescents, Brian came to see me, saying he now understood how his parenting style had severely damaged his relationship with his daughter. He greatly feared the same was beginning to happen with his son. But now, like many parents, the more Brian understood the steps he needed to take, the more he was also discovering a real battle within himself. Several times he had left my office with a plan for giving more control and responsibility to his kids, but he had completely failed to follow through. More than once, he had even announced some area of responsibility that would now be left to his teenagers' judgment, only to take it back at the first hint that they might not be handling it the way he thought they should. This seemed only to have added to his teenagers' resentment toward him.

Brian is not unusual among Christian parents. Over the years, I've learned that most parents come to their task armed with the tools of parenting knowledge and dedication that they expect will guide them through all stages of their child's life. But at the foundation of parenting, more important than all the resources parents may utilize, there are two tools all parents must have. Without these tools, all our parenting efforts will be shot through with fear. Above all else, fear is the cancer that puts our relationships and all our efforts toward our children at risk. Although these tools are necessary for parents of children at any age, their absence becomes most apparent during the adolescent years.

Brian had learned many of the tools he could use to influence and guide his teenage children, but his fear kept him paralyzed. The tools I knew Brian didn't have were the *fire* and the *knife*.

Fundamental Truths

God said, "Take your son, your only son, whom you love— Isaac—and go to the region of Moriah. Sacrifice him there as a burnt offering on a mountain I will show you."

Early the next morning Abraham got up and loaded his donkey. He took with him two of his servants and his son Isaac. When he had cut enough wood for the burnt offering, he set out for the place God had told him about. On the third day Abraham looked up and saw the place in the distance. He said to his servants, "Stay here with the donkey while I and the boy go over there. We will worship and then we will come back to you."

Abraham took the wood for the burnt offering and placed it on his son Isaac, and he himself carried the fire and the knife.

GENESIS 22:2-6, NIV

Try to picture this scene. In the dim, shadowy light of dawn, an old man is walking up a mountain with a teenage boy by his side. It's cold, and the wind occasionally whips around the hillside as they slowly trudge upward, the boy laden with a large bundle of wood on his back. The white boulders they climb over have a bluish hue in the dim light. All that stands out is the blazing torch in the old man's hand and the occasional glint from his knife.

What I like about Old Testament history is that so much of it is not only historically true, but also many of the stories are so fundamentally true as to represent common human experience. The story of Abraham and Isaac is just that sort of story. It not only tells an essential story in Jewish history of a man and his son living in Canaan (a region encompassing modern-day Israel, Palestine, and parts of Lebanon, Jordan, and Syria), but it also tells the story of an archetypal struggle among all parents. For Abraham was not just a father. In many ways, Abraham can be seen as the "father of all fathers." Therefore, this story reveals something important about all parents.

To me, this scene not only depicts the historical events, but it's also a scene that's continually played out within parents. In many ways, Abraham is the ideal parent, and Isaac is the ideal child. The journey we go through in raising our children is always accompanied by this inward, archetypal journey of the ideal we have of ourselves as parents and the ideal we have of our children. How the scene plays out can mark the difference between parenting success and failure. The presence of the fire and the knife calls us to examine carefully what we consider success as a parent.

Abraham, the Quintessential Parent

Abraham was always meant to be a parent. Even his name, Abram, given by his parents, meant "exalted father." The expectations that went along with such a name had become somewhat of an embarrassment as he grew older, and he and his wife, Sarai, remained childless. To make matters worse, when God blessed Abram and revealed that he was chosen for a special purpose, God changed Abram's name to Abraham, which means "father of many." Abraham's confusion and self-consciousness were wonderfully erased at the age of one hundred when God gave him a son. The joy of his son's arrival was shown in his name, Isaac, which means "he laughs."

Now, I love my children very much, and I'm sure you love yours as much as I do mine. But I believe Abraham loved his boy even more than we do ours. Isaac was not only Abraham's child, but he was also the core of Abraham's future. Isaac was both the fulfillment of a parent's desire for a child and the key to God's blessings to Abraham and the fulfillment of his lifelong purpose.

It's noteworthy that the first time the word *love* appears in Scripture is in Genesis 22:2, when God is talking to Abraham about his son. By this point, the Bible has already told us about Creation, Adam and Eve, Noah, the tower of Babel, and Abraham's whole life. But the word *love* isn't needed until God is referring to Isaac. Isaac was Abraham's son, his only son, whom he loved.

Half of Wisdom Is Just Getting Tired

The story of God's call for Abraham to sacrifice Isaac has always been difficult for us to understand. As Christians, most of us have come to know more of the mysterious ways of God. But as parents, it can be difficult to understand Abraham's response to such a command. Did Abraham struggle with it? Did he plead with God to let his son live?

My answer to this conjecture is *Why do we have to imagine it?* Genesis 18 devotes ten verses to describing Abraham's pleading with God to spare Sodom for the sake of the righteous in the city. We assume Abraham resisted such a command because we can't imagine a parent responding the way Abraham did. But apparently, Abraham's response to God's call to sacrifice his beloved and only son was something like "Well, we'd better get an early start."

We must remember that by this time, Abraham was an old man and had wrestled with God over and over. Like many of us, he had already seen the disastrous effects of his own efforts to "help God out" in fulfilling His purposes. Abraham's first big plan to help God fulfill His blessings to him was to make his servant Eliezer his heir (see Genesis 15). Then, of course, there was the whole Ishmael debacle, in which Abraham thought having a child with his wife's slave would fix God's problem of their childlessness.

> Apparently, Abraham's response to God's call to sacrifice his beloved and only son was something like "Well, we'd better get an early start."

There's a scene in the movie *Harry Potter and the Half-Blood Prince* when Professor Dumbledore asks Harry to meet him late one night. Dumbledore says, "You are, of course, wondering why I brought you here tonight."

But Harry answers, "Actually, sir, after all these years, I just sort of go with it."[1]

Abraham's response was sort of like Harry's. He had seen God's power to fulfill glorious promises and the futility of his own efforts in trying to make things work out as he thought they should.

In my own life, I've begun to use the adage "Half of wisdom is just getting tired." By now, Abraham was tired—tired of uselessly trying to figure things out for himself, and tired of resisting the power of God in fulfilling His wonderful purpose in Abraham's life. He had learned to "just sort of go with it." Abraham heard God's command and knew only that he had to get an early start.

"We Will Worship and Return to You"

We do get a glimpse into Abraham's motives and thoughts when he arrived at the place of sacrifice. He told his servants, "We will worship and return to you" (Genesis 22:5, NASB). This was a surprising statement for him to make. First, Abraham referred to the act he was about to carry out, sacrificing his son, as *worship*. Second, he made the surprising prediction that "*we* will return."

The word *worship* is derived from the old English *worth-ship*—that is, to ascribe worth to something. Abraham knew that God's purpose in this command was not a capricious desire to see His handiwork destroyed. God's desire was for Abraham to display what he valued most—Isaac, God's gift to Abraham, or God Himself. The Westminster Shorter Catechism, written in the 1640s and widely considered one of the greatest doctrinal statements to come out of the English Reformation, states that the chief end of man is to "glorify God, and to enjoy him for ever."[2]

Abraham knew, as many of us have forgotten, that God's purpose for our lives is found in communion with Him, not in trying to help God out by being good parents to our children. How long will we continue to wear ourselves out trying to raise our children according to our ideals? Why does it so often seem God isn't doing His part in helping us achieve this goal? Half of wisdom is just getting tired!

But how did Abraham know both he and Isaac would return? There's no question that when Abraham raised the knife, he fully intended to cut the boy's throat. Genesis 22:11 tells us the angel of the Lord had to call Abraham's name twice just to get his attention. The writer of Hebrews answered this for us when he wrote, "[Abraham] considered that God was able even to raise [Isaac] from the dead" (Hebrews 11:19). Without ever having seen or heard of someone raised from the dead,

Abraham expected God would restore his son to him, even after death. How much more basis for faith in God's power, as Christian parents, do we have than Abraham had?

Three Lessons

Lesson One: Who Is More Important to You—God or Your Child?

Asking us to choose between God and our children can seem unfair. Even Christian parents might consider the choice of our children's welfare over *anything* as a noble one. In a recent series on people losing religious faith, National Public Radio interviewed one mother whose twenty-one-year-old son had been meaninglessly shot and killed by an acquaintance. When the priest at her Catholic church told her, "We all have our crosses to bear," she decided that "a priest couldn't possibly understand the pain of losing a child."

"I just remember thinking, 'That's it. I'm done with the Catholic religion,'" she said. ". . . [W]hat kind of God lets a child be shot?"[3] As tragic as this story is, it reveals that, for this woman, God was worthy only in so far as He protected her child.

Most of us will not have to face the tragedy of losing a child. And yet, when we come face-to-face with releasing control over our children, including the ideals we have for them, we have to confront the reality of who our children belong to. For that matter, whose child are *you*?

In his essential book *The Knowledge of the Holy*, A. W. Tozer lamented the degraded view of God and His glory that dominates the modern Christian church. Tozer made the fundamental observation, "What comes into our minds when we think about God is the most important thing about us."[4] Too many of us have so reduced our knowledge of God as to assign Him the role of a helper in our all-important job of raising children. We have, too often, become so utilitarian in our understanding of our faith that we forget our purpose as parents and as God's creation to "glorify God, and to enjoy Him for ever."

We must come to see that raising our children is just one of the paths

God has placed before us to aid in accomplishing our true purpose—union with Him. We must let go of our ideals, both for us as parents and for our children, to enter into God's work. For many of us, this means confronting the deep, sinful reality that we may not trust God to want good things for our children. It means acknowledging that we may hold to the idea that the outcome of our children's lives is up to us, not God. Ours is the God who reminds us, "Can a mother forget the baby at her breast and have no compassion on the child she has borne? Though she may forget, I will not forget you! See, I have engraved you on the palms of my hands"(Isaiah 49:15-16, NIV). Do we think we love our children and desire the best for them more than our God does?

> Too many of us have so reduced our knowledge of God as to assign Him the role of a helper in our all-important job of raising children.

Lesson Two: Sacrificing to God Means Giving Up Nothing

If letting go of our parenting ideals is an appropriate act of worship that is often an essential struggle to draw us toward God, what is the real cost of this sacrifice? Abraham trusted that God would restore life to his son, even if Isaac were to be sacrificed. What do we expect would be the outcome if we let go of our ideals and absolutes for ourselves and our children?

At the end of the Abraham and Isaac story, it wasn't Isaac who was sacrificed but a ram provided by God—a scapegoat, if you will. In the same way, it's not our children that God usually asks us to let go of. It's our ideal image of our children that must be sacrificed. In this sacrifice, our image of ourselves as great parents must also be destroyed.

Our ideal image for our kids blinds us to seeing who they really are. Our ideals define both our goals for them and those things we find unacceptable in them. This plays out in my office all the time. I've seen this blindness in a father who considers himself close to his son simply because of his constant pronouncements that "He's just like me" while remaining unaware that the boy shares more of his mother's temperament than his. I've seen it in a mother who panics at her daughter's average school performance because scholastic achievement is a huge part of her own self-worth. And I've seen parents overreact to their son's first incident of drinking alcohol because they have a family member who had serious substance abuse issues.

To let go of our ideal image is to open our eyes to our children as God sees them. It means seeing them as they are. To do this, we must trust that God has created these children with exactly the strengths and weaknesses that will ultimately fulfill His purposes in their lives. Sacrificing our ideals means trusting that God knows them better than we do. More importantly, when we begin to see our children as they are, we begin to learn what Abraham learned. Like Abraham, we realize that what God will return to us are children with lives of better purpose and deeper meaning than we could ever have planned or accomplished. Sacrificing to God means giving up nothing!

Lesson Three: A Place of Sacrifice Is Holy Ground

Lest we're tempted to see this sacrifice of our ideals as an exception—an ordeal for the few that we hope we aren't called on to endure—we must remember the eternal importance of that place in our lives where we choose His purpose over ours. Abraham's sacrifice occurred in roughly 2,000 BC. At that time, the mountain God "told him about" was named Mount Moriah. As far as anyone was concerned, it was an unimportant place in the wilderness. But to God, it was highly significant.

A thousand years later, King David reigned over the nation of Israel at the height of its power and prosperity. But David had a census taken of all Israel, knowing that a man is only allowed to take a census of what belonged to him. Just as our pride as parents may lead us to consider our children as belonging to us, not God, David began to see Israel as his creation. In righteous indignation, God sent an angel to bring a great plague on all the people. But at one particular spot, something unexpected happened:

And when the angel stretched out his hand toward Jerusalem to destroy it, the LORD relented from the calamity and said to the angel who was working destruction among the people, "It is enough; now stay your hand." And the angel of the LORD was by the threshing floor of Araunah the Jebusite.

2 SAMUEL 24:16

Although seemingly unimportant to the people, Araunah's (also called Ornan) land was on the top of Mount Moriah, the very place of Abraham's sacrifice. King David bought this land, and it was inherited by his son Solomon. It was this site that God chose for His Temple: "Then Solomon began to build the house of the LORD in Jerusalem on Mount Moriah, where the LORD had appeared to David his father, at the place that David had appointed, on the threshing floor of Ornan the Jebusite" (2 Chronicles 3:1).

This is the same site, the Temple Mount, from which Jesus would be taken out and crucified a thousand years later. The place of sacrifice is holy to God because it echoes His own sacrifice for us.

I've known many Christian parents who have struggled to see God's hand in the lives of their children. These parents are looking for God to support their own goals and ideals for their children. When we consciously sacrifice our desires for our children to God and His will, it opens a place in our hearts that's precious to Him. It's a place that moves the Spirit of God in us to compassion for our children and for ourselves as parents. It's a place that opens our eyes to the ongoing, loving work of God in the lives of our children.

Conclusion: Fear and the Christian Parent

Christian parents can sometimes be the most fearful parents around. This should come as a surprise, but it has become so common as to be almost cliché. Too many parents sign their kids up for a Christian school, with less regard for the spiritual teaching they receive than for a hoped-for haven from struggles and temptations. In too many churches, a fearful, overcontrolling protectiveness is lauded as godly parenting. And yet, the number one command in all the New Testament is *Do not fear*! The Bible makes the source of fear plain: "There is no fear in love. But perfect love drives out fear, because fear has to do with punishment. The one who fears is not made perfect in love" (1 John 4:18, NIV).

Our lack of faith in God's love as revealed in grace through His Son keeps us in fear. I understand we all struggle with fear. What I don't understand is how fear can sometimes be held in such high esteem by Christian parents. The only way to actively combat this false image of a godly parent is by sacrificing our expectations and ideals for our children to the God who loves completely.

But this is a book about parenting teenagers. Your teenagers are watching you, and they understand what your fear means. Adolescents are past the stage of listening to what you say you believe. They're watching your actions to see what you *really* believe. To teenagers, nothing screams *I don't believe what I say I believe* like displays of fear.

I once had a father come to see me who was a leader in his church and carried numerous important responsibilities. He told me he was concerned about his fourteen-year-old son's lack of spiritual interest. During his angry tirade about his disappointing son (men often express anger when they're afraid), he mentioned, in passing, that a recent argument they had about church attendance resulted in his throwing his boy to the ground and punching him. Instead of his son going to church more, child protective services had been called!

> Christian parents can sometimes be the most fearful parents around.

Fear can cause parents to lose all sense of perspective, and adolescents are too aware not to notice it. This is precisely why parents must work hard to confront these fears for what they are, lack of faith. By letting go of our ideals, we can more fully cooperate in the ongoing work of God in our teenagers' lives. Parenting adolescents can be maddening. Sometimes teenagers say and do things deliberately to prey on our fears, just to watch us squirm. Nothing is more effective with teenagers than the calm demeanor of a loving parent who regularly tosses up the prayer "Thank You, God, that this kid is really Yours and not mine!"

CHAPTER 30

Marriage and Parenting

The secret of a happy marriage remains a secret.
HENNY YOUNGMAN

It's common for parents to disagree about how best to parent their children. The problem is not that you don't agree. Disagreements about parenting cannot cause marital conflict. Instead, parenting is one of the "big three" important areas of life that couples inevitably stumble across. The other two are money and religion.

You may be surprised by how much you and your spouse differ in your approach to these areas. You need to know that these topics are not the *cause* of your conflict, they're challenges that test a couple's ability to deal with their differences.

Adolescence is not a time to put aside marriage issues "until you've finished raising the kids." This strategy is not only dangerous for your marriage, but it's not good for your teenager either.

"Will My Parents Be Okay if I Leave?"

As adolescents prepare for life on their own, they're mostly asking themselves, *Will I be okay without my parents?* Another unconscious question they need an answer to is *Will my parents be okay when I'm gone?* When adolescents sense that their parents won't emotionally survive their departure, it's hard for them to feel permission to move on. This is particularly true for more emotionally sensitive teenagers and those with an especially close relationship with one parent.

Throughout their development, children need to feel a close, supportive relationship with their parents. Many parents I work with already know that. What they may not know is that children of all ages need to feel there's an extra bond between Mom and Dad that's deeper than that shared with their children. Remember when your five-year-old pushed the two of you apart when you tried to get affectionate in front of him? This bond can be threatening to children during the period of life when security is their primary need. They want Mommy or Daddy all to themselves. Denying children that central place may be more difficult when they are small, but teenagers are comforted by it.

> Trying to find fulfillment in parenting as a substitute for disappointment in marriage, however, doesn't solve anything.

Many couples avoid growing tensions in their marriage by pouring themselves into parenting. A lifelong, romantic love relationship involves far more personal and emotional risk than parenting. It's a common temptation to avoid the risk of a relationship that constantly asks, "Am I loved above all others?" (i.e., marriage) by substituting a relationship that offers the more certain but less desirable answer, "At least I'm needed" (i.e., parenting). This is a far greater temptation for mothers, and we'll talk about that more soon.

Trying to find fulfillment in parenting as a substitute for disappointment in marriage, however, doesn't solve anything. At best, this strategy can be used to fake your way through your kids' childhood years. Then they hit adolescence and things begin to fall apart; especially when your youngest becomes a teenager. When one parent (typically a mother) becomes increasingly panicky about withdrawing control of the teenager, there's usually a marriage problem. You must keep your marriage a priority in your life. If you're having conflicts (even old, unresolved conflicts), now is the time to see a counselor or pursue some other strategy to make your marriage the priority it needs to be.

It's good for teenagers to hear parents ask, "Don't you have somewhere to go Friday night? Your mother and I need some time without you around." Just ignore the "Oh, gross, Dad" responses. In the long run, adolescents are comforted by the knowledge that their parents will be just fine after they're gone.

Staying on the Same Page

The other important reason not to neglect your marriage during your children's teen years has already been discussed. In chapter 11, we learned the fourth law of disciplining adolescents: Lack of parental unity seriously undercuts effective limit setting. I've known parents who thought they were hiding the tensions and differences in their marriage from the kids, but teenagers can always tell. Adolescents pay attention to what's allowed or not allowed when their father is present compared to when Mom is in charge. Even worse, when a teenager can sense serious, unspoken tension between parents, he won't say anything, but his respect for parental authority can be seriously undercut.

Poor Marriage Examples

Following this advice to stay on the same page would be easy except for one problem: Marriage can be tough! You already know that. If you're a single parent, you know that love relationships don't always work out as you planned. If you're married or remarried and worried that you're the only one having a tough time, relax. I've worked with married couples for more than thirty years, and I can tell you that periods of real struggle (e.g., "I don't even *like* this person.") are pretty much the norm. The marriage relationship requires work, and almost all of us are working without a blueprint.

When working with married couples, one of the first things I do is ask the husbands, "What advice did you get from your father about marriage?" The vast majority answer either "None" or something similar to "I wouldn't have listened to anything that guy said anyway." I ask the same question to wives and receive comparable results. Fewer and fewer married people were raised around an intact couple; they don't even know what that looks like. Of those whose parents remain married, much of what they saw in their parents' marriage was not what they wanted for their own.

This book isn't here to offer marriage advice. What's important here is the effect your marriage has on parenting. Since most people learn so little about marriage and its challenges from their parents, it shouldn't come as a surprise that many couples don't know what to do to improve their marriages.

Spending Time Together

Whether you're having conflicts, the issue of prioritizing marriage is easily seen in how you use your time. Almost all parents of teenagers complain they "just don't have time" to spend together. This is a real struggle, and it doesn't have easy solutions. When our children were small, our decisions regarding the use of time involved choices between good uses of time and bad uses, such as wasting time. Now, with teenagers, careers, and civic and church involvement, parents' time-use decisions involve differentiating good uses of time and better uses of time. Wasting time is a luxury few parents can afford.

And yet, what we spend our time on inevitably reveals our priorities. When parents read or hear that their kids need focused time and attention from their mom and dad, everyone seems to get that. Parents I work with either proudly outline the kind of intentional focus they give to being there with their children or they lament that they know they should be spending more time than other stresses allow. None of the parents confidently tell me they can't find enough spare time to be with their children. We seem to know that time in parenting relation-ships must be a priority.

When I ask about focused time together in marriage, couples always express a longing to do so. But this longing is much the same as long-ing to take a trip to Hawaii. Simply spending time together as a couple almost seems like something extracurricular or that can only happen after everything else is done. It's as if time together is a luxury they just can't afford. They're too busy taking care of the things that they think have to be done.

> No intimate relationship can grow without significant time dedicated to it. We all knew that when we dated, right?

This common attitude reveals our lack of understanding about how to make marriage work. No intimate relationship can grow without significant time dedi-cated to it. We all knew that when we dated, right? Having adolescents should be a signal to get back to the real priority of marriage. You need that kind of time together, and your teenagers need to see you take time for each other.

Married Couples Are *Not* Just Co-Parents

If you and your spouse were some sort of professional child raisers who happened to be working the same shift, you'd probably be able to man-age your differences easier than married people. The most common problem married parents have when they try to resolve their parent-ing differences is ignoring the sensitivities inherent in marriage. In a relationship as intimate as marriage, you can't expect to resolve parent-ing differences by producing some book and saying, "Well, this expert says . . ." The feelings of both husband and wife need to be considered, especially each other's fears.

"Tell Me Your Fears, and I'll Tell You Mine"

At the base of most significant parental differences are fears of what may happen. Say, for example, a couple is trying to decide whether to send their kid to a private school. The mom thinks it's essential to make this switch, but the dad thinks they can't afford it. This difference won't be resolved by articles on how bad public schools are, nor by spreadsheets about future income potential. It won't even be best resolved by a wealthy grandparent willing to foot the bill. The basis of this disagreement is that Mom and Dad fear different things. And both fears should be taken seriously. This calls for a "tell me your fears and I'll tell you mine" series of discussions.

The best way to navigate this scenario would be for the husband to ask his wife, "What do you fear will happen if we keep our kid in public school?" He must listen to her answer and avoid using her words as fodder for his own argument. The important part is that she feels her husband has heard her. By listening, he's communicating to her, "That makes sense," rather than "Now wait a minute, that's not how it is!"

The next step is for the wife to ask, "What are you afraid will happen if we put our kid in private school?" Again, it's important to listen to his concerns.

After this kind of discussion, the best answer is usually something that causes the least fear in both parents. The best solution is found in *how* the couple arrived at the answer, more so than *what* was decided. I can tell you hundreds of stories of couples who came to some insensitive solution that didn't please either of them. Good discussions of difficult marriage disagreements happen at intimate dinners or on long walks while holding hands. Remember, these kids are going to be gone someday, but it's your spouse you will be buried next to.

CHAPTER 31

Single Parenting

*When your children are teenagers, it's important to have a dog
so that someone in the house is happy to see you.*
NORA EPHRON

Being a single parent presents a significant challenge in providing for the same needs discussed in the marriage chapter. In case you skipped that chapter, while adolescents consciously focus on the question "Will I be okay without my parents?" a less conscious part of them is wondering, *Will my parents be okay when I'm gone?* For married parents, this means strengthening their marriage. For single parents, this means strengthening your support system to meet your emotional needs when your parenting job is done.

Most of the single parents I work with (and they're almost always moms) are strong individuals who have had to go it alone. Truly shared, postdivorce parenting can make the job easier, but sadly, this arrangement remains the exception to the rule. Being a strong individual makes for a good, steady parent in a child's life. Unfortunately, those same strengths can make it harder for a single parent to seek out the supportive relationships that signal to a teenager that you'll be fine when he or she is gone. It's not enough to remain dedicated to your job and parent like always while adding the occasional public service announcement: "Don't worry about me." Teenagers are smart, and they know you better than you think they do.

Strange as it may seem, this means that to be a good single parent, you need to take care of yourself. That means doing more socially, especially spending time with family and friends who love you and whom you can count on to be there for you. Very often this is found in another single parent. Sometimes it's found in family members. If someone is a member of your support team, she should know she's on that team. Simply having a lot of friends at work doesn't count. Support people are the ones who call you when the weather is bad or when you're sick. Those of you who are strong single moms may be getting uncomfortable even reading this. But this isn't just for you. Your teenager needs this as well.

You may have noticed that I haven't mentioned dating when it comes to finding support. Dating while you're a single parent is a good thing, and you should pursue it. Putting off dating because of your kids may be advisable when they're young, but as you should know by now, it isn't necessary if you have teenagers. However, dating relationships are often more of an emotional drain than they are a support. Most of you single parents don't need me to tell you that dating after you're older and have children is a tricky business. The ups and downs of trying to match your complicated life with someone else's can be frustrating; it may include some real excitement, but dating relationships can't be counted on to provide the lasting and consistent emotional support a single parent needs.

Most teenagers are okay with their parents dating, but they may have mixed feelings and find the subject hard to discuss. Often, the overlap between your dating and their doing the same thing brings out a kind of pseudo-maturity in their responses, and you may find your teenage daughter giving you advice (often bad advice, but still). It's important that you talk to your teens and try to get their honest feedback about your choice to date. While their discomfort should be taken seriously, you should be careful about giving inappropriate assurances (e.g., "I would never marry again if you don't want me to."). They may have mixed feelings about how you get there, but they do want you to end up being okay when they leave.

Don't introduce your teenagers to everyone you go out with. Remember, you're not asking their permission anyway. Adolescents find it hard enough just to come to terms with the concept of you dating, and there's no need to add to that confusion by putting them through getting to know a series of people whom you may only be in short-term relationships with. It's best to wait until you're at least near engagement before bringing your teenagers into it. This also reduces the risk of your teenagers' getting to know and like someone who will be out of their lives in a few weeks or months.

> Don't introduce your teenagers to everyone you go out with.

While dating and eventual remarriage can provide a good way to assure your adolescents you will emotionally survive their departure, it's not the only way. Some creativity in family and friend relationships may be necessary, but single parents can still do a good job of giving their teenagers the needed message that their growing up and moving on will not leave behind an emotionally bereft parent. And the time for single parents of teenagers to start taking care of themselves emotionally is now!

Planned Emancipation and Single Parents

The only unique aspect of managing Planned Emancipation for single parents has to do with your emotional resources as discussed above. It can be difficult to maintain an orderly retreat if your teenager is one of your closest emotional relationships. This is especially true for single parents with only one or two adolescents remaining at home.

I've seen many single parents drift into a kind of roommate relationship with their teenager. This is particularly true if your teen is relatively well-behaved and a good communicator. The appearance of a mutually supportive relationship between a single parent and a teenage child can be appealing. Most of the time, the parent and teen float along with intertwined schedules, seemingly sharing their lives. This compatibility is usually disrupted by regular parent-teen tensions that can often be resolved by talking it out.

Then something big happens. When a single parent and teen have this kind of relationship, it's jolting when the teen comes home drunk or is disciplined at school for cheating. Suddenly what seemed like a mutually agreed truce in the "When do I become an adult?" process comes to a halt. The single parent feels she must exercise some sort of discipline, but her adolescent is outraged at this apparent patronizing response. This usually results in either the single parent backing off the discipline she should be implementing or a teenager who, overnight, wants nothing to do with a parent he seemed so close to.

The alternative is for single parents to maintain a visible program of Planned Emancipation. These parents need to maintain clear expectations and consequences when their rules are violated, while regularly handing over freedoms even to a teenager who seems to be a good kid. Single parents who maintain vigilance with Planned Emancipation while taking care of their own relationship needs may feel like they're sacrificing a level of intimacy with their teenager. In reality, they're ensuring a close connection far into their teen's adult life.

CHAPTER 32

Divorce and Blended Families

Divorce isn't the child's fault. Don't say anything unkind about
your ex to the child, because you're really just hurting the child.
VALERIE BERTINELLI

Co-parenting after divorce is *hard*. Don't let anyone tell you different.
However, co-parenting teenagers can be easier than when they're young.
It's time to assess the burdens that are now lifted because your kids are
no longer children.

Finding Their Own Voice

It's not uncommon for a divorced parent to have serious concerns about
how his or her ex is parenting the kids. Often, a parent has to hear the
complaints of his sweet children, who may dislike how they're treated
when they're at the other parent's house. This often motivates a parent's protective instinct, and he feels he must advocate for the child.
Since relations with the ex are often strained, these attempts are stressful
and complicated and seem fruitless. If the concerns rise to the point of

possible abuse, expensive lawyers become involved, and things can get incredibly messy. Short of clear proof of danger to the child (which is rare), the issue of protecting the child from the other parent can be a huge source of stress.

When kids reach adolescence, it becomes increasingly important that these young adults find ways to speak up for themselves with both of their divorced parents. At this stage, it's unhelpful for a parent to continually step in on behalf of a teenager. When a teen complains about your ex, it's often best to offer a response such as "Did you tell your father/mother that?" Overt abuse is, obviously, an exception here and calls for the intervention of a counselor or even the police, but that's rarely what divorced parents are dealing with.

Things get complicated when the divorced parent remembers her own experience when married. A mom may find herself identifying with her teen's feeling of helplessness in trying to communicate with the other parent. However, parents need to remember that a child's struggles with a parent are very different from struggles in marriage, even if they sound the same. Married people voluntarily begin their marriage as adults. Children don't choose their parents and must grow into adult relationships with their parents regardless of the pitfalls.

> A child's struggles with a parent are very different from struggles in marriage, even if they sound the same.

It's important that parents not express an overidentification with their teen's struggles in communication or relationship with the other parent. Agreeing with your teen's sense of helplessness only hurts her sense of competence. Communicating agreement that the other parent is impossible to deal with only reinforces a message that your teenager is powerless.

Instead, divorced parents must recognize this unstated freedom they need to release to their teen: "Use your own judgment in handling difficulties with your other parent, regardless of my history with him [or her]."

Adolescents Need a Relationship with Both Parents, if Possible

Where possible—regardless of the difficult history you may have with your ex—it's better for your teenager to maintain a good relationship with both parents. This means you must try not to discourage your adolescent from spending time with the other parent. This does *not* mean you're responsible for somehow making their relationship a good one. If your ex is a "rat," you don't have to advocate for him, but it's probably better that your young-adult child find her way in that relationship.

A common struggle with divorced parents is a father who blames all their children's unhappiness with him on their mother. These fathers need to know that while a mother can exert considerable influence over her children's views, this influence decreases significantly in adolescence. When a five-year-old is angry because "Daddy was mean to Mommy," that may or may not indicate a mother who is bad-mouthing her ex. When a fifteen-year-old is angry because "You never listen to me," that's a different situation entirely.

By adolescence, kids can develop their relationships with both parents with less interference from the side effects of divorce. Again, these are young adults who deserve to be respected as such.

Planned Emancipation in Different Households

When adolescents divide their time between their parents' households, Planned Emancipation can be tricky. Often, one household has far fewer expectations than the other. Teenagers gravitate toward fewer restrictions without regard to whether this freedom is given due to respect for their age or just because no parent is watching. Young children may feel safer with clear expectations and consequences, but adolescents push back against what can feel like one parent who still sees them as incompetent.

The best solution is to try to get on the same page as your ex, but in my experience in working with divorced couples, this is often not possible. There's a reason you and your ex are divorced. Still, it's worth the effort. Sometimes a therapist you both trust can help you and your ex-spouse reach an agreement. If not, you (the parent reading this book) will need to make those compromises yourself.

Many parents report experiencing extra turmoil when their teenagers return from a weekend with the other parent, during which they were given much more freedom. Trying to tell your adolescent, "Well, that's not how we do it here in this house" is ineffective and only stokes resentment. The overall effect will be to undercut both parents' authority. (See the fourth law of disciplining adolescents in chapter 11.)

If you're a parent who is following Planned Emancipation, you already know the positive impact this can have on your relationship with your teenager. The message of respect that a clear Freedoms list communicates should increase your ability to communicate with and advise your adolescent. But you'll need to tread carefully when responding to your teenager's complaints about his other, overly controlling parent.

If the other household is providing far less oversight than you think is best (even though you're giving over freedoms where you can, right?), communicate openly about that. Telling your kid, "Look, you know I don't think it's good for you to have your phone as much as your mom/dad does, but I understand this is hard for you" is a good start. You'll be more effective if you allow that freedom in your household as well or find some compromise position. Remember that teenagers do *not* secretly think, *I know Mom is stricter than Dad* or *I know Dad is stricter than Mom*, or *I know they have my best interests at heart, and they're right to restrict me.* Teenagers just think that the more restrictive parent doesn't get it.

Dealing with separate households can be complicated with children of all ages. But with teenagers, some of the complications can be eased if you pay attention to their need for autonomy. Remember that the goal of Planned Emancipation is to communicate and demonstrate, where possible, that you recognize their young-adult status and that you're on your way out of controlling their life. This message can still be given even when the situation is complicated by differences with your ex.

CHAPTER 33

Adoption, Foster Care, and Teenagers

Adoption is complicated, but also rich with narratives of strength.
JILLIAN LAUREN

Negotiating Planned Emancipation with adopted adolescents can be challenging. Often, parents feel they must go slower with giving over freedoms due to the struggles these teenagers may be having. The truth, however, is quite the opposite. Clear and orderly releasing of freedoms is more important with adopted teens.

Individuation and Adoption Awareness

As stated earlier, adolescence is a period of identity development as well as of cognitive advances that allows these young adults to review their own lives in ways they were previously incapable of. It can be hurtful when an otherwise compliant adopted teenager suddenly declares, "You aren't my real parents!" to parents who have invested everything into the teenager's life. These parents shouldn't consider this new awareness as a rejection of them. All young adults must prepare for their own lives, and touching base with their origins is just a natural part of that process.

In many cases, this ability to think more deeply about adoption and their sense of identity is a bit overwhelming and can contribute to acting out in heretofore unknown ways. Therapists with training in adoption issues can help. Even if your adopted teenagers show no signs of rethinking their adoptions, it's a good idea to talk to them about these things anyway.

Circumstances of Adoption

The family's road to adoption matters. Parents who adopted their children very young or even straight from the hospital tend to think the complications of their child's entering their family can be minimized. Many kids who were adopted young seem uninterested in their adoption history. This often changes in adolescence, however, and can be surprising to parents. Those who adopted their teenager when he was older may not feel quite as jolted by their teen's focus on his adoption, but it can still be disappointing or feel like some kind of criticism.

As mentioned, parents who adopted their teenager in infancy may be tempted to minimize the impact adoption can have. But all adoptions involve some circumstance that leads the biological parents to place their child. As an adopted child approaches adulthood, parents may be surprised to see characteristics in their teenager that were part of her biological parents' struggles in life. Mood swings and a proclivity toward risky or addictive behaviors may emerge. Often, adoptive parents feel these tendencies are a result of a failure in their parenting.

> Parents of adopted teenagers need to assess the effectiveness of their parenting by asking, "Where would this child be if we hadn't adopted him?"

It can be helpful for parents of adopted teenagers to think, *Where would this child be if we hadn't adopted him?* Ironically, this can seem disappointing for parents who set their expectations for their young, adopted child just as if he or she were their biological child. By adolescence, this expectations reality check is necessary and comforting. After all, in many cases, their adopted adolescent might even be dead if it weren't for them.

Grandparents who have adopted their grandchildren have a particular need to be careful about their expectations. It's common for these grandparents to set out, consciously or unconsciously, to fix any mistakes they made with their child (their adopted teen's parent). This can result in a fearful rigidity that can push away their teenage grandkids.

Adoption and Planned Emancipation

The bottom line for parents of adopted teenagers is that you need to be even *more committed* to giving the Planned Emancipation message. Teenagers who have been adopted may display alarming behavioral problems that are new or now worse than long-standing behavior patterns. Dealing with these situations can be scary for parents and, if they're not careful, can result in constant restrictions that accidentally send the message to their teenager *You're never going to grow up in this house.*

Adopted teenagers can have a complicated relationship with their own need for individuation. This is especially true in homes where grandparents have adopted their grandchildren. When the kids feel grateful to their grandparents, they tend to keep their resentments quiet. This can result in a lot of sneaky rebellion. Planned Emancipation can provide needed feedback to help an adopted teenager avoid panicking when she feels resentment toward people she loves. Telling your adopted thirteen-year-old that she's now an adult doesn't threaten her sense of connection to your family. Since individuation is inevitable, this message can calm her fears by identifying her desire for autonomy and positioning yourself as in favor of this change.

Planned Emancipation also opens opportunities for communication about difficult topics. If your adopted teenager is experimenting with drugs or alcohol and you know addiction was part of why he was adopted in the first place, how do you bring that up? Planned Emancipation can ease the tension from constant control battles and give the right context to have this kind of adult-to-adult conversation.

Many times, the support of a therapist can help navigate the adolescent years with adopted teenagers. Having open discussions about their approaching adulthood and the tensions that may be part of their adoption history can help teens make use of a psychologist or other therapist to work through these things.

The onset of adolescence brings big changes as childhood comes to an end and teenagers prepare for adulthood. For teenagers who have been adopted, this shift in identity can set off deep insecurities that might have been unseen before. There's no disrespect intended when newly developing adults begin asking hard questions such as "Who am I, and how did I get here?" Parents of adopted teenagers need to remind themselves of the advantages they've provided for their adolescents—not so they can make *You owe me* speeches but to have the patience needed to guide these adolescents into adulthood. Without you, where would they be?

Foster Teenagers

Teenagers who have come to your house through foster care require even more of the Planned Emancipation message than other teenagers, including adopted teens. I emphasize this because foster parents often must hit the ground running in dealing with behavior issues and mistrust on both sides of the foster-parent-and-teenager relationship. Chaos and uncertainty often cause foster parents to reflexively pull back from respecting the freedoms these adolescents need. Additionally, the need to establish a sense of security for foster teenagers can run counter to Planned Emancipation. A kind of balancing act is needed to give these adolescents a strong message of *You belong here* but also *We're not trying to control your whole life.*

Foster parents have usually undergone a lot of parent training, and I don't want to add to your burden. I remember teaching at a foster parenting conference and seeing the looks of training fatigue on many faces that said, *Do you really have something to say, or is this just another hoop we have to jump through?* Experienced and generous foster parents sometimes must endure a system that assumes they know very little.

For our purposes, I will keep it short. Foster parents should reassure the adult part of an adolescent that you see them as a young adult. This means being clear about the Freedoms list, especially the freedoms you can't control anyway (e.g., music, friend choices, their own opinions about things). This can be difficult when an adolescent has arrived with a list of previous behavior problems or conflicts. While being honest about trust concerns you may have, I still recommend you wave the banner of upcoming emancipation and your overall support of that day.

Some foster teens will need a period of establishing trust. If you have reasons for caution in giving freedoms to a newly fostered teenager, you might try letting him know that you expect to grant him freedoms as soon as you and he have gotten used to each other. This shouldn't be more than a month in most circumstances. Remember, he doesn't know you, either, and words that promise future freedoms may not be trusted early in your relationship.

The Expectations and Consequences list is also very important for foster teenagers. With the kind of attachment problems many foster teens have, it's not unusual for them to act out to test the relationship. Foster parent training covers discipline with children, but I'm not sure how well this training differentiates between disciplining children and adolescents. You need to be extremely clear about what's required and what's *not* required by you as the parent. Adolescents respond best to clearly stated behavioral expectations accompanied by predictable consequences if not followed.

This is where knowing how to be a judge and not a police officer (see chapter 11) is important. The foster parents I've known who have worked best with adolescents know instinctively how to avoid getting into useless control battles. When basic trust hasn't been established in a relationship, consistency and laying out options will help (e.g., "If you choose to _____, then we will _____.").

Finally, I want to remind foster parents that your goal is to be able to show generous love and support for these teenagers. It's not uncommon that generous, loving foster parents can feel patronizing to an adolescent who doesn't know you well and has likely gone through poor parental experiences before you. Remaining clear in what you cannot control helps reduce a foster teenager's fear and allows her to relax a bit in a warm environment.

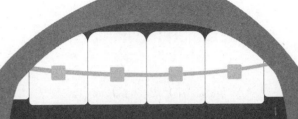

PART EIGHT

After You're Done

Life with Adult Children
and Grandchildren

CHAPTER 34

Adult Children Living at Home

The best way to keep children at home is to
make the home atmosphere pleasant,
and let the air out of the tires.
DOROTHY PARKER

"So . . . our twenty-two-year-old daughter is living at home. Is that okay?"

Parents who know about Planned Emancipation are sometimes sheepish when they talk to me about their adult children living in their homes. They seem to think I'm going to tell them they've done wrong because all post–high school kids should be living on their own. But that's not the case at all.

All my children spent some time after high school living at home with me and their mother. Overall, Sally and I enjoyed our time with our adult kids. Sure, there was some occasional tension (e.g., "Are you going to be home in time for dinner or not?"), but it was mostly fun . . . at least for us. Now, with nine grandchildren, we've all but given up on having extended alone time with any one of our adult kids. That's just not the stage we're in.

I've worked with many families, however, who were having major problems with their adult children living at home. Some parents had frequent, angry arguments with their children or had to struggle with a kind of ghost who rarely left his room or seemed to disappear to mysterious destinations. Sometimes these parents felt as though their adult children had no regard for them or their home. They didn't help around the house and acted resentful when asked. How is it that some parents seem to get along well with adult children living at home, while others suffer?

Whose Home Is This?

Believe it or not, a major factor in the relationship between parents and adult kids living at home is the implied answer to the question "Whose home is this?" Many parents have taught their children of any age that they're always welcome. How could that be a problem? Aren't parents supposed to always be a safe place for their children? By now, readers of this book can see where this is going. When parents feel they must always provide a home for their children, regardless of their age, they run the risk of communicating not only *We love you* but also *We don't respect you.*

As we discussed in chapter 7 on the endpoint of parenting, it's not overly burdensome to expect a high school graduate to be working for his living or to be working hard at further education or training toward the goal of making his own way. Continuing to provide food and shelter for an adult who isn't pursuing these goals is disrespectful and sends the wrong signals. The exception to this, of course, is a young adult with serious intellectual or other disabilities. By serious, I mean a young adult that your civil and legal community would agree shouldn't be required to carry his own weight. If your adult child's surrounding community doesn't see him as an exception, neither should you.

This means that after your child graduates high school, you may wish to (but are not required to) invite her to continue to live in *your* home. An adolescent who's appropriately individuated will not view her parents' home as her home. Think back to when you were finished with high school. Did you feel warm and cozy in your parents' home? Is that where you wanted to spend your days?

Adults living in your home for an extended period are expected to be working full-time, going to school full-time, or some combination that adds up to something approaching a forty-hour workweek. If that sounds overly demanding of your adult kid, you might be inadvertently influencing him to agree with you. I have reminded many parents that there's nothing pathological about an adult who doesn't pursue a career if he doesn't have to. Even at the height of my career as a psychologist, if my mother had called and said she would happily pay my bills and provide me with whatever I needed, I might not have quit my job, but I would have been a lot lazier. Trust me, my parents would *never* have offered such a thing, and I'm grateful they didn't.

The Problems of Adults Living with Their Parents

Even when it's going well, there are pitfalls to adult children living for years with their parents. Few parents expect their adult children to pay for all their food and expenses while living with them. Fathers may uniquely struggle with this. Sally and I have had instances when she's asked me, "Why did you pay for that?" It's certainly not because my wife is cheap. The problem is that I like to play the part of the wealthy dad being magnanimous to these ever-grateful kids. The practical problem is, of course, I'm not super wealthy, and my overplaying Daddy Warbucks can send a message of disrespect to my very capable adult children.

Another difficulty occurs in everyday living. Parents often enjoy taking care of little extras for their adult children, like paying bills, grocery shopping, cooking, or going to restaurants young adults can't afford. Even if your adult child is grateful and doesn't expect these things from you, it's a bad habit that's easy to fall into. Living on your own is the only way to learn the hard realities of adult life—boring, mundane tasks; calling professionals to help you when you need them; or even just learning to do without.

Lastly, remember that although you've worked hard to launch your kids into adulthood and are likely reaping the benefits of a good relationship, they need to establish and maintain emotionally supportive relationships with their peers. In her excellent article "How to Land Your Kid in Therapy," psychotherapist Lori Gottlieb writes about the depressed and anxious young adults she saw who, surprisingly, reported very good relationships with their parents: "Back in graduate school, the clinical focus had always been on how the *lack* of parental attunement affects the child. It never occurred to any of us to ask, what if the parents were *too* attuned? What happens to *those* kids?"[1]

> Living on your own is the only way to learn the hard realities of adult life—boring, mundane tasks, calling professionals to help you when you need them, or even just learning to do without.

I've had that same experience with my young-adult patients. Having adult children who consider their parents as best friends can make parents feel like parenting superheroes. That's a good thing, right?

Like everything else in *Feeding the Mouth* parenting, the answer depends on the goal of independent adulthood. If parental closeness is interfering with an adult child's connection with same-aged adults, that's a problem. Too often, young adults leave their parents' homes and try to live by themselves or with an almost randomly chosen roommate. Conversely, parents who signal to their adult kids living at home that they should be thinking about finding a place with friends aren't threatening their child's security but signaling a very natural step in their child's adulthood.

Time to Leave vs. Being Kicked Out

Sometimes well-meaning parents and their adult children living with them just don't get along. Maybe the kids are working, but not as much as they should be. There might be constant blowups, or the children may not be overtly mean, but they don't seem to like being around their parents, and they don't participate in household management without being asked. These are several of many situations where parents and their kids love each other, but they just don't like each other right now.

Remember, it's your home, not theirs. There's nothing wrong with clearly stating the nature of your relationship and letting them know they should look for another place to live. There's real power in calmly stating, "Listen, it's obvious you don't like us much these days, and we're not too pleased with you either. You should probably find somewhere else to stay. Are we still having lunch on Sunday?" This kind of message can remove the implied pressure of parents who feel they must care for their adult children's needs, and also the pressure of young adults who feel their parents make unfair demands. No one is doing anything wrong; it's just time to go.

This is when some parents will ask, "But where will he go?" Again, *that's not your problem*, and your adult child must see you believe that. For Christian parents, these are times when we find out if we trust God.

Adult children living with their parents is not antithetical to Planned Emancipation. But these situations work best when they're limited to set periods of time in which parents have graciously allowed their adult kids to live in *their* homes. Moving away from parents should be expected and seen as the norm.

CHAPTER 35

Teenagers and Grandparents

Grandparents are both our past and our future. In some ways they are
what has gone before, and in others, they are what we will become.
FRED ROGERS

The role grandparents play in family life has become more important
than ever. Sometimes that's hard to see, but other times it's obvious.

> The girls had fallen asleep, but now they woke up. I think it's
> 2:00 p.m. They haven't had anything to eat since last night.
> There's no light, and we don't have cell phones anymore, so we
> can't even show them our faces, and there's one sentence that is
> keeping them from falling apart and starting to cry—I'm telling
> them: "Grandfather is coming."[1]

Among the harrowing stories coming out of Israel after the Hamas
terrorist attack in 2023 was that of one family who, when they had
lost all hope of rescue, knew the people they could count on—their
grandparents.

Amir Tibon, an Israeli journalist who lived with his wife and two
young daughters in the southern Israel kibbutz of Nahal Oz, found

As teens spend more time with no deep connections to peers or parents, grandparents often find themselves called upon to lessen their pain.

himself locked in his family's safe room with no food and little water. With little cell phone battery left, Amir texted his parents, "There are terrorists outside." Without hesitation, Amir's father, a sixty-two-year-old retired general, and his mother got into their car and started the hour and twenty-minute drive to find them. They rescued several soldiers and civilians on the way, and then joined the firefight to free the people of Nahal Oz and his son and his family.

> And at 4 p.m., after 10 hours like this, we hear a large bang on the window, and we hear the voice of my father. Galia, my oldest daughter, says, "*Saba higea*"—"Grandfather is here." And that's when we all just start crying. And that's when we knew that we were safe.[2]

Grandparents are important. Parents who are now grandparents have been raised in a culture with little thought toward graduating into adulthood. This limited experience may lead to significant misconceptions about the importance of grandparents in the lives of their grandchildren. As teens spend more time with no deep connections to peers or parents, grandparents often find themselves called upon to lessen their pain.

Return to the Importance of Grandparents

Many people of the Greatest Generation came back from WWII, started their families, raised their kids, and looked forward to retirement. They viewed the role of grandparents as a sort of side job, swooping in occasionally to spoil their grandchildren, then taking off for more retirement heaven. Historically, this was an anomaly and doesn't represent the role grandparents have played in the past or that they play in other cultures.

Before the benefits of wealth and mobility, grandparents have always played a key role in the extended family.

Most grandparents I work with have a more significant role in the lives of their grandchildren than their parents did. They're usually happy with this because they long to be involved with their grandkids. Many wish they had more involvement than they currently have. Conversely, dual-career couples often count on grandparents for much-needed childcare. Some grandparents find themselves in the unexpected role of being the primary parent of their grandchildren, a family system sometimes referred to as *grandfamilies*. Whatever the circumstances, there are important considerations when your grandchildren become teenagers.

Many of us grandparents dreamed of having grandkids. Pictures of my parents and my in-laws holding our newborns, and their grand-babies, are precious to my wife and me. Grandparent-aged friend groups tend to tell stories of spoiling their cute, little grandkids, giving gifts, and taking them to fun places.

But what about when grandchildren reach adolescence? As a grand-father myself, I'll be honest with you, I'm not as good a grandparent as I thought I would be. Little kids make me nervous. I do okay with them, but I enjoy my grandchildren more as they get older. I'm not proud of this; it's just the way I am. Grandparenting teenage grandkids can be empowering to both the grandparents and their young-adult grandchildren.

Deepening Involvement with Teen Grandchildren

When grandchildren are adolescents, grandparents can focus more on connecting directly with them and not rely solely on indirect communication through their parents. This means grandparents would benefit from getting on at least some of the social media channels their grandkids are on. This is easy for some grandparents, but others might need to adjust their disdain for technology. If that's where your teenage grandkids are, that's where you need to be. If you don't know how to get on these apps, ask your grandchildren! They know this stuff, and they'd be happy to teach you a few things.

The key here is to find the best ways to have direct communication with adolescent grandchildren. This is one of the advantages of communication technology. Grandparents who are separated from grandchildren can maintain a more day-to-day relationship. Remember that real-time communication (e.g., talking on the phone) is not preferred by most teenagers. Texting and other forms of messaging may be more effective. Also remember to keep your messages short. Your goal is to strengthen your daily contact. Deeper communication can be had, but that's best when they're physically with you.

When teenage grandchildren are sullen and distant, grandparents can be particularly helpful, but they need to have confidence in their role. This seems particularly true for the Christian grandparents that I see. In his book *Aging with Purpose*, Hal Habecker encourages grandparents to remember, "We are here to tell the story of God's faithfulness, abiding presence, and joy. . . . To encourage our adult children and grandchildren who need this desperately in the world they are facing."[3]

Grandparents need to believe in the experience they can share with their grandkids. Without lecturing, grandparents can encourage adolescents with stories and reminders learned from their own lives. Remember to talk about your failures as much as your successes. No one wants to hear from an older person who constantly complains that things aren't like they used to be, or to hear stories of how successful they were "back in the day."

Patient, carefully worded moments of wisdom tend to have the most effect. As I've said before, "Half of wisdom is just getting tired." When I was younger, I had the energy to be worried more, make more plans, and dream big futures for myself and my kids. Being older has the advantage of perspective . . . and fatigue. That perspective is an important foundation of wisdom. When teenage grandchildren are falling apart and their parents are too, we grandparents can provide helpful grounding by reminding everyone that we've seen a lot and learned that things turn out okay.

Babying Your Teen Grandchildren

Grandparents, especially those who don't see their grandchildren regularly, often flood their grandkids with love, affection, and cookies. Teenagers may allow such babying behavior from grandparents far longer than they'll take it from their parents. Teenage grandchildren rarely have similar control battles with their grandparents. This dynamic can be uplifting to sour and withdrawn teenagers. During periods of a toxic relationship with parents, grandparents can be a reliable source of love and encouragement.

Not all teenagers are tolerant of grandparents, however, whose love and attention can feel patronizing. It's best if grandparents pay attention to these dynamics and adjust accordingly.

Teenage grandchildren who feel overcontrolled by their parents may feel uplifted instead by grandparents who allow them to make suggestions and decisions about activities they're planning. Where possible, grandparents can encourage their teen grandchildren's autonomy by scheduling visits without their younger siblings. Since many grandparents gravitate toward nurturing, little-kid-type interactions, time with "just us adults" can be an important way to strengthen the relationship.

Whatever your goal as a grandparent of teenagers, you must be aware of the relationship your grandkids see between you and their parents. Adolescents watch everything. They know, for instance, if there are tensions between you and Mom and Dad. And remember, teens are now on the adult side of the equation. They are very aware of whether their parents are receiving the kind of respect from you that they strongly desire from their parents.

Respect Your Grandchildren's Parents

Remember that your relationship with grandchildren must inherently go through their parents. I've worked with many well-meaning grandparents whose concern for what they felt was best for their grandchildren caused them to disregard the power and influence of the parents. Unless these concerns rise to the point of criminal abuse on the part of the parents, grandparents who assume some sort of partial parental role run a high risk of being ineffective in their grandchildren's lives as well as undermining the effectiveness of the parents.

Most of the tensions that arise between adult children and grandparents are the predictable results of never letting your children grow up in your eyes. This is where successful Planned Emancipation with your children pays significant dividends. Releasing control of your children allows for an adult-to-adult relationship with your grandchildren's parents. Just as you communicated with Planned Emancipation, grandparents should look for opportunities to communicate to their adult children, *We want you to know we will respect your decisions with your children, not because we'll always agree with what you do, but because we know you're an adult and these are your children.* That's not always an easy line to hold.

I remember telling my wife before our adult children started having children that we needed to prepare ourselves to bite our tongues when we watched our kids parent their kids. This turned out to be prophetic, even though our adult children are doing a fine job in parenting their children. There are just some things that my wife and I think our adult kids should do differently with our grandchildren. How should we handle this? We keep our mouths shut!

> To have an impact on your adolescent grandchildren's lives, you must be careful not to step over the line of respecting their parents (your children).

One good resource for dealing with adult children comes from Jim Burns, PhD, and is subtitled "Keep Your Mouth Shut and the Welcome Mat Out" He reminds parents, "Withholding advice goes against our nature as parents, but unsolicited advice is usually taken as criticism."[4] *Feeding the Mouth* parents understand this completely. To have an impact on your adolescent grandchildren's lives, you must be careful not to step over the line of respecting their parents (your children).

This doesn't mean you can never talk to your children about how they're parenting, but you must be extremely careful if you do. Most of us have experienced or know someone who has experienced the common tension and resentment that springs up when parents freely offer suggestions and criticisms to their children. If you have understood the message of this book and have taken steps to release your children into adulthood, you will have an easier time than most when it comes to offering feedback about how your grandchildren are being raised.

First, giving constructive feedback should be extremely rare. Even when your adult child is expressing frustration about your grandchildren, your response should mostly remain in the realm of encouragement and recognition.

Your kid: "Will these kids ever sleep through the night?!"

You: "I know. I remember thinking your brother would never go to sleep!"

If your comment is followed by the question "What finally worked?" then go ahead and tell him. If not, just keep your supportive spirit open and your critical mouth shut. Maintaining a baseline level of communication that reinforces the message *We're all adults who have struggled with parenting* can help you be more effective with the few times you may feel compelled to give feedback.

Second, if you feel you must give constructive feedback, review the rules of advice giving outlined in our discussion of communication. Grandparents commenting to their kids about parenting is super touchy business. Usually, I recommend this feedback be given to your child rather than her spouse. Use your own judgment about this, of course. You don't want to appear secretive to your son- or daughter-in-law, but you want to avoid coming across as critical of your adult child's spouse.

When Teen Grandchildren Complain about Their Parents

It can be tempting for grandparents to bond with disgruntled teenagers by agreeing with them when they complain about their parents. This kind of talk should be avoided. It's disrespectful to your kids, and ultimately, this sort of "enemy of my enemy" bond is shallow and short-lived. Since you're hearing these complaints from young adults, however, grandparents don't necessarily need to always defend and explain their own children's actions to adolescent grandchildren. It may be best to listen and perhaps help your teenage grandchild put his frustrations into words. The most important advice to give is to encourage your grandchild to talk to his parents about his frustrations.

This kind of discussion can be like other types of communication with teenagers. When they express an "it won't do any good" kind of helplessness, grandparents should remind them they're not children, and you believe they're capable of taking the risk of talking to their parents. Caution should be observed regarding whether you should always inform your children of your grandchildren's complaints about them. It's best to find a balance between appearing to keep secrets from your kids and feeling obligated to share every detail of what your teen grandchildren are saying.

Grandparents who understand the principles of Planned Emancipation can increase the impact they have on teenage grandchildren. Being relieved of the control battles that often sour a parent's relationship with an adolescent, grandparents can feel the freedom to speak adult-to-adult with their grandkids. By being able to listen without judgment and withhold speeches, grandparents can give a teenager a safe place to talk through some of her biggest conflicts. In these times of ever-increasing isolation, grandparents can be essential in rescuing their teenage grandchildren from loneliness and despair.

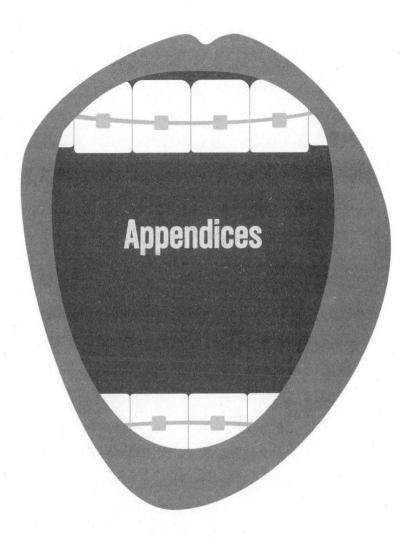

Appendices

APPENDIX 1

Freedoms List Examples

For the next few sections, I'll cover the typical areas of freedom I suggest parents consider progressively granting to their teenagers. This list isn't meant to be comprehensive, and you may find some issues that won't apply to your teenager. These examples were chosen because they come up time and again in my practice, but in the end, you know your kid better than I do. If you don't like these examples, change them up.

The areas of autonomy mentioned are also listed in a generally suggested order of withdrawal. For example, granting autonomy over how teens keep their room is listed first because it's a freedom that can be granted to young adolescents with few life-altering consequences. The freedom to no longer have a curfew is usually granted last.

FREEDOM	BOUNDARIES
Use your own judgment in keeping your room as clean or as dirty as you see fit.	• Do your own laundry. • No food in your room. • No odors beyond your room.

For some of you, I can see your face and hear your thoughts (because I've often seen similar faces and heard similar thoughts in my office). With a scrunched-up face, you're thinking, *Do you know what you're saying? We have no idea where the floor is in my teenage daughter's room.* I've even had mothers bring me photos of what looks like a bomb site and tearfully plead, "You mean this room?"

To which I would answer, "Yep. I do." We parents of teenagers have a special bond when it comes to the messes and smells that seem to be attached to our adolescent loved ones.

But I want to ask you to move past your initial shock and seriously consider what I'm suggesting.

When Should I Grant This Freedom?

Granting your teenager freedom over the cleanliness of his room is one of my favorite areas of autonomy for several reasons:

- It can be granted to young adolescents, for example, thirteen-year-olds.
- You don't have to clean their room anymore.
- Insanity-inducing, never-ceasing "Clean your room!" battles cease.

The main reason this ought to be one of the first areas of autonomy is that the natural consequences of a dirty room are felt, but they're not devastating. (And don't start with the "But he has asthma!" argument. Remember what we said about fear?)

In my thirty-plus years of seeing parents of adolescents, so far not one teenager has died as a result of a dirty room.

What Are the Boundaries of This Freedom?

Now, here's why this works, both for you and your adolescent: With adult freedom comes adult responsibility. You are no longer responsible for the mess in her room. While I wouldn't recommend saying it that way to your teenager, there are certain ways (besides the list itself) you can let her know she has this new freedom and responsibility. After saying, "Now that you're old enough, you can begin to keep your room as clean or as messy as you'd like" (and after watching your young teenager pick her jaw up from the floor), consider explaining the following boundaries of this newfound freedom:

1. *They do their own laundry.* ("You don't want your mommy coming in to gather up your stuff and invade your privacy. At your age, it's time you take charge of caring for the stuff in your room—and that includes your laundry.") Treat his laundry like you would at a laundromat. Throw his left-in-the-dryer or left-in-the-washer laundry on the floor, in a spare basket, or in a sack. Mildew isn't your problem; it's a real-life consequence of forgetting your laundry in the machines. Don't warn him about what could happen to his clothes. Let it happen. Conversely, let your adolescent know that he may not treat your clothes the same way. Why? Because you own the laundromat.

2. *No food in their room.* ("Your room happens to be attached to our house, so unless you can afford an exterminator, there will be a fine for any food-related items seen in your room.")

3. *No odors emanating from their room.* The rest of the family shouldn't have to endure bad smells from your teenager's poor choices. Give her a couple of days to fix the problem (e.g., a can of Lysol bought by the teenager, not you). Otherwise, a one-time cleanup may be required.

4. *Don't clean for them.* Fight your inner urges to "just tidy up the mess." If you have a housecleaning service, tell them to skip your teenager's room.

5. *Don't help with finding lost items or other consequences of their own choices.* This is a reminder for you and doesn't need to be put on the list for your adolescent to see. You must remind yourself not to rescue your teenager from the natural consequences of keeping his or her room messy. One messy room crisis is worth twenty of your "Cleanliness is next to godliness" lectures.

It's that last part that many parents struggle with the most. Let them reap the consequences. Don't nag them or give them reminders such as "Remember that you leave for camp in two days, so if you have any laundry, you'd better get to it today." This is exactly the kind of help adolescents hate.

Granting them authority over this small area of their lives allows them to begin to feel the burdens that accompany adult-level responsibilities. If they fail to remember to do their laundry before leaving for camp, they won't win the Most Popular Camper award, but they'll have learned an invaluable lesson about grooming and proper self-care.

And whatever you do, don't exacerbate the problem by bluntly asking them upon their return home, "So, did they have a washer and dryer at camp?" You want to let them experience real-world consequences; you don't want to goad them into better behavior next time. That's for kids; you're raising an adult-in-training. You may be surprised at how your teenager responds to his new freedoms.

However, you must prepare yourself (especially moms of male teenagers) to watch them go a long time without doing any laundry. (Some of you are now going online to search for allergy masks.) They will wear dirty clothes. They will go a long time without washing their sheets. This may be hard to watch, but such a laissez-faire attitude toward cleanliness commonly occurs among college freshmen. You're just giving them a head start on this life experience.

But let me reiterate: Granting freedom does not mean losing influence. Don't be afraid to occasionally comment on their increased shabbiness or new musky cologne smell. Just be sure to make a joke out of it by reminding them, "Hey, that's your business now." Don't ever take this autonomy back. They will need time to experience real-life consequences. For many adolescent boys, all it will take is the first time a cute girl asks, "What's that smell?" Next thing you know, they'll be asking for a primer on how to use the washer and dryer.

Above all, if they come dashing out of their room one day in a panic and say, "Quick, I'm supposed to have this shirt ironed for my concert," you must stand there, drink your coffee, and say, "Bummer. What are you gonna do?" If you rescue them from the consequences of their irresponsible choices, all is lost. You cannot iron for them now, because you are finishing your coffee.

One of my other favorite responses for parents to say is "I always hang up my shirts after washing them, but that's just me." Or address your spouse in your teenager's presence and say, "Hey, honey, remember that time when you forgot to iron your shirt before that big interview?" Lastly, consider the useful age reminder: "What are you, six? You can figure this out on your own."

Overly nurturant moms always think this is unloving behavior toward a child in trouble. My answer is that this is respectful behavior toward a capable adult. By not rescuing her, you show support for her creative ability to figure out her problems like an adult.

Now let's consider another avenue for individuation.

FREEDOM	BOUNDARIES
Use your own judgment in choosing your friends.	• Objectionable friends may not be allowed in our home. • Guilt by association will be your problem.

Ever try to tell your teenager that he or she shouldn't be hanging out with this or that friend? How'd that work for you? Many times you'll hear a loud protest: "You don't even know her!" Teenagers may even respond to your feedback by defending a friend that you know they don't even like. By now you should be able to guess why they do this. Let's make it a multiple-choice question.

Teenagers get very defensive when parents try to tell them to stop hanging around with certain friends for one of these reasons:

a. They know this friend well and can see the saintly soul just underneath their flawed exterior.

b. They aren't defending the friend but are defending the use of their own judgment in choosing friends.

c. They were just tired and seemed upset, but they secretly realized the wisdom of their parents' words.

The answer is *b*. Even sound advice about choices in friendships often falls flat. The need for individuation in teenagers causes them to hear this advice as criticism of their judgment. If you want to talk about friends in a way that an adolescent will listen to, you first have to ask yourself the question *Is her choice of friends up to her or still under my control?*

I know some of you may be worried about considering this freedom as one of the earliest ones to be granted. Many parents are fearful about giving over control of friends because they fear the dire consequences of teenagers hanging out with the wrong crowd. I would respond to these fears in three ways.

First, bad crowds don't just walk up and accost unsuspecting teenagers. Adolescents choose their friends, and they need to be held accountable for those choices. Overemphasizing the role of bad influences is demeaning to young adults and paints them as passive agents.

Second, it's very hard to monitor and control whom teenagers spend time with. This only gets harder as they get older. Granting teens the freedom to choose their friends allows parents to gain influence. Mom and Dad become allies in their teenagers' decision-making in their social lives.

Lastly, the biggest fear parents have about negative peer influences usually involves drug or alcohol use. I would argue that in such cases it's even more important that freedom to choose friends is granted early in adolescence. Chronic involvement with friends who party may well require restriction from certain friends, but this restriction must be tied to the boundary "Substance use will not be tolerated" and not misunderstood as meaning "You don't know how to pick friends." There's nothing worse than teenagers who purposefully gravitate toward substance-using friends just to win the *When will you say I can choose my own friends?* control battle.

When Should I Grant This Freedom?

Remember that your teenager's basic question of individuation—*When will you say I'm an adult?*—is always beneath the friend argument. It just takes on more specific forms: "When will you say I'm old enough and responsible enough to choose my friends?" "When will you grant me the freedom to make my own choices regarding my friends without your snap judgments, dismissive remarks, and vain attempts at controlling my relationships?" That's overstated, but you get the point. Adolescents want to know when they can be trusted with an area of their life that feels so integral to their identity.

You should consider granting this freedom in early adolescence (around thirteen) for two reasons: (1) freedom over choice of friends sends a powerful message of growing autonomy and (2) your ability to monitor and control friendships is weak and getting weaker.

For many of you, choice of friends hasn't been a problem with your teen, but you should grant it anyway. Phrase it in your way, but it's time to tell your thirteen-year-old, "By the way, you know we like Andrew and those other guys you hang around with. But we want to let you know that, at your age, we wouldn't interfere with whom you hang around with even if we didn't happen to like them. They're your friends, not ours." Even though you're more likely to get a blank stare and a "Yeah, okay" response, that doesn't mean it didn't register.

What Are the Boundaries of This Freedom?

While I'm suggesting a retreat from the territory of friendship choices, I'm not encouraging you to be wholly uninvolved or to grant your child immunity when friends drag him into trouble. With freedom comes accountability, and all freedoms have limits. If you've heard bad reports about someone he's hanging out with, you might specifically mention that you won't vouch for him if he gets caught doing something he shouldn't while with a known delinquent friend. Remind yourself that he will only truly learn a lesson if the real world is his teacher. Again, if alcohol or drugs become an issue, see chapter 22.

Feel free to also set boundaries on whether certain friends can come over to your house. It's still your house, after all. "You can hang out with Suzie if you'd like, but not at our house, not after she talked that way to your mother last week." I wouldn't expect this to be an oft-used boundary, but you still retain the right to control situations that affect the household as a whole.

I understand it can be challenging to know how to respond when you've heard negative things about your teenager's friends. If you've heard through the parents' grapevine that Suzie got drunk at a party once, that may be cause for concern, but it's not a reason to forever label her as a delinquent. Remember that communication will be most important once you've granted this freedom. Try to avoid painting any of her friends as *bad*. Listen to what your teenager likes about this friend, and don't be afraid to share your fears or concerns. Just be sure to clarify that they are your concerns; she can disagree.

Withdrawing your troops from the territory of friendship choices will result in unforeseen outcomes and possibly hard lessons for your adolescent, but granting her such freedom can open lines of communication that you may have never thought possible.

FREEDOM	BOUNDARIES
Use your own judgment in deciding when to go to bed.	• You must be in your room and quiet by __:__. • All screens off by __:__. • You must wake yourself up and be ready on time. • We will not help you with fatigue-related problems.

Like room cleaning, the battle over getting adolescents to go to bed at a certain time is too often a big strain on your relationship with them. There's something about being told when to go to bed that feels very childish to teenagers. If you want to push it, try telling them, "You look tired. I think you'll need to go to bed early tonight." They love that! (Not!) The constant battle over bedtime will hurt the relationship more than it changes your teenagers' habits.

Believe it or not, with a little creativity in making sure they're held accountable for their choices, autonomy in choosing bedtime can be given early in adolescence. In our home we often withdrew this around our children's thirteenth birthdays, and sometimes even earlier.

I've placed this area of autonomy later than the territory of clean rooms because while you can choose to give over both at an early age, there's a major difference in terms of consequences between these two territories. Adolescents need sleep, and a lack of sleep can cause real problems for most teenagers.

When Should I Grant This Freedom?

How can you tell when your adolescent may be ready to choose his bedtime? First, assess how well your current control methods are doing in helping him get enough sleep. If your adolescent isn't fighting you on this and regularly goes to bed when told, feel free to wait on granting this particular autonomy. (Remember, it's never a question of *if* you'll give over autonomy, but *when*.)

However, as is often the case, if your adolescent still finds ways to avoid going to bed at a decent hour despite your nagging or yelling, "Go to bed," consider granting her autonomy over her bedtime. As always, giving autonomy to decide for herself only means you'll be getting out of the way of her real-world consequences. Your next step is to make sure that your teenager—and not you—feels these consequences.

What Are the Boundaries of This Freedom?

You Must Be in Your Room and Quiet by [Time]

You've given autonomy in deciding when to go to bed, not the freedom to wander around the house until all hours. The reason they don't get freedom to wander about should not be linked to "the importance of being quiet and still in the evening" or anything like that. Again, that's kid stuff. The reason is that it's your house, and you don't want people wandering around after you've gone to bed. It's a burden to your sense of security ("Is that Timmy or a burglar in the kitchen?") and might—depending on the layout of your house—deprive you of sleep. Your adolescents probably won't like this either. However, there's something less offensive and less childish about requiring that they be in their room because it affects you rather than you telling them when they should sleep.

All Screens Off by [Time]

I recently added a new boundary that I recommend parents consider when granting bedtime freedom: setting an "all screens off" time. By this I mean you may need to require that they turn off all devices with screens (cell phones, tablets, computers, e-readers, video game consoles, TVs, etc.) by a certain time. This is a tricky boundary to require because it's one of those "because it's good for you" types of limits. I recommend it because a growing body of research links the blue light from these screens to serious disruptions in sleep patterns. Just google *screens before bed*, and you'll see what I mean.

To ease this tension, parents should first implement such a ban for themselves. Allowing yourself the freedom to practice this detrimental behavior only adds to the message that grown-ups are allowed to do this, but teenagers are not. Remember, no one is talking about whether you have the right to use screens before bed while restricting your teenager. That's up to you. However, setting an example in this area will make the boundary less offensive to an adolescent's individuation needs.

You Must Wake Yourself Up and Be Ready on Time

The real issue in allowing your teenager her choice of bedtime doesn't happen at night; it happens every morning. The most important accountability that goes with setting one's bedtime is waking oneself up. This is a big responsibility that must be tied to autonomy in going to bed. The main signal that an adolescent's body gives to the child that she's not getting enough sleep is difficulty waking up in the morning. If you continue to shoulder the burden of awakening her, she won't feel the weight of fatigue in her life.

You can't imagine how common this struggle is in households with adolescents. Scores of parents begin to dread the coming of morning, as the rising sun seems to bring a new life-or-death battle into view. Parents try all kinds of weapons:

- a gentle voice and back stroking
- the flip-on-the-light-and-yell method
- turning on the shower for their kid
- bringing breakfast to their kid's bed (I know, but some actually try this)
- Super Soaker squirt guns
- loud stereos blaring music the kid hates

These tactics are inevitably used in some combination because multiple repetitions are invariably needed. Some working parents are up at four o'clock in the morning because they have to set aside a good hour or more just to "get this kid up and going!"

All this dramatic parental behavior is carried on before teenagers, who appear either comatose or very angry that this crazy parent is putting them through all this. They display an attitude of unconcern that seems to say, "Getting up in the morning? Oh, I have someone who does that for me." In growing your adult-in-training to be an adult in the world, this attitude reveals an immaturity that can be dangerous later on. If they don't develop inner motivation to wake up on time while they're still under your direct influence, they may become quite incapable of getting to that eight o'clock college course on time.

Yes, I can hear many of you telling me, "But my son really does have some sort of sleep disorder!" Though adolescent boys do tend to sleep longer, it's not likely that he has a diagnosable sleep disorder. Getting up on time is about inner motivation. For instance, if you tell a typical teenage boy that the cheerleaders need his help this Saturday for a photo shoot, but he has to be at the gym by six o'clock in the morning, how do you think he will react? His motivation for getting up on time would exponentially increase, and he'd likely place three alarm clocks in his room and ask a friend to call him that morning. He may even wake early enough to take a shower.

While sleeping, our brains are still working. If his sleeping brain keeps telling him *not my problem* regarding when he has to wake up, he'll remain comatose for as long as possible. Even if some sort of sleep disorder does exist, there's a huge difference between an adolescent asking to see a doctor for help versus a parent dragging a disinterested kid in for tests.

For older adolescents, and especially seniors in high school, it's best to let all the natural consequences fall on them. Younger adolescents are not yet ready to shoulder all the natural consequences of not waking up in the mornings. No responsible parent can stand back and tell a thirteen-year-old, "Well, don't come crying to me if you drop out of school and have to live on the streets." For them, you will have to fill in with your expectations and consequences.

We Will Not Help You with Fatigue-Related Problems

This is more of a reminder for you. It doesn't matter if you're right that he wouldn't have punched that hole in the wall if he wasn't so tired all the time. It's his problem, not yours!

Balancing bedtime freedom with appropriate levels of consequences does require some creativity on your part, but I'm serious about eventually giving over complete autonomy, especially by the time he's a senior. He'll have to deal with real-world ramifications in a few short months as it is, so you may as well make the most of your influence while he's still under your roof.

FREEDOM	BOUNDARIES
Use your own judgment in handling school.	• Minimum grades must be maintained. • We are available to help if you ask, but not at all times.

"Do you have any homework?"

"Nope," fourteen-year-old Kevin quickly replies without taking his eyes off his video game.

"Are you sure? I thought you said you had that project due Friday."

"She said we can work on that in class and that it's no big deal."

"That doesn't sound right. What did she mean by 'No big deal'?"

Kevin's voice rises a little, and his mom can tell he's getting agitated.

"I don't know! She just said not to worry too much about it, okay?"

"I'm just asking because her last email said your last test didn't go so well, and . . ."

"Look, I told you. That test wasn't fair, because nobody knew what was gonna be on it! I'm doing fine. Now can I just finish my game?"

Kevin's mom walks away, feeling defeated and a bit helpless, thinking, *Doesn't he know how his grades could affect his future? Why doesn't he care?*

This is a parent trying to help a teenager manage his schooling when he doesn't believe he needs that help. Yet Mom or Dad may keep harping on their teen's grades because they don't know what else to do.

Someone has to care about how he does in school, right? Yes, but that somebody needs to be him. You've finished high school, remember? You may be thinking, *But he doesn't care, and I don't know how to make him care.* Again, a helpful approach lies in your teenager's need for individuation and autonomy.

I often ask teenagers, "If your parents disappeared tomorrow, do you think your grades would go down?" The vast majority will answer no, even when their parents are confident that if they backed off from helping, their teenagers would fail. This demonstrates teenagers' lack of insight into their school problems.

When parents continue to push through escalating control battles about schoolwork, they may interfere with a teenager's insight into her own academic needs. It's not enough for adults-in-training to be surrounded by helpful parents and teachers if the adolescent herself doesn't see the need for it. Giving freedom to manage schoolwork as she sees fit can be an important step in increasing a teenager's insight into her education.

When Should I Grant This Freedom?

Managing schoolwork often needs to be granted to younger adolescents, primarily for one reason: Parents' attempts to micromanage their teenagers' schooling can quickly turn into increasing control battles, with decreasing degrees of success in helping the adolescents keep their grades up.

In other words, inflicting such help on reluctant teenagers is like giving medicine with side effects that are worse than its ability to cure the disease. You can likely imagine the warning label on such a bottle: "Micromanaging school has been known to increase the risks of heightened control battles, heated arguments, and the need for private-detective-level snooping to discover your teenager's assignments and grades." For some parents, the trade-off in grade performance may be worth the momentary headaches of arguing over grades, but for most, the cure isn't worth the side effects.

If you've suffered too many ill side effects in the ongoing wars over grades, you must change your approach. You must grant your teenager a certain amount of autonomy over his schoolwork.

Fear not. You're not handing over complete autonomy to your adolescent in the territory of school (though that should come by the senior year). What I'm suggesting is that you only give him autonomy in how he handles schoolwork. You'll still need to give consequences if he doesn't keep his grades to a minimally acceptable level.

To grant your adolescent autonomy over her schoolwork, you must no longer micromanage her academic career. Neither must you implement such freedom in a "We'll see how it goes" six-week trial. A trial of being left alone is a privilege, not a freedom. Such a trial period doesn't address your adolescent's underlying drive for autonomy, and you won't get credit from her for your seeming generosity of spirit. If you try leaving her alone for a semester and she fails to perform well, she's never going to say, "Wow, you were right, Dad. I guess I do need your help."

As for the words you *ought* to say, remember this short but critical phrase that's useful for every area of autonomy you'll eventually grant to your adolescent: "At your age . . ." These three simple words remind your teenager that he's growing up and that doing so requires more responsibility. When it comes to schoolwork, you might say, "I understand that at your age you don't want our help with your schoolwork anymore. Maybe it's time for you to take on that responsibility yourself, so long as your grades are acceptable."

What Are the Boundaries of This Freedom?

Minimum Grades Must Be Maintained

Be specific in telling your teenager what those minimum grades are and when they will be assessed. For example, you might say, "You can't have more than two Cs on any given six-week report." The time frame will vary based on school grading periods. You may want to use report card grades (every six to nine weeks) or even midterm grades (every three to four-and-a-half weeks). For younger teenagers, consider midterm grades. This shortens the length of any crashing but also reduces the length of restrictions (assuming they bring their grades up).

Parents Are Available to Help if Their Teenager Asks, but Not at All Times

If your teenager asks for help with homework or a school project, feel free to do so, but don't make a habit of offering help before you're asked. And don't rescue him out of poor planning. If he comes to you at ten thirty at night, saying, "I'll fail if I don't finish this before tomorrow," feel free to respond by saying, "The help desk is closed for the day. Why don't you try us again tomorrow?" As the cliché goes, "A failure to plan on your part does not constitute an emergency on my part." That's not a nurturing thought, but that's the point. With adolescents, we're past nurturing. We want to be firmly respectful.

TUTORING SHOULD BE MADE AVAILABLE, BUT NOT IF THE TEEN DOESN'T WANT IT

Too many parents fail to realize the mixed message they send when they respond to bad grades by making their adolescent go to tutoring. Also, parents who press this issue underestimate their teenager's ability to undermine the effectiveness of tutoring by his passivity, like supposedly getting lost while driving to sessions and the like.

WHAT ARE MINIMALLY ACCEPTABLE GRADES?

Don't set minimally acceptable grades at or too near your teen's best-achievable grades. An adolescent has to be internally motivated to make her best grades. There aren't enough external rewards or punishments you can supply to force her to do her best. Parents who proudly announce, "We don't accept any grades below your best!" clearly show they know nothing of adolescents. That's a fine message to give to children, but you can't pay or threaten an adolescent enough to do her best.

Besides, *doing your best* is impossible to measure with a teenager and doesn't prepare him for the real world. ("Well, Tom, you missed your sales quota again this quarter, but you seem to be trying hard, so we'll go ahead and give you that promotion.") On the other hand, applying consequences for poor grades can be a good motivator for him to at least perform acceptably. To put it another way, you can't punish an adolescent into doing his best, but you can punish him into getting minimally acceptable grades.

Consider dividing your expectations into three categories:

1. Grades you know they could make if they applied themselves.
2. Grades they make that are okay, but you know they could do better.
3. Grades that are unacceptable.

Minimum grade requirements should be just that: minimum. You want to convey an attitude that says, *We're trying to leave you alone here and not manage your schoolwork, but these grades aren't even average for you. They're just not acceptable.*

For the A student, you should consider giving her a maximum number of Bs you will accept for each grading period. You might also insist that no more than one C is made per year. Secondary education, especially if you consider math, involves a lot more than just motivation. Even smart kids with average motivation levels pull at least one bad grade per year. You must ask yourself if you can still leave your teenager autonomous, even with an occasional C. If the answer is yes, let it go.

For the B student, you might consider the maximum number of acceptable Cs per grading period. For all students, the absolute bottom line is failing a class—Ds or worse. This isn't unacceptable just to you; it's unacceptable to their school. You'll have to make your own decision if your kid goes to one of those schools that consider a score below seventy to still be passing (which I never understood). If you're paying for a private school, it's also acceptable to expect somewhat higher grades. However, you may want to prepare a response for when your teen says, "Fine, then send me to public school!"

Consequences for earning below-minimum grades should include restricting electronics and other distractions, or grounding if necessary.

DON'T REVERT TO MICROMANAGING

Here's one of the more difficult but most important parts about granting autonomy in schoolwork: You must never go back to micromanaging. Doing so violates your teenager's need for autonomy. Adolescents who struggle in school need to figure out what problems they're having and what they're going to do about them.

More often than not, teenagers seem to be sure of only one thing: They don't need your help. Teenagers whose grades continue to slide will end up with virtually all their privileges removed, which should be motivation enough. Going back to the battles of micromanaging won't add to their motivation; it just complicates your message.

Some parents worry that setting expectations below the adolescent's best teaches him that lower grades are acceptable. If you've been paying attention so far, you should already know the answer to this. Parents teach acceptable expectations to their *children*. *Adolescents* are now deciding which parental expectations they will agree with and which they won't. If you tell a fifteen-year-old that there will be no consequences as long as he doesn't get more than two Cs, he's not going to answer, "Oh, I thought Cs weren't as good as As. You mean Cs are good too?" Grant him the benefit of the doubt to know what's acceptable.

Also, tell your teenager of any contact you have with her teachers. Now that school management is her responsibility, you want to avoid all appearances of adults getting together to decide what they'll do about her grades. This undercuts the autonomy you're trying to grant and makes it seem as if you're sneaking around behind her back to still check up on her. Once your teenager discovers that, she'll likely believe you never granted her schoolwork freedom in the first place, because, well, you didn't.

Remember, we live in a confused culture, and parents can't always expect that teachers will respect an adolescent's need for autonomy. In fact, most teachers expect to be dealing with parents who still treat their teenagers as children. You may need to consider explaining to your adolescent's teacher what you're doing so you don't look like an absentee parent. If a teacher emails you with concerns about your teenager's performance in class, forward the message to your teen. If a meeting is suggested, plan for your adolescent to attend. Unless things are falling apart, do not contact teachers if your adolescent doesn't want you to.

A Note of Caution about Motivation and School

While it's proper for parents to seek the best ways to motivate their adolescents to apply themselves to their schoolwork, we must also be careful not to assume that all poor grades are a result of laziness. To be sure, teenagers can be quite lazy, but you should also know that learning differences and other academic struggles are often misdiagnosed as laziness, even by adolescents themselves.

So if you've always encouraged good performance in school and given consequences when your kid appeared not to be putting forth effort, there's likely something else going on besides stubborn laziness. If you're not sure what that is, it's always good to seek an evaluation of your teenager's IQ and learning styles to rule out any underlying problems. Too often, parents use punishment, speechmaking, and other forms of coercion as a hammer that turns every school problem into a nail.

For example, when I see an adolescent who has been recently diagnosed with attention deficit disorder (ADD), I first have to challenge the teenager's fixed assumption that he just needs to try harder. In such cases, the parents have assumed laziness to be the main cause, and this leads to an adolescent who doesn't understand herself. ADD is just one learning difference that can look like laziness, even to the adolescent who has it.

Other potential learning issues include auditory processing problems, dyslexia, dysgraphia, and more. Discovering the presence of a learning problem doesn't mean the adolescent isn't ever lazy, but it does mean that even when motivated to do better, he will still struggle to apply himself when and where he needs to. If your teenager spends much of every school year grounded and still doesn't bring his grades to a minimum level, he probably suffers from more than just a lack of motivation.

FREEDOM	BOUNDARIES
Use your own judgment in setting style of dress.	• We will still limit provocative clothing. • We will not pay extra for objectionable clothing.

You don't need a professional to tell you appearance is a big deal during adolescence. If you haven't already, spend some time unobtrusively observing your teenager when he or she walks by a mirror or other reflective surface. At least by mid-adolescence (if not sooner), most teenagers can't resist taking a look at themselves. It's not vanity. It's more like trying to figure out what they look like. With all the fast changes puberty brings, they're probably trying to get a fix on their appearance. Even when a teenager (especially a girl) doesn't regularly check out her look, it's probably related more to unhappiness with what she sees rather than lack of concern.

Not surprisingly, clothes can become an important issue for teenagers. While you may not be having conflicts about how your adolescent dresses, it's worthwhile to stay aware (as best as you can) of your teen's relationship with his or her appearance. If there *is* conflict, it's best to be careful about what boundaries you set and why you set them. Fast-changing bodies are sometimes tough to inhabit, especially when one's ability to think more critically about oneself is developing just as quickly. Clothes and appearance are too important to be tossed off with a few parental decrees like "You look like a homeless person!" or, far worse, "You're dressed like a prostitute!"

These insecurities about appearance can erupt in intense control battles over what to wear. Teenagers often need guidance while they work out their appearance issues. Parents who steadfastly deliver decrees from on high about appropriate clothing run the risk of ensuring their views will be ignored or fought against at every turn. Like the issues we've already discussed, it's important that you seek the earliest opportunity to give over as much freedom in the area of appearance and dress as you can without placing your teenagers (especially girls) in situations they may not be ready to handle.

Consider this sobering thought too: When teenagers are asked why they want to drink alcohol, they often answer, "To feel grown-up." Granting them freedom in clothing style seems a small sacrifice to make to help them feel grown-up without their resorting to more drastic measures. A well-behaved teenager who feels the freedom to wear a T-shirt and jeans to church, or to wear that heavy metal shirt to school, has greater confidence in the fact that he or she is growing up—confidence that's very useful in fending off more dangerous temptations.

When Should I Grant This Freedom?

Though it's not fair to girls, parental arguments over what their teenage daughters wear occur much more often than similar arguments with teenage sons. Sons may be slobs and may need to be reminded to bathe once in a while, but a daughter's choice of dress is a hot-button issue in many households. Consequently, different limits are often necessary based on your adolescent's gender.

I've purposely worded this freedom as *style of dress* to allow parents to grant a necessary freedom in appearance while still maintaining some control over teenage girls who choose to wear provocative clothing. Parents who try to maintain control over all their teenagers' choices fail to communicate important differences in why some things are appropriate and others are not.

Remember: More Control Often Results in Less Influence

Sure, you may forbid your daughter from wearing that too-short dress, but you may lose the ability to influence her as to why it's inappropriate. Parents need to communicate that there's a distinct difference between clothing that makes the statements *I'm unique* or *I'm rebellious* and clothing that indicates *I'm sexually available.* An all-black outfit that covers her body is not the same as a pretty-colored outfit that covers only a few inches. Giving your adolescent daughter the freedom to choose styles, even if you don't like them, is an important means of communicating this.

With our children entering puberty at an earlier age than ever, parents must communicate their awareness that a teenage girl is not a child. Fathers and older brothers—those who can be trusted to give good advice—can play a key role here. With a confident sneer, adolescent girls will sometimes say that their mothers "just don't know what looks good today." But no matter what know-it-all airs she puts on with her mom, feedback from the world of men tends to command more authority. While being careful to avoid the "guys only want one thing" cliché, fathers can give valuable feedback to their daughters about the effect certain clothing choices will have on guys in general. Note that the impact of such feedback will vary greatly based on the strength of the father's relationship with his daughter.

These same principles also apply to hair and makeup—similar areas of autonomy that likewise need to be given over to your teenage daughter's judgment sometime during her adolescence. No matter how objectionable the look is that she wants for today, never fail to remind her that there will come a day while still in your house when her appearance choices will be up to her. Overcontrolling tirades about how you'll never agree to that style of dress, amount of eye makeup, and so on don't give extra emphasis to your opinion. They just mean you won't see her look that way until you stumble across her social media page when she's in college.

Granting autonomy to a teenage boy for his style of dress often concerns issues like appropriateness, rattiness, and cleanliness. Some may dress in all black with a new holey T-shirt every day. Others may forget to have done their wash and use the age-old explanation "It smells clean to me." But even though their specific problems differ from the clothing choices of teenage girls, the underlying question remains the same: *When will you say I'm able to choose my clothing styles?*

This could mean being embarrassed in public because of his appearance (or smell!). But it could also mean an unexpected opening to better communicating with your son about his clothing choices. Ceding control often leads to earning trust, and that trust can often be seen in better dialogue that you don't even have to initiate.

Our confused culture often makes giving over this freedom a bit harder. Walking into a restaurant or church with a teenager who looks like he just woke up can be embarrassing to parents. A culture that still regards adults-in-training as just big children means that a lot of parents will look at a ratty-looking teenager as a sign of poor parenting. An adolescent who's still figuring out how to manage his appearance may look to the uninitiated like a big, disobedient child.

As noted earlier, you may need to help other parents understand the difference between respecting a young adult and being too permissive with a child. Remember, we've been confused about this for three generations or so.

Having said that, giving freedom to choose his style of dress does not mean you have to pretend to like what he picks. Giving freedom creates space for open communication. Feel free to express your dislike of his choices, but be sure and own this as your opinion. You'll even want to be careful in how you react if he happens to choose clothing you think is appropriate.

Telling a teenager, "You can wear that to the reception if you want. That's your call. Just don't be surprised if I sort of act like I don't know you," isn't necessarily as rude as it sounds. If he gets defensive, just remind him, "You're too old for me to tell you how to dress, but I just don't think it's respectful, that's all." This kind of feedback won't make an adolescent happy, but I would argue that it has more potential for impact than a blanket "Because I said so" kind of reaction.

What Are the Boundaries of This Freedom?

As before, autonomy comes with responsibility. When you grant your teenager the right to choose her clothing, consider these two boundaries.

We Will Still Limit Provocative Clothing

This relates primarily to girls. Defining which clothes are too tight, too low cut, or too short are judgment calls, so make sure both mother and father are on the same page before you tell her no. Again, hearing this message from a strong male influence can be helpful.

We Will Not Pay Extra for Objectionable Clothing

This usually means setting a clothing budget for your teenager. Establishing a clothing budget helps you avoid fights over what he chooses to spend his money on. It also takes you out of the decision loop on objectionable but expensive clothes: "It doesn't matter if I like it, honey, as long as you're willing to spend that much on one pair of jeans." Furthermore, a clothing budget provides important financial planning experience: "Sorry, I guess you'll have to wait until next month's allowance. Maybe you could sell something . . . or even get a job!"

Beyond provocative and questionable clothing, few other limits ought to be placed on your adolescent's style of dress. Remember, too, that during this sometimes difficult time, your teenager is often trying on identities more than trying on clothes. While she may be wearing a style you detest, just wait a few months. If you make a fuss about her choice, she may stay with that identity (and style) just to irk you. However, if you give up control and gain influence, she might just start taking your advice when it comes to clothing (and identity!).

Some appearance-related issues, however, should certainly have set limits. The freedom to get a tattoo or extra piercings should usually be left until after they turn eighteen. These require parental consent from a licensed practitioner anyway, and they're rather invasive changes to the body. Even if you don't object to the look of tattoos and piercings (and most parents do object), the fact that they're permanent should give you pause.

If your teenager turns eighteen before finishing high school, you could still try to make it off-limits until after he graduates, but I don't recommend it. Forbidding tattoos and piercings after an adolescent turns eighteen is a weak control maneuver. "If you get a tattoo, I'm not paying for college" is one of the most anemic rules given to post-eighteen-year-olds. You probably won't follow through with that threat. ("Oh no, fifteen years ago we spent our daughter's college money on a round-the-world vacation because she got a Mickey Mouse tattoo on her ankle.") Or, more likely, you just won't know she got it. I've completely lost track of how many adolescents have shown me some tattoo or piercing their parents had never seen. If you follow Planned Emancipation and invest in communication, your advice has a greater possibility of influencing what will mark them for life.

Now that we've considered the major territories that your teenagers believe you've been encroaching upon for far too long, let's consider the last territory, one I don't recommend you fully withdraw from until the day after they've graduated from high school.

FREEDOM	BOUNDARIES
Use your own judgment in deciding when to come in at night.	• Please don't wake us up. • If you're going to be out past __:__ or not coming home at all, let us know.

"Tough night?"

Kevin raises his face out of his cereal bowl. A few flakes stick to his chin.

"Yup."

"What time did you get in?"

"Don't ask."

"When you choose to come home is your business. I'm not asking because you'll be in trouble. I'm just curious."

"Three o'clock in the morning."

Kevin's dad chuckles. "Work's gonna be a pain today, isn't it?"

Before you start writing a letter to me, let me clarify that the story above features a senior who's just graduated high school. Because his dad knows his son will be making these choices himself when he leaves for college in ten weeks, he's granted his son the freedom to set his curfew. But with that freedom comes the responsibility of working a summer job and facing the real-world consequences of making poor curfew choices.

A high school graduate is certainly too old to still expect any money from his parents over the summer, right? Speaking of jobs, you'll also want to outline the amount of spending money (if any) you'll provide when your teenager starts college. It's best if you make sure it's not enough for their needs so they know how much they must save over the summer.

When Should I Grant This Freedom?

For almost all teenagers, I recommend you allow them full curfew autonomy after they've graduated from high school. You may wait a day and set a curfew for graduation night, considering the parties or other events they may be invited to, but the sooner you can grant them full control over their time to come home, the better. After all, if your teenagers are planning to go to college or move out, you likely only have two or three months left with them. Wouldn't you rather they learn hard lessons while you're still close by instead of when they may be hundreds of miles away?

This is one of the reasons curfew autonomy is the last territory from which you should withdraw your troops. They're going to have this autonomy handed to them in a short while as it is, so it would behoove you to exert some influence over them during that short amount of time when they have full control of their schedule but still live in your house.

Additionally, granting them the right to set their curfew does come with higher risks than the other territories of autonomy we've already discussed. But if you've been progressively withdrawing from those other territories, you've been showing your adolescents a growing trust in their ability to make better and better decisions. Hopefully, such a trend would carry over to their decisions when it comes to curfew, especially if they have real-world responsibilities to live up to while setting their schedules.

The Final Frontier

There may be few sweeter words to a teenager's ear than "At your age, it's up to you when you come in at night." The words may conjure visions of majestic eagles flying in front of a waving American flag as "God Bless America" blares in the background and your adolescent thinks, *Free at last! Free at last!*

That may be a bit exaggerated, but as you hand over the last vestige of your parental control, your adolescent may finally and fully feel like an adult. To him, getting the right to choose his curfew is one of the more conclusive answers to the question he's been asking for years: *When will you say I'm an adult?*

After you've granted the freedom to come in when she pleases, what other freedoms are left to grant?

None.

But that doesn't mean *her* new freedom should impinge on *your* freedom.

What Are the Boundaries of This Freedom?

When giving teenagers autonomy for setting their curfew, be specific about how their decisions shouldn't adversely affect the household. These responsibilities are similar to what we covered in the sections on setting their bedtime and choosing their friends.

Please Don't Wake Us Up

While these teenagers have the right to come in when they want, you certainly can expect them not to wake up the household. If they should use a different entrance so as not to disturb the household, be clear about which entrance that is. If your house has some sort of mega–alarm system or there's just no way for them to come in without disturbing everyone, you could set the rule "If you're coming home after midnight, please stay somewhere else." That's a logical option, but most parents don't like suggesting it.

If You're Going to Be Out Past [Time] or Not Coming Home At All, Please Let Us Know

While this is a reasonable request for most adults living in a house together, you may want to be careful with this one. While this curfew freedom is still new, asking your young adults to let you know anything about their plans may still feel like checking up.

I put the word *please* on these boundaries because you must not try to give consequences if they fail to follow them. It makes no sense to ground an adult living in your home because he failed to let you know he wasn't coming home. He won't be informing you about his whereabouts in a few weeks, so why should you insist on knowing now?

Oh, and don't try the old "I can't sleep until I know you're home" argument. You'll sleep fine when she's 150 miles away in six weeks and you won't know when she got to her room. What's the difference? You still feel that this kid is on your watch, or that her safety is still your job, or maybe it's just that you'll feel guilty if something happens to her. These are all the leftover natural feelings of parents who grew up in a culture that doesn't know when to tell parents their kids are no longer children.

Because your adolescent is so close to being an adult living on his own, the consequences you bring upon him for curfew issues (or any other issues, for that matter) should be slim to none. Now the consequences he faces will come from the same sources from which you face consequences—your job, your boss, your relationships, and so on. One late night coupled with one early morning job is a quick and efficient teacher.

Issues of young adults not respecting their parents' needs for sleep should be the subject of serious communication, not threats. If your adult child doesn't respect your need for sleep, or for a house that's not littered with her stuff, there's only one real-world consequence you can give: You may need to insist that she move out.

Adults don't have a right to live with their parents. It's a privilege. They're guests, and it's appropriate for you to expect that they respect your home. If you've followed Planned Emancipation with even a reasonable amount of consistency, this shouldn't be a problem.

Examples of and Issues with an Expectations and Consequences List

Up and Ready in the Mornings

EXPECTATION	CONSEQUENCE
Must be in the car and ready for school by 8:00 a.m.	• If you're not already up, we'll wake you at 7:45 a.m. If we have to wake you, you'll have an early bed restriction of 10:00 p.m. • Fatigue will not be accepted as an excuse for disrespect, etc.

Let's look at practical ways to withdraw your troops from your teenager's choice of bedtime:

1. Find a wake-up time that's later than he wants to wake up. (He should already have bedtime freedom, which means waking himself is his responsibility.) This should leave him barely enough time to get ready and go.
2. Tell her you're not willing to wake her before this time, and that as long as she has risen before that time, there will be no consequences from you.
3. Explain to him that if he's not awake by that time, you will come and wake him. The cost of your wake-up call is that he must go to bed that same night at the time he's usually required only

to be in his room. In other words, if you're responsible for his wake-up call, wake him with a reminder: "Good morning! You have an early bedtime tonight" (not "Oh my gosh, you're still in bed!").

Do you see what this does? For the younger adolescent, you may still have to wake her up occasionally, but the responsibility shifts when she is a teenager. Your wake-up call is no longer her right, but more of a backup measure you're willing to offer (at a cost!).

The advantage of using an early bedtime as a consequence is that if your adolescent is truly too tired to wake up because he's making poor bedtime choices, he will at least have to be in bed at a reasonable time for every morning he fails to wake up. With this consequence, you won't ever have to take back the autonomy and set a bedtime. (And you never want to take back autonomy.) If he continually fails to wake up in the mornings, he'll automatically revert to a set bedtime—one day at a time. By the way, late wake-ups on Friday mornings should equal an early bedtime that next Sunday night.

Don't write fake excuse notes to cover for consequences at school, either. Neither should you become her de facto taxi. If she's constantly asking favors of you—"I forgot my homework. Can you bring it up to school?"—charge a five-dollar taxi fee. In doing so, you work against what seems like a swelling tidal wave of entitlement that courses through so many of today's teenagers. Again, you want to shift your adolescent away from thinking, *I have people who do things for me.*

One way to incentivize your older teenager's bedtime decisions is to charge him money if his lateness negatively affects the family in some way. For instance, when my son was a senior in high school, he had autonomy regarding his bedtime, but he had to wake up early enough to drive his sisters to school. If he left even thirty seconds later than what we had agreed upon, I'd fine him two dollars. If he was so late that my wife or I had to take our girls to school, the fine was five dollars.

In exercising my "Dad-ness," I'd sometimes stand next to the clock in our kitchen while my son scurried about, trying to get ready and out the door with his sisters. I'd playfully announce, "I'm smelling two dollars coming my way soon." He'd fly by me with a loud shout: "No you're not!"

My favorite story about that particular consequence happened on one of those chaotic mornings. He left so late that I contacted the principal to say that my son was likely going to be late and that whatever consequence the principal decided on was between him and my son. (We live in a small school district where I could just call the principal.) Much to my chagrin, my son somehow made it to school on time that day.

It was very disappointing to me. I don't think he received even one tardy that year.

Chores and Allowance

EXPECTATION	CONSEQUENCE
Empty the dishwasher on Mondays, Wednesdays, and Fridays by 8:00 p.m.	• After 8:00 p.m.: $2 fine • If not done by 9:00 p.m.: 24 hours without phone • If still not done by next morning: grounded for 24 hours

Money and household chores often get tangled up in the Expectations and Consequences list. Children often learn about responsibility by being given household tasks and then receiving money as a reward: "You did a good job vacuuming. Here's five dollars." By the time adolescence rolls around, that system may need to change:

"Did you remember to vacuum?"

"I'm going out. You can just keep your five bucks and do it yourself!"

While fining a teenager may be a useful consequence for failing to do a household chore, you may need to redefine the connection between money and your behavioral expectations for your (now) young adult. You're not paying your teenager to do the household chores you've assigned her. She's required to do the chore, and the fine is the consequence. If that doesn't get her to comply, the consequence will increase, whether through a greater fine or another consequence altogether. If you get into regular fights about these expectations, you might need to construct a progressive consequence system like the one we saw for curfew in appendix 1.

Note that the previous example is for fairly extreme circumstances. This would be for a teenager who often forgets to do a given chore, but who also seems to resist doing it even after a consequence is given. This escalation of consequences allows for occasional forgetting but makes clear that the chore needs to be done. You might also note that if you wake up and it's still not done, feel free to empty the dishwasher yourself and avoid the unnecessary control battle of trying to make him do it. You may end up doing the chore occasionally, but he's lost two dollars, has no phone, and is grounded for a full day!

Remember that with chores, just as with any other expectation, don't remind her about it. You could say, "It's eight o'clock, so you owe me two dollars" rather than "Honey, it's seven thirty. You need to get going on that dishwasher!" Constant reminders sound like a parent who's demanding obedience from a child, not a parent who's holding a teenager accountable for his or her choices.

Disrespect

EXPECTATION	CONSEQUENCE
No disrespect: • No cussing. • No name-calling. • No giving direct orders (e.g., "Get out of here!). • No threats.	$1 fine

Few things are more annoying to parents than a teenager who speaks or acts disrespectfully toward them. Many of you will need to add something about respectful behavior to your Expectations and Consequences list. Failing to do so is a common cause of parental blowups with their adolescents. But this issue can be tricky and requires finesse on your part.

First, it's easier than you think to accidentally create the expectation that your teen cannot be angry with you for no good reason. Adolescents long for autonomy, and it's common for them to become quite angry as they navigate their parents' involvement in their lives. If expressing anger is equivalent to being disrespectful, however, you have put a major hurdle in your teenager's ability to communicate honestly with you. Your expectation regarding disrespect must be clear and yet allow your teenager to talk to you even when she's angry. For example, if you're married, you probably know that a limit like "no yelling" is hard to define:

"I wasn't yelling!"
  "You're doing it right now!"

Second, a large percentage of teenagers seem to have a sixth sense of finding passive-aggressive ways to display their lack of respect. Trying to chase each of these behaviors down and punish them usually results in parents looking silly:

"Did I just see you roll your eyes at me?"
  "No, I was looking at a spot on the ceiling!"

Since the goal of these under-the-radar behaviors is to upset the parent, it can be quite powerful for Mom and Dad to learn the art of ignoring or even joking about them: "Seems to be a lot to look at on the ceiling."

When parents get down to clearly defining what they consider disrespectful, only a handful of behaviors can be used. The most common ones I've seen include no cursing, no name-calling, no giving parents direct orders (e.g., "Shut up" or "Get out of here"), and no threats. If you must include yelling on your list, I would recommend you add "after one warning" or something similar so your teenager isn't too afraid to talk when angry.

Curfew

EXPECTATION	CONSEQUENCE
Must be home by 11:00 p.m. on non-school nights	• 1 to 15 minutes late: 10:00 p.m. curfew next non-school night • 16 to 30 minutes late: grounded on next non-school night • 31 or more minutes late: grounded for more than 1 day depending on how late you are (we'll let you know)

In appendix 1, I go into more detail about granting your teenager the freedom to decide when to come home at night. But before your teen is ready for that, you'll need to set and enforce a curfew in your Expectations and Consequences list.

I mentioned earlier the need for clarity and action in implementing the Expectations and Consequences list. I used the example of curfew because it can create a common little problem. You need to issue a consequence the minute your teenager is late, but a few minutes late isn't that big of a deal. Curfew is a good example of an expectation that should have *progressive* consequences. The later the teenager is, the more severe the consequence should be.

In this example, notice that "I was only three minutes late!" should be answered by reiterating the consequence: "It's only one hour earlier the next time." Violating the expectation does have a consequence. Also notice that as the violation gets more serious (e.g., more than thirty minutes late), you've left yourself leeway to significantly increase the consequences if the circumstances call for it. If your teenager is considering blowing off curfew, you've only clarified the minimum he or she can expect.

In my opinion, mathematically cleaner options like "one minute late equals one minute earlier the next time" don't communicate the seriousness of curfew. Also, consequences for missing curfew on non-school nights should be applied to the next non-school night, not to school nights. However, if I were you, I wouldn't worry about whether the consequence happens to fall on a non-school night when they weren't planning anything anyway. You're not trying to ensure maximum pain for each consequence.

Starting Planned Emancipation in Your Home

The Ideal Start: Thirteenth Birthday

When my son turned thirteen, we had a party. This was a celebration with a purpose. I wanted to emphasize that he had reached a milestone in his life. He was now a young adult and no longer a child. If we were Jewish, this would have been his bar mitzvah. Since we were in Texas and Christians, we went with the next best thing—barbecue.

If you have at least one child who hasn't yet turned thirteen, I would recommend you consider some kind of event marking the importance of that day. Your son or daughter is no longer a child (in your household at least). This is a great way to kick off Planned Emancipation.

If you ever get the chance to attend a bar mitzvah or bat mitzvah, you should go. It's an event filled with pride, service to the community, and family support. Too often, however, I've known the newly minted Jewish adult to leave this coming-of-age ceremony, only to go back to a home where there is no apparent change in status. In these cases, I find that it doesn't matter how elaborate and sacred the ceremony is if no real change occurs afterward.

I celebrated my son's birthday along with his cousin's, who is one day younger. His father and I reached out to uncles, grandfathers, and other interested men in our sons' lives and asked them each to write a letter congratulating our sons and making any observations or offering words of wisdom they thought important. We put these letters in a scrapbook for each son and presented them at the birthday barbecue gathering. Both young men were pleased and a bit overwhelmed when they walked into the restaurant where many of these men had gathered in support.

Over the years, I've heard other creative ideas for such a gathering. Most of these tend to focus on ceremonies for boys. These include hunting trips (of course), gathering in secret, and always food. I would argue, however, that our girls may be in more need of their own ceremonies than ever. The increasing isolation in the lives of our girls accentuates the importance of their gathering with the women who want to support their transition into adulthood.

As you may have noticed, I see no benefit in some sort of obligatory inclusion of opposite-sex family members in these ceremonies. If circumstances dictate that a single mom will be planning this ceremony for her son, that's fine, of course. But virtually all coming-of-age ceremonies around the world and through history emphasize different experiences for girls and boys.

The important part, however, should occur in private. This is when both parents (if present in the home) give a thirteen-year-old his or her first Freedoms list. This should be presented as part of the whole "now that you're an adult" theme of the ceremony or party you just gave. This isn't the time to also give the Expectations and Consequences list. You can do that in a week or two. This is the time to show that this celebration and ceremony actually mean something in your home. As I've said before, be sure and emphasize the *freedoms* part.

For example, the freedom to make their own choices with music sounds like "You're too old to be answering to us about what music you listen to." If you sound more like "Okay, you can listen to whatever music you want, but *we'd better not catch your little sister listening to that junk*!" you're probably doing it wrong.

Starting Late

Many parents ask me, "We didn't do this when our kid turned thirteen. What do we do now?" This really isn't a big problem. For most parents, it just means they might have saved themselves some headaches, but *it is never too late to start Planned Emancipation*. Remember, *Feeding the Mouth* parenting isn't some magic bullet such that if only you had started earlier, all would be well by now. (See chapter 3, on the burden of parenting.)

The best way to start late is to make a little announcement signaling you want to make a significant change in how you treat your teenager. It's important to announce this change, because simply letting go a bit more or even quietly adding a few freedoms will not have the effect you're looking for. The Freedoms list is there to reinforce a broader message that you, as the parents, see that your child is growing up and more in charge of his or her own life.

It's probably best to start with an honest summary of what you're learning in this book and why you want to make a change. I suggest you start with something like "So, we read this book about parenting teenagers, and this guy says that when we try to be helpful, you probably feel like we're treating you like a child. If so, we're sorry about that. We know you're not a kid anymore, and we don't want you to feel disrespected."

Then you present the Freedoms list. Obviously, older teenagers' Freedoms lists will be longer than if you'd started at thirteen. Don't be at all surprised if this whole presentation is met with a blank stare or even suspicion. It usually takes some time for your meaning to sink in.

Remember that however you've begun Planned Emancipation, it's vital that you look for lots and lots of little ways to remind your child of this change in his or her status. ("Why did you only eat half your sandwich at lun—oh, sorry. You're not a kid anymore.") Obviously, you need to stick with the freedoms you've given, but when you start late, you'll want to really pour on the "You're an adult now" messaging.

When your older teen complains that their younger teenage sibling is being given freedoms she didn't have at that age, just say, "Yeah, we didn't know this stuff back then." You don't owe your child an apology for finding new information and improving your parenting.

Whether you start on time or late, the key is to start as soon as you realize the value of Planned Emancipation. Even if your kids are well past high school and maybe not even living with you, giving the message that you see them as adults can be healing. Taking ownership for not seeing this earlier isn't the same thing as seeking some sort of absolution from your children. Remember, most of you reading this book never received a clear message that you had entered adulthood either.

Notes

CHAPTER 2 | THE INVENTION OF TEENAGERS

1. G. Stanley Hall, *Adolescence: Its Psychology and Its Relations to Physiology, Anthropology, Sociology, Sex, Crime, Religion, and Education* (New York: D. Appleton, 1904).
2. Robert Epstein, *The Case against Adolescence: Rediscovering the Adult in Every Teen* (Sanger, CA: Quill Driver Books, 2007), 23.
3. Alice Schlegel and Herbert Barry III, *Adolescence: An Anthropological Inquiry* (New York: Free Press, 1991).
4. R. G. Condon, "Adolescence and Changing Family Relations in the Central Canadian Arctic," *Arctic Medical Research* 49, no. 2 (April 1990): 81–92.
5. Joseph Allen and Claudia Worrell Allen, *Escaping the Endless Adolescence: How We Can Help Our Teenagers Grow Up before They Grow Old* (New York: Ballantine Books, 2009), x.
6. Philippe Ariès, *Centuries of Childhood: A Social History of Family Life*, trans. Robert Baldick (New York: Vintage Books, 1965), 30.

CHAPTER 3 | THE BURDEN OF PARENTING

1. Alison Gopnik, "A Manifesto against 'Parenting,'" *Wall Street Journal*, July 8, 2016, https://www.wsj.com/articles/a-manifesto-against-parenting-1467991745.
2. Ylonda Gault Caviness, "What Black Moms Know," editorial, *New York Times*, May 2, 2015, https://www.nytimes.com/2015/05/03/opinion/sunday/what-black-moms-know.html.
3. Ibid.
4. Robert Epstein, *The Case against Adolescence: Rediscovering the Adult in Every Teen* (Sanger, CA: Quill Driver Books, 2007), 5.

CHAPTER 5 | UNDERSTANDING PLANNED EMANCIPATION

1. *Kung Fu*, season 1, pilot episode, "The Way of the Tiger, the Sign of the Dragon," directed by Jerry Thorpe, written by Ed Spielman and Howard Friedlander, aired February 22, 1972, on ABC.
2. *Gandhi*, directed by Richard Attenborough (Columbia Pictures, 1982).

CHAPTER 7 | THE ENDPOINT OF PLANNED EMANCIPATION

1. Amanda Jackson, "A Judge Sides with Parents and Rules Their 30-Year-Old Son Must Move Out," CNN, updated May 23, 2018, https://www.cnn.com /2018/05/22/us/judge-rules-son-must-move-out-new-york-trnd/index.html.

CHAPTER 11 | LIMIT SETTING WITH ADOLESCENTS

1. *Postcards from the Edge*, directed by Mike Nichols (Columbia Pictures, 1990).

CHAPTER 15 | FRIENDSHIPS AND GROUP ACTIVITIES

1. "Protestant Churchgoer Views on Livestreaming" (Nashville: Lifeway Research, June 2023).

CHAPTER 16 | DATING AND SEX

1. *The Big Bang Theory*, season 6, episode 1, "The Date Night Variable," directed by Mark Cendrowski, aired September 27, 2012, on CBS.
2. Janette Rallison, *How to Take the Ex out of Ex-Boyfriend* (New York: Speak, 2009), 79.
3. Tina Fey, *Bossypants* (New York: Reagan Arthur Books, 2011), 15.

CHAPTER 19 | SOCIAL MEDIA

1. Jennie G. Nolla et al., "Association of Maltreatment with High-Risk Internet Behaviors and Offline Encounters," *Pediatrics* 131, no. 2 (February 2013) e510–17, https://pubmed.ncbi.nlm.nih.gov/23319522.
2. Danah Boyd, *It's Complicated: The Social Lives of Networked Teens* (New Haven, CT: Yale University Press, 2014), 5, 20.
3. Katie Davis, "Friendship 2.0: Adolescents' Experiences of Belonging and Self-Disclosure Online," *Journal of Adolescence* 35, no. 6 (December 2012): 1527–36, https://onlinelibrary.wiley.com/doi/10.1016/j.adolescence.2012.02.013.
4. Jean Rhodes, "Adolescents' Digital Media Use and Friendships," *Chronicle of Evidence-Based Mentoring*, December 10, 2013, https://www.evidencebased mentoring.org/adolescents-digital-media-use-and-friendships.
5. Ibid.
6. Ibid.

CHAPTER 20 | VIDEO GAMES

1. "Gaming Disorder," World Health Organization, Health Topics, accessed January 30, 2024, https://www.who.int/standards/classifications/frequently -asked-questions/gaming-disorder.
2. American Psychiatric Association, *Diagnostic and Statistical Manual of Mental Disorders, Fifth Edition*, Text Revision (DSM-5-TR) (Washington, DC: American Psychiatric Association Publishing, 2022), 783.
3. Marja Leonhardt and Stian Overå, "Are There Differences in Video Gaming and Use of Social Media among Boys and Girls?—A Mixed Methods Approach,"

International Journal of Environmental Research and Public Health, 18, no. 11 (June 2021): 6085.

4. Ibid.
5. Andrew K. Przybylski, "Electronic Gaming and Psychosocial Adjustment," Pediatrics 134, no. 3 (September 2014): e716–22, https://pubmed.ncbi.nlm.nih.gov/25092934.
6. Ibid.
7. "Average Daily Time Spent Playing Games and Using Computer for Leisure Per Capita in the United States from 2019 to 2022, by Age Group," August 30, 2023, Statista, https://www.statista.com/statistics/502149/average-daily-time-playing-games-and-using-computer-use-by-age.
8. Przybylski, "Electronic Gaming."

CHAPTER 21 | THE SHAME-BASED POWER OF PORNOGRAPHY
1. Erik H. Erikson, *Childhood and Society* (New York: W. W. Norton, 1993), 253.

CHAPTER 25 | ADHD AND AUTISM SPECTRUM ISSUES
1. Russell A. Barkley, PhD, recognized authority on attention deficit hyperactivity disorder (ADHD/ADD), russellbarkley.org. See *ADHD and the Nature of Self-Control* (New York: Guilford Press, 1997), 314.
2. Dr. Stephen Shore, autistic professor of special education at Adelphi University, drstephenshore.com. Also see "Interview with Dr. Stephen Shore: Autism Advocate and on the Spectrum," International Board of Credentialing and Continuing Education Standards (IBCCES), March 23, 2018, https://ibcces.org/blog/2018/03/23/12748.

CHAPTER 26 | BRAIN SCIENCE, TRAUMA, AND OTHER RABBIT HOLES
1. "Teen Brain: Behavior, Problem Solving, and Decision Making," Facts for Families Guide, no. 95, American Academy of Child and Adolescent Psychiatry, September 2017, https://www.aacap.org/AACAP/Families_and_Youth/Facts_for_Families/FFF-Guide/The-Teen-Brain-Behavior-Problem-Solving-and-Decision-Making-095.aspx.
2. Dan Romer, "The Impulsive 'Teen Brain' Isn't Based in Science," *Smithsonian Magazine*, October 31, 2017 https://www.smithsonianmag.com/science-nature/impulsive-teen-brain-not-based-science-180967027.
3. Soo-Hyun Im, Keisha Varma, and Sashank Varma, "Extending the Seductive Allure of Neuroscience Explanations Effect to Popular Articles about Educational Topics," *British Journal of Educational Psychology*, 87, no. 4 (December 2017): 518–34, https://pubmed.ncbi.nlm.nih.gov/29124752. Diego Fernandez-Duque et al., "Superfluous Neuroscience Information Makes Explanations of Psychological Phenomena More Appealing," *Journal of Cognitive Neuroscience*, 27, no. 5 (May 2015): 926–44, https://pubmed.ncbi.nlm.nih.gov/25390208.

4. Alexis Madrigal, "Scanning Dead Salmon in fMRI Machine Highlights Risk of Red Herrings," *Wired*, September 18, 2009, https://www.wired.com/2009/09/fmrisalmon.

5. Frances E. Jensen with Amy Ellis Nutt, *The Teenage Brain: A Neuroscientist's Survival Guide to Raising Adolescents and Young Adults* (New York: Harper, 2016), 2–3.

6. "About the CDC-Kaiser ACE Study," Centers for Disease Control, last modified April 6, 2021, https://www.cdc.gov/violenceprevention/aces/about.html.

7. Jessica Bennett, "If Everything Is 'Trauma,' Is Anything?," editorial, *New York Times*, February 4, 2022, https://www.nytimes.com/2022/02/04/opinion/caleb-love-bombing-gaslighting-trauma.html.

CHAPTER 27 | SEXUALITY AND GENDER IDENTITY

1. Gilbert K. Chesterton, *Orthodoxy* (New York: John Lane, 1909), 85.
   G. K. Chesterton was a writer, philosopher, Christian apologist, and literary and art critic (1874–1936).

2. *The Twilight Zone*, season 3, episode 8, "It's a Good Life," directed by James Sheldon, aired November 3, 1961, on CBS.

3. Jeffrey M. Jones, "U.S. LGBT Identification Steady at 7.2%," Gallup News, February 22, 2023, https://news.gallup.com/poll/470708/lgbt-identification-steady.aspx.

4. Caitlin O'Kane, "9-Year-Old-Boy Asks Pete Buttigieg Advice for Coming Out as Gay," CBS News, February 24, 2020, https://www.cbsnews.com/news/pete-buttigieg-answers-9-year-old-boy-about-being-gay-at-democratic-presidential-candidate-rally-colorado.

5. "What Is Gender?," Gender and Health, World Health Organization, May 24, 2021, https://www.who.int/news-room/questions-and-answers/item/gender-and-health.

6. Varun Warrier et al., "Elevated Rates of Autism, Other Neurodevelopmental and Psychiatric Diagnoses, and Autistic Traits in Transgender and Gender-Diverse Individuals," *Nature Communications* 11, no. 1 (August 7, 2020): 3959, https://pubmed.ncbi.nlm.nih.gov/32770077.

7. Jeff Amy, "Georgia House OKs Ban on Some Gender-Affirming Care for Kids," Associated Press, March 16, 2023, https://apnews.com/article/georgia-transgender-care-teens-children-0084539772e778aaf4ad67d8f5138baa.

8. "Suicide Facts and Myths," Transgender Trend, accessed January 1, 2024, https://www.transgendertrend.com/the-suicide-myth.

9. Leor Sapir, "Reckless and Irresponsible: The ACLU Pushes the Potent but Misleading 'Affirm or Suicide' Narrative," *City Journal*, March 17, 2023, https://www.city-journal.org/article/reckless-and-irresponsible.

10. Jasmine Andersson and Andre Rhoden-Paul, "NHS to Close Tavistock Child Gender Identity Clinic," BBC News, July 28, 2022, https://www.bbc.com/news/uk-62335665.

Notes

CHAPTER 29 | THE FIRE AND THE KNIFE: LESSONS FROM FATHER ABRAHAM

1. *Harry Potter and the Half-Blood Prince*, directed by David Yates (Warner Bros. Pictures, 2009).
2. Westminster Assembly, *Westminster Shorter Catechism*, 1647.
3. Barbara Bradley Hagerty, "After Tragedy, Nonbelievers Find Other Ways to Cope," *Morning Edition*, NPR, January 16, 2013, https://www.npr.org/2013/01/16/168563480/after-tragedy-nonbelievers-find-other-ways-to-cope.
4. A. W. Tozer, *The Knowledge of the Holy* (New York: HarperOne, 1978), 1.

CHAPTER 34 | ADULT CHILDREN LIVING AT HOME

1. Lori Gottlieb, "How to Land Your Kid in Therapy," *Atlantic*, July/August 2011, https://www.theatlantic.com/magazine/archive/2011/07/how-to-land-your-kid-in-therapy/308555.

CHAPTER 35 | TEENAGERS AND GRANDPARENTS

1. Yair Rosenberg, "We're Going to Die Here," *Atlantic*, October 9, 2023, https://www.theatlantic.com/ideas/archive/2023/10/amir-tibon-how-his-family-survived-hamas-massacre/675596.
2. Ibid.
3. Hal Habecker with Philip Rawley, *Aging with Purpose: 7 Essentials for Finishing Well* (Plano, TX: Finishing Well Ministries, 2023), 61.
4. Jim Burns, *Doing Life with Your Adult Children: Keep Your Mouth Shut and the Welcome Mat Out* (Grand Rapids: Zondervan, 2019), 39.

YOU'VE FINISHED!

Now you've got the road map to your teenager's planned emancipation, right? Fantastic, but let's be real, this journey will still be filled with lots of sharp **curves** and unexpected **bumps** in the road.

→

Focus on the Family has got you covered! We are your ally. **We are your go-to resource** when you encounter those unexpected obstacles in your parenting journey, no matter your child's age! With our useful resources for parents preparing their children for adulthood, we'll help you smooth out those curves and bumps.

HELP FOR PARENTS

7 TRAITS OF **EFFECTIVE PARENTING** ASSESSMENT

FOCUS ON THE FAMILY'S AGES & STAGES
GROWING UP AND
GROWING TOGETHER

THE **LIVE IT CHALLENGE**™ BY **FOCUS ON THE FAMILY**

plugged in
BY FOCUS ON THE FAMILY

FOCUS ON THE FAMILY. | PARENTING

Q & A Articles

GET THESE
RESOURCES
HERE